WHO NEEDS THE PAST?

ONE WORLD ARCHAEOLOGY
Series Editor: P. J. Ucko

WHO NEEDS THE PAST?

Indigenous values and archaeology

Edited by Robert Layton

Department of Anthropology, University of Durham

London and New York

First published by Unwin Hyman Ltd in 1989

First published in paperback 1994
by Routledge
11 New Fetter Lane, London EC4P 4EE

Simultaneously published in the USA and Canada
by Routledge
29 West 35th Street, New York, NY 10001

Typeset in 11 on 11½ Bembo by BookEns, Saffron Walden, Essex
Printed in Great Britain by TJ Press (Padstow) Ltd, Padstow, Cornwall

British Library Cataloguing in Publication Data
Who needs the past? – (One world archaeology: 5).
1. Archaeology
1. Layton, Robert II. Series
930.1

Library of Congress Cataloging in Publication Data
Who needs the past?/edited by R. Layton.
p.   cm. – (One world archaeology: 5)
Bibliography: p.
Includes index.
1. Archaeology and history. 2. History – Philosophy. I. Layton, R. (Robert).
II. Series.
CC77.H5W46 1988
901–dc19

ISBN 0–415–09558–1

List of contributors

Jack Anawak, Kivallia Consulting, Northwest Territories, Canada.

John Baines, Oriental Institute, Oxford, UK.

A.K. Chase, School of Australian Environmental Studies, Griffith University, Brisbane, Queensland, Australia.

Margaret Clunies Ross, Department of English, University of Sydney, NSW, Australia.

Kathy Emmott, Multicultural Festival Project, Argyle Centre, Southampton, UK.

Robert Layton, Department of Anthropology, University of Durham, UK.

Antonio Males, Centre for the Investigation of Social Movements in Ecuador, Otavolo, Ecuador.

Patrick Mbunwe-Samba, Provincial Pedagogic Inspector, Bamenda, Cameroon.

Daymbalipu Mununggurr, Yirrkala Community, Northern Territory, Australia.

D.K. Ndagala, Ministry of Labour and Manpower Development, Tanzania.

Elias Nwana, Ecole Normale Supérieure Bambi, Bamenda, Cameroon.

Deena Bandhu Pandey, SBB Degree College, Varanasi, India.

João de Pina-Cabral, Faculty of Social Sciences, University of Lisbon, Portugal.

Rai Gyan Narain Prasad, Independent Researcher, Gorakhpur, Uttah Pradesh, India.

Victor Raharijaona, Musée d'Art et d'Archéologie, Antananarivo, Madagascar.

Joanne Rappaport, Department of Modern Languages, University of Maryland, USA.

Brian Sparkes, Department of Archaeology, University of Southampton, UK.

Peter G. Stone, Education Section, English Heritage, London, UK.

Nancy M. Williams, Australian Institute of Aboriginal Studies, Canberra, ACT, Australia.

N. Zengu, Ministry of Labour and Manpower Development, Tanzania.

Foreword

This book is one of a major series of more than 20 volumes resulting from the World Archaeological Congress held in Southampton, England, in September 1986. The series reflects the enormous academic impact of the Congress, which was attended by 850 people from more than 70 countries, and attracted many additional contributions from others who were unable to attend in person.

The *One World Archaeology* series is the result of a determined and highly successful attempt to bring together for the first time not only archaeologists and anthropologists from many different parts of the world, as well as academics from a host of contingent disciplines, but also non-academics from a wide range of cultural backgrounds, who could lend their own expertise to the discussions at the Congress. Many of the latter, accustomed to being treated as the 'subjects' of archaeological and anthropological observation, had never before been admitted as equal participants in the discussion of their own (cultural) past or present, with their own particularly vital contribution to make towards global, cross-cultural understanding.

The Congress therefore really addressed world archaeology in its widest sense. Central to a world archaeological approach is the investigation not only of how people lived in the past but also of how, and why, changes took place resulting in the forms of society and culture which exist today. Contrary to popular belief, and the archaeology of some 20 years ago, world archaeology is much more than the mere recording of specific historical events, embracing as it does the study of social and cultural change in its entirety. All the books in the *One World Archaeology* series are the result of meetings and discussions which took place within a context that encouraged a feeling of self-criticism and humility in the participants about their own interpretations and concepts of the past. Many participants experienced a new self-awareness, as well as a degree of awe about past and present human endeavours, all of which is reflected in this unique series.

The Congress was organized around major themes. Several of these themes were based on the discussion of full-length papers which had been circulated some months previously to all who had indicated a special interest in them. Other sessions, including some dealing with areas of specialization defined by period or geographical region, were based on oral addresses, or a combination of pre-circulated papers and lectures. In all cases, the entire sessions were recorded on cassette, and all contributors were presented with the recordings of the discussion of their papers. A major part of the thinking behind the Congress was that a meeting of many hundreds of participants that did not leave behind a published record of its academic discussions would be little more than an exercise in tourism.

Thus, from the very beginning of the detailed planning for the World Archaeological Congress, in 1982, the intention was to produce post-Congress books containing a selection only of the contributions, revised in the light of discussions during the sessions themselves as well as during subsequent consultations with the academic editors appointed for each book. From the outset, contributors to the Congress knew that if their papers were selected for publication, they would have only a few months to revise them according to editorial specifications, and that they would become authors in an important academic volume scheduled to appear within a reasonable period following the Southampton meeting.

The publication of the series reflects the intense planning which took place before the Congress. Not only were all contributors aware of the subsequent production schedules, but also session organizers were already planning their books before and during the Congress. The editors were entitled to commission additional chapters for their books when they felt that there were significant gaps in the coverage of a topic during the Congress, or where discussion at the Congress indicated a need for additional contributions.

One of the main themes of the Congress was devoted to 'Archaeological "Objectivity" in Interpretation', where consideration of the precirculated full-length papers on this theme extended over four and a half days of academic discussion. The particular sessions on 'Archaeological "Objectivity" in Interpretation' were under my overall control, the main aim being to focus attention on the way that evidence of the past – including archaeological evidence – has been used and viewed by particular groups (whether local, regional or national) at different times. Essential to this aim was the exploration of the reasons why particular interpretations might have been chosen, or favoured, by individual societies and traditions at specific points in their development, or at certain stages in their activities. The whole theme attempted, therefore, a unique mix of critical assessment of the basis of archaeological methodology with critical awareness of the social contexts of the use (and possible manipulation) of the evidence of the past.

Central to this re-evaluation of the strengths and weaknesses of archaeological approaches to the interpretation, and indeed 'display', of the past – whether through academic articles or by means of formal or informal curricula, or through museums or site presentation – is an assessment of the methodologies and approaches to the significance of material culture. This has long been a core issue in archaeological discussion, but it badly needed re-examination. Throughout the history of archaeology as a discipline material culture, or at least the repetitive association of distinctive material culture objects, has been taken to reflect activities of specific social groups or 'societies' whose physical movements across a geographic stage have often been postulated on the basis of the distribution patterns of such objects, and whose supposed physical or ethnic identity (see also *State and society*, edited by J. Gledhill, B. Bender & M. Larsen) have often been assumed to correlate with such artefactual groupings. More recently archaeologists have been forced to recognize, often through lessons gained from ethnography, that a distinctive material culture complex may represent the activities of a vast variety of social groupings and subgroups, and that archaeological classification may often serve to camouflage the more subtle messages of style and technique (see also *Animals into art*, edited by H. Morphy, and *Domination and resistance*, edited by D. Miller, M. J. Rowlands & C. Tilley) which probably symbolize complex patterns of behaviour, as well as individual aspirations – within any society.

If the very basis of the equation between a material culture complex and a social grouping is ambiguous, then much of archaeological interpretation must remain subjective, even at this fundamental level of its operations. Whenever the archaeological data of material culture are presented in museums, on sites, in literature, in schools or in textbooks, as the evidence for the activities of 'races', 'peoples', 'tribes', 'linguistic groups' or other socially derived ethnic amalgamations, there should be at least scepticism if not downright suspicion. In a large number of such cases, what we are witnessing is the none-too-subtle ascription of racial/cultural stereotypes to static material culture items.

The overall theme therefore took as its starting point the proposition that archaeological interpretation is a subjective matter. It also assumed that to regard archaeology as somehow constituting the only legitimate 'scientific' approach to the past needed re-examination and possibly even rejection. A narrow parochial approach to the past which simply assumes that a linear chronology based on a 'verifiable' set of 'meaningful' 'absolute' dates is the only way to tackle the recording of, and the only way to comprehend, the past completely ignores the complexity of many literate and of many non-literate 'civilizations' and cultures. However, a world archaeological approach to a concept such as 'the past' focuses attention on precisely those features of archaeological enquiry and method which archaeologists all too often take for granted, without questioning the related assumptions.

Discussions on this theme during the Congress were grouped around seven headings, and have led to the publication of five books. The first subtheme, organized by Stephen Shennan, Department of Archaeology, University of Southampton, which lasted for almost a day, was concerned with 'Multi-culturalism and Ethnicity in Archaeological Interpretation' and the second, under the control of Ian Hodder, Department of Archaeology, University of Cambridge, which occupied more than a day, was on 'Material Culture and Symbolic Expression'. The fourth subtheme, 'The Politics of the Past: Museums, Media, and other Presentations of Archaeology', was organized by Peter Gathercole of Darwin College, Cambridge and also lasted for more than a day. Each of these subthemes has led to a separate book: *Archaeological approaches to cultural identity* (edited by S. J. Shennan), *The meanings of things* (edited by I. Hodder), and *The politics of the past* (edited by P. Gathercole & David Lowenthal, until recently of the Department of Geography, University College London). The fifth subtheme, on 'The Past in Education', was organized by Robert MacKenzie, until recently of the Department of Adult Education, University of Southampton, and discussion of this topic (which lasted formally for half a day at the Congress and informally throughout the week by means of displays and educational events) has been expanded into the book *The excluded past*, under the editorship of Peter Stone (of English Heritage) and R. MacKenzie. David Bellos of the Department of French, University of Manchester, was responsible for a short discussion session on the sixth subtheme 'Mediations of the Past in Modern Europe', and contributions from this subtheme have been combined either with those from the third on 'Contemporary Claims about Stonehenge' (a short discussion session organized by Christopher Chippindale, of the Department of Archaeology, University of Cambridge), or with those from the seventh subtheme on 'Indigenous Perceptions of the Past' which lasted for almost a day. Robert Layton of the Department of Anthropology, University of Durham, was in charge of this seventh topic and has also edited the two resulting books, the present volume and *Conflict in the archaeology of living traditions*. The latter also incorporates several contributions from a one-day discussion on 'Material Culture and the Making of the Modern United States: Views from Native America', which had been organized by Russell Handsman of the American Indian Archaeological Institute, Washington, and Randall McGuire of the Department of Anthropology of the State University of New York at Binghamton.

The whole of the 'Archaeological "Objectivity" in Interpretation' theme had been planned as the progressive development of an idea and the division of it into subthemes was undertaken in the full knowledge that there would be considerable overlap between them. It was accepted that it would, in many ways, be impossible, and even counter-productive, to split, for example, education from site presentation, or literary presentations of the past from indigenous history. In the event, while each of the books resulting from this overall theme has its own coherence, they also share a concern to make explicit the responsibility of recognizing the various ways of interpreting humanly created artefacts. In addition they recognize the social responsibility of archaeological interpretation, and the way that this may be used, consciously or unconsciously, by others for their own ends. The contributions in these books, directly or indirectly, explicitly or implicitly, epitomize the view that modern archaeology must recognize and confront its new role, which is to address the wider community. It must do this with a sophisticated awareness of the strengths and the weaknesses of its own methodologies and practices.

A world archaeological approach to archaeology as a 'discipline' reveals how subjective archaeological interpretation has always been. It also demonstrates the importance that all rulers and leaders (politicians) have placed on the legitimization of their positions through the 'evidence' of the past. Objectivity is strikingly absent from most archaeological exercises in interpretation. In some cases there has been conscious manipulation of the past for national political ends (as in the case of Ian Smith's Rhodesian regime over Great Zimbabwe, or that of the Nazis with their racist use of archaeology). But, apart from this, archaeologists themselves have been influenced in their interpretation by the received wisdom of their times, both in the sort of classificatory schemes which they consider appropriate to their subject, and in the way that their dating of materials is affected by their assumptions about the capabilities of the humans concerned. Nowhere is archaeological explanation immune to changes in interpretative fashion. This is as true of Britain as of anywhere else – Stonehenge especially has been subjected to the most bizarre collection of interpretations over the years, including all sort of references to it having been constructed by Mycenaeans and Phoenicians. Although, at first sight, it is tempting to assume that such contentions are different from attempts by politicians to claim that the extraordinary site of Great Zimbabwe was constructed by Phoenicians using black slaves, the difference is not very easy to sustain.

Realization of the flexibility and variety of past human endeavour all over the world directs attention back to those questions that are at the very basis of archaeological interpretation. How can static material culture objects be equated with dynamic human cultures? How can we define and recognize the 'styles' of human activity, as well as their possible implications? In some contexts these questions assume immense political importance. For example, the archaeological 'evidence' of cultural continuity, as opposed to discontinuity, may make all the difference to an indigenous land claim, the right of access to a site/region, or the disposal of a human skeleton to a museum, as against its reburial.

All these factors lead in turn to a new consideration of how different societies choose to display their museum collections and conserve their sites. As the debates about who should be allowed to use Stonehenge, and how it should be displayed, make clear, objects or places may be considered important at one time and 'not worth bothering about' at others. Who makes these decisions and in what contexts? Who is responsible, and why, for what is taught about the past in schools or in adult education? Is such education based on a narrow local/regional/national framework of archaeology and history, or is it oriented towards multiculturalism and the variety of human cultural experiences in a world-wide context? What should the implications be for the future of archaeology?

The main themes in *Who needs the past?* have been discussed in detail in its editorial introduction (pp. 1–20). My aim in what follows is to examine a few of the points which have struck me personally as being of particular note or fascination.

In this book Robert Layton and his contributors analyse varying frameworks for understanding the past which are drawn from an impressive variety of contexts including the modern Americas, Aboriginal Australia, the Arctic, Europe, Cameroon, Madagascar and India, as well as ancient Greece and Egypt. Some of these frameworks are based on indigenous oral histories and others on the archaeological record or written documents. In several cases these approaches to the past appear so different as to have at least the potential for confrontation and conflict (see also *Conflict in the archaeology of living traditions*, edited by R. Layton), but in others they appear to be tangential to each other, or parallel, or possibly even complementary to each other. *Who needs the past?* is not a book which sets out to make judgements about which sort of approach to the past may be more, or less, 'correct' – although the editor does attempt to identify the criteria of reliability on which different approaches rely. Rather, the aim of this book is to present the sophistication and basis of all attempts to conceptualize the past, and the role of the past in the present, from whichever culture of the past or of the present such conceptualizations derive. Almost every chapter offers a unique view of the insights of individuals into their own society and the role that the past should, or does, play in it. As a result, *Who needs the past?* serves to highlight the fact that the past is indeed a foreign country (see also *The politics of the past*, edited by P. Gathercole & D. Lowenthal), and by recognizing and honouring the importance of *all* attempts to navigate through this foreign country, it constitutes a very important statement about the common humanity of all human beings (see also *What is an animal?*, edited by T. Ingold). One of the strongest messages to come from this book is that the common assumption that a real interest in the past is exclusively the preserve of Western historians and archaeologists is totally misconceived. The acceptance of this message raises difficult questions about the archaeologists' assumption that they have automatic and prior rights to the material evidence of the past.

Who needs the past? makes several important points about the nature of literacy, a subject also discussed in some detail in *State and society* (edited by J. Gledhill, B. Bender & M. Larsen). Many of the claims, by anthropologists and others, that literacy marks a distinctive mode of thought, or at least facilitates the development of a new and different means of conceptualizing and 'anchoring' the past within time, appear to be dispelled by the accounts of the past presented by several of the authors in this book. There are fascinating glimpses of cultural parallelisms between such diverse situations as the Hadza of Tanzania and some of the varying social groups which make up the Britain of today. There is, in both, a binary conceptualization of the past into the recent past and the distant past, but it is also clear from the various contributions dealing with Australian Aboriginal cultures in this book that such a basic dichotomy does not exclude complex subdivisions of a time-perspective, and that the normal English short-hand of the Australian Aboriginal concept of 'the Dreamtime' is a caricature of the complexity and sophistication of the concept involved. It is also clear that whatever the similarities and differences of attitudes and conceptualizations of past time that there may be between cultures, they do not seem to be dependent on the facility to read and write.

Who needs the past? reveals, for instance, that Australian Aborigines and Portuguese peasants both categorize the past in somewhat similar ways, confirming that cyclic and linear models of time can, and do, co-exist in diverse cultures. This is an important addition to our understanding of views of the past, as it has usually been thought that cyclic concepts, which view the present as a re-embodiment of the past, were incompatible with linear ones, which view time as progress, or decline, from a 'golden age'. For example, contemporary East African hunter-gatherers and ancient Hindu texts both conceive of man's history as one of increasing cultural sophistication, whereas Australian Aborigines regard (and the Greeks of Homer's time regarded) the past as a prototype which the present strives to replicate. Personal reflection on the character of the past is also not unique to the West, but is documented in ancient Egypt and contemporary West Africa.

Who needs the past? clearly reveals that knowledge of the past is a political resource in many societies, and its control undoubtedly varies with the political structure of the community and with the level of the social hierarchy which is engaged in any dispute. It is not surprising, therefore, that the visible material remains of the past are also often highly valued, because they may often be the evident means of control of that past (see also *The meanings of things*, edited by I. Hodder). Archaeologists and anthropologists have often ignored the symbolism and value that archaeological material may hold for their host communities. A wide range of examples is documented in this book and they serve to stress the social context of the practice of archaeology itself. *Who needs the past?* shows that indigenous views about the past, whether from Britain or from the so-called Third or Fourth Worlds, are riddled with vested interests, partial experiences, and differing commitments depending on the particular point at issue. In some cases, as reported from Ecuador, the views of the 'same' past may be almost opposed, depending whether the interpreters are the Amerindians or their European conquerors, and yet both are fundamentally involved with 'Ecuadorian nationality'. For children in Britain, interest in the past may be formed and greatly influenced by their own past cultural experiences, whether by equating it with fictitious heroes and extinct animals or by running it together with relatively recent events of their own, or their parents', migrations. For British adults, interest in the past may be differently expressed depending on whether or not their own financial contribution to its preservation is involved. There is no doubt that for many, in whatever culture, reference to the past, where it is more than simply a token obeisance, is synonymous with tradition and conservatism. The young and the rebellious, in any culture, are likely to reject, or at least to ignore, the received version of the past, in the interests of a new future – whether for individual or national reasons (see also *The politics of the past*, edited by P. Gathercole & D. Lowenthal). They, in their turn, choose a version of the past which will bolster their claims to legitimacy and personal or group identity (see also *Conflict in the archaeology of living traditions*, edited by R. Layton).

In a strangely provocative way, *Who needs the past?* asks many of the questions which should be the basis of those national and regional pieces of legislation which form the basis of *Archaeological heritage management in the modern world* (edited by H. Cleere) but whose rationales are rarely presented to the public except in gross terms of 'world', 'national' or 'regional' importance. Such legislation is often conceived and implemented by those steeped in a Western tradition of archaeology with its own Western conceptualization of the past, and such legislation often lacks much, or any, regard for the complexities of the views of the past held by the very people who inhabit the countries or areas concerned. Whatever the merits or demerits of such practices, no-one who reads this book can continue to believe that non-Western societies typically live in a timeless world. In all cultures the value and importance given to the past and its remains depend on its significance for the present. As one of the Cameroon authors in the book puts it: 'There is no greater treasure for the modern man than to know his past well as a basis for assessing and understanding the future'.

P. J. Ucko
Southampton

Contents

Preface

Robert Layton, *Durham*

Apart from the Introduction, all but one of the chapters in this book are based on precirculated papers presented at the World Archaeological Congress in Southampton within the theme 'Archaeological "Objectivity" in Interpretation'. The chapter by Clunies Ross was commissioned after the Congress. The papers by Emmott and by Stone were contributions to the sessions on 'The Past in Education'. The remainder were contributions to the sessions on 'Mediations of the Past in Modern Europe', and 'Indigenous Perceptions of the Past'. Most have been revised by the authors in the light of discussion at the Congress, but they retain the style of the original versions. Only Anawak and Mununggurr were unable to attend the Congress.

Many people were involved in the initial organization of these sessions, and in disseminating advance information about the Congress to potential participants; the book is the result of collective effort by its contributors and the Congress organizers, including Peter Ucko, Jane Hubert, Robert MacKenzie, David Bellos, Olivia Harris and myself. I would particularly like to thank Olivia Harris and Daniel Ndagala for chairing discussion sessions during the Congress.

The passage quoted from *Ion*, from the Bacchae and other plays by Euripides, translated by Philip Vellacott (Penguin Classics, 1954) which appears on pages 125–6 is reproduced by permission of Penguin Books Ltd. Figure 7.1 was prepared by Julie Perlmutter, National Museum of Natural History, Smithsonian Institution, Washington, DC. The Royal Anthropological Institute has kindly given permission for the inclusion of Pina-Cabral's chapter, a longer version of which is published in *Man*, December 1987.

Recent developments

Several studies of oral history have recently been published, including Connerton (1989), Finnegan (1991) and Tonkin (1992). The conference proceedings edited by Tonkin include the papers by Hugh-Jones and Collard cited in the Introduction to this volume. The issue of collecting and interpreting the property of other cultures is debated in Greenfield (1989), McBryde (1985, 1988) and Messenger (1989). John Baines has asked me to note a new volume in German by Jan Assmann (Assmann 1992) and recommends Stock (1990).

A more fundamental question is posed by Swain, who argues that Native Australians conceive of being in terms of space, but not time. History is an alien construction to Native Australian thought which deals rather with 'rhythmed events' (Swain 1993, p. 19). While Swain's study breaks new ground in attempting to characterize Native Australian philosophy without resort to familiar Western categories, contributors to *Who needs the past?* provide case studies which challenge Swain's radical thesis.

It is undoubtedly the case that Western Colonization gives new significance to the pre-colonial past. In a project which parallels Jack Anawak's efforts to document Inuit settlement history described in this volume, the Beringian Heritage International Park of Alaska has relied on Gideon Barr, a Native elder, in its ethnoarchaeological study of reindeer herding and landscape history on the Seward and Chukotsa Peninsulas. Between the ages of 6 and 10, Barr lived in a Chukchi village, now being destroyed by rapid sea erosion. Barr collaborated with architects, ethnographers and archaeologists to ensure that the village was correctly visualized from the sea and provided details about the placement of dog yards, seal nets, skin boats and house construction. An appreciation of the early 20th-century reindeer herd management strategies described by Barr is assisting current studies of reindeer within the Park. The University of Alaska Fairbanks has produced a thirty-minute videotape narrated by Barr (Schaaf 1992). Similar projects have been undertaken by the Catabwa (Tippitt & Haire 1993) and Makah (Ledford 1993).

On the other hand, Antonio Males writes, updating his contribution to this volume, conflict over land has increased along the Andean corridor and in the region of the Amazon. Paramilitary groups have been created to support large landowners and, in the resulting confrontations between these groups and the indigenous people, indigenous leaders have been assassinated without their killers being brought to justice. The people of the Otavalo region continue to promote and reaffirm their culture and ethnic identity, but have to fight against the individualism and desire to accumulate wealth introduced by the dominant society. Indigenous organizations have responded under the umbrella of CONAIE, the Confederation of Indigenous Nationalities of Ecuador. In June 1990, he writes, a national uprising of indigenous peoples took place, in support of demands that the government give immediate attention to the acute social, economic and political problems of the Indian population.

'For more than a week the country was immobilized, the Indian communities closed all the main roads and made barricades along the Panamerican Highway . . . Ecuadorian society was shaken. After realizing the legitimacy and the justice of the Indian uprising, many of the non-Indian people showed solidarity and support towards the Indian cause.'

UNESCO has recently revised its criteria for the inclusion of sites on the World Heritage List, to include what it calls 'cultural landscapes', whether they be designed by humans or are the object of powerful religious, artistic or cultural associations, providing national governments can guarantee their protection (UNESCO 1993). The Tongariro National Park in New Zealand has already been accepted for the List under these new criteria, and the nomination of Uluru in Central Australia is currently under consideration. Unfortunately, the criteria are couched in terms of landscapes which represent 'stages' in history and cultural traditions which have disappeared; both reflecting an outmoded theory of cultural evolution as progress toward a (Western-defined) goal. The specification of criteria by which cultural landscapes are to be judged has, moreover, been accompanied by the removal of references to human agency from UNESCO's criteria for the Natural Heritage. This seems particularly unfortunate when it is increasingly recognized that 'the human presence . . . has always been part of the wilderness experience' (see Layton and Titchen, *in press* and US Department of the Interior 1993).

Probably the most controversial event to have occurred recently in Australia concerning the preservation of indigenous artefacts was the repainting of ancestral figures in the rock art of the Western Kimberleys. According to Mowaljarlai and Peck, who co-ordinated the project, young Ngarinyin people have had little chance to learn the traditions of their own culture 'because of European settlement of this part of the Kimberley. We have decided not to complain about this but we are doing our best to teach them' (Mowaljarlai & Peck 1987, p. 71). The Wadang Ngari community association obtained Community Employment Programme funds to repaint faded paintings, in the presence of an elder who told the stories of the place and showed the young people how to carry out the repainting. Despite reliable evidence that the retouching of such paintings is a continuous tradition (summarized in Layton 1992, p. 21), their initiative provoked an outcry among those who sought to appropriate the paintings as part of a 'national heritage'. In the words of one Australian anthropologist, the result was 'a "startling case" of "bad Aboriginal art" . . . producing a result claimed by some to be rather more like tea-towel kitsch than the original 5,000-year-old designs' (Michaels 1988, p. 63). A special session of the First Congress of the Australian Rock Art Research Association, held in Darwin in 1988, was given over to debating this event; David Mowaljarlai was among those delivering papers to the session (published as Ward 1992).

Byrne (1991, p. 275) points out that 'Heritage Management', as we understand it, is a Western concept and a product of the Enlightenment. Other cultures have different concepts of how to manage their heritage. He compares the Kimberley repaintings to the continual restoration and enlargement of the Chinese Confucian temple of Qufu; first constructed in 478 BC, but enlarged and rebuilt over fifty times since: 'Although the physical form may change, the spirit and purpose of the original is not only preserved as a continuity, but can be enhanced through the contributions of succeeding generations' (Byrne 1989, p. 275, quoting Wei and Aass 1989). Byrne's observations serve to remind us that the past is culturally conceived, and that even when highly valued, the appropriate form of respect will depend on cultural premises.

References

Assmann, J. 1992. *Das kulturelle Gedachtnis: Schrift, Erinnerung und politische Identitat in fruhen Hochkulturen.* Munich, C. H. Beck.

Byrne, D. 1991. Western hegemony in archaeological heritage management. *History and Anthropology* **5**, 269–76.

Connerton, P. 1989. *How societies remember.* Cambridge: Cambridge University Press.

Finnegan, R. 1991 *Oral traditions and the verbal arts: a guide to research practice.* London: Routledge.

Greenfield, J. (ed.) 1989. *The return of cultural treasures.* Cambridge: Cambridge University Press.

Layton, R. 1992. *Australian rock art, a new synthesis.* Cambridge, Cambridge University Press.

Layton, R. and S. Titchen, *in press.* Uluru: an outstanding Australian Aboriginal cultural landscape. To be published in H. Plachter (ed.) Proceedings of the International Expert Meeting 'Cultural landscapes of outstanding universal value'.

Ledford, J. 1993. A lifetime with the Makah collections. *Federal Archaeology Report* **6(2)**, 5–7. Washington, US National Parks Service.

McBryde, I. (ed.) 1985. *Who owns the past?* Melbourne: Oxford University Press.

McBryde, I. 1988. 'Spoiling the past?'. *The Cambridge Review*, **109(2301)**, 62–8.

Messenger, P. M. (ed.) 1989. *The ethics of collecting cultural property.* Albuquerque: University of New Mexico Press.

Michaels, E. 1988. Bad Aboriginal art. *Art and Text* **28**, 59–73. Paddington, New South Wales, City Art Institute.

Mowaljarlai, D. and C. Peck 1987. Ngarinyin cultural continuity: a project to teach the young people the culture including the repainting of Wandjina rock art sites. *Australian Aboriginal Studies* **1987(2)**, 71–8.

Schaaf, J. 1992. The Shared Beringian Heritage Program. *Federal Archaeology Report* **5(2)**, 1–3. Washington, US National Parks Service.

Stock, B. 1990. *Listening for the text: on the uses of the past.* Baltimore, John Hopkins University Press.

Swain, T. 1993. *A place for strangers.* Cambridge, Cambridge University Press.

Tippitt, V. A. and W. Hare 1993. Tradition and innovation. *Federal Archaeology Report* **6(2)**, 1, 6. Washington, US National Parks Service.

Tonkin, E. 1992. *Narrating our pasts: the social construction of oral history.* Cambridge: Cambridge University Press.

UNESCO 1993. Bureau of the World Heritage Committee, Seventeenth Session, 21–6 July 1993. Item 4 of the provisional agenda: examination of the revised version of the guidelines for the implementation of the Convention. WHC-93/Conf.001/2. Paris: United Nations Educational, Scientific and Cultural Organization.

US Department of the Interior 1993. *Archaeology in the wilderness.* Federal archaeology report **6(3)**.

Ward, G. (ed.) 1992 *Retouch: maintenance and conservation of Aboriginal rock art imagery.* Melbourne, Australian Rock Art Research Association, Occasional Publication No. 5.

Wei, C. and Aass, A. 1989. Heritage conservation: East and West. *Icomos Information*, **1989(3)**.

Introduction:
Who needs the past?

ROBERT LAYTON

It is not just archaeologists who value knowledge of the past. That is the message of this book, repeated by contributors from Europe, North and South America, Africa, India and Australia. 'I like roots. Plants don't grow well without them. People are the same' wrote a Southampton parent quoted by Emmott in Chapter 1. Mbunwe-Samba (Ch. 9) writes of West Africa 'Our present is a re-embodiment of the past for, although some values have changed and are still changing, the past is with us today'. Anawak (Ch. 2) writes that the harsh environment of the Inuit (Arctic Eskimo) demands 'actively practising the traditional skills and attitudes and coping mechanisms . . . these skills are only attained through incorporating the past into the present'. Pandey (Ch. 4) challenges the Western assumption that the study of prehistoric times in India was a British innovation. Contributors show that there are a number of reasons for attempting to preserve an accurate record of the past.

Such declarations are at variance with both Functionalist and Structuralist dogma in anthropology, and question the assumption that archaeologists have a privileged interest in the past's remains. The Functionalist approach is encapsulated in Malinowski's theory of myth. For Malinowski myth existed almost entirely to validate contemporary behaviour. Non-Western peoples are not given to reflecting on their past (Malinowski 1954, p. 144). On the contrary, myth 'is always made *ad hoc* to fulfil a certain sociological function' (*ibid.*, p. 125) which can be achieved equally well by historical fact, semi-historical legend and pure myth (*ibid.*, p. 126). Goody & Watt have perpetuated Malinowski's position in their recent work on literacy, writing that little distinction is made between myth and history in oral cultures (Goody & Watt 1968, p. 47), and that the selective retention of oral lore promotes the 'homeostatic organization of the cultural tradition' (*ibid.*, p. 30) – that is, a tendency to forget how the past differed from the present. The concept of homeostasis is repeated in Goody (1977), although there Goody concedes that the opposition of magic and myth to history and science is a simplistic one (*ibid.*, p. 148). Goody's approach has been comprehensively criticized by Street (1984) and his most recent work represents a further modification of Goody's original position (Goody 1987).

For Lévi-Strauss myth appears equally timeless, but for a different reason. The purpose of myth is to encapsulate enduring, culturally established cognitive oppositions such as incest versus exogamy, delayed versus immediate reciprocity, in particular imagery. These oppositions may equally well be represented in myth as possibilities which exist at one moment, or as possibilities which replace one another through time (for example, Lévi-Strauss 1973, p. 153).

Both Malinowski and Lévi-Strauss arrived at these positions for methodological reasons. Malinowski reacted against the earlier use of mythology to reconstruct a people's history, because there were generally insufficient means available to test such reconstructions. Indeed, he felt that there was some probability that Trobriand myths of origin accurately recorded events spanning three chiefly reigns, and that they might well contain information about successive waves of settlement on the Trobriand Islands over a much longer period (Malinowski 1954, pp. 117–25). However, he dismissed such speculation as 'a mental game, attractive and absorbing . . . but always remaining outside the field of observation and sound conclusion' (ibid., p. 125, cf. Henige 1982, Ch. 5). Lévi-Strauss is interested in elucidating the constant features of human cognition. For him the content of imagery in myth is less important than the structured thought it discloses. History, for Lévi-Strauss, can throw light only on the accidents that result in enduring cognitive structures acquiring a particular, contingent symbolic content (Lévi-Strauss 1973, pp. 474–5). Both assumptions demand critical scrutiny.

Had Malinowski and Lévi-Strauss been content to accept that their treatment of history was the result of limitations in their own particular methodology, rather than being inherent in the character of tribal society, no great harm would have been done. Were it possible to corroborate oral tradition through parallel written records or archaeological excavation, then Malinowski's objection would be unnecessary. Allen & Montell (1981, Ch. 4) have written a detailed defence of oral history, identifying a number of criteria for assessing its veracity. Lévi-Strauss, to be fair, presents a different view of history and exotic cultures elsewhere (Lévi-Strauss 1958). Of more immediate significance is Hugh-Jones' research in North-West Amazonia. Hugh-Jones (1987) concludes that myth and history constitute alternative ways of representing the past among the same people. White colonists figure in both; on the one hand, caught up in the structural oppositions of myth as emblems and, on the other hand, as individuals, whose presence is independently attested by documents, in oral history. Myth, argues Hugh-Jones, presents a static view and englobes the present. In myth, groups and categories of people are represented by single characters. History, on the other hand, depicts individuals and embodies the idea that human agency can change the state of affairs (compare Rappaport 1987). Sahlins argues for a different type of interaction between mythological structures and historical events in Hawaiian culture. He shows how, through the circumstances of his arrival, Captain Cook was identified with the deity Lono, and infers from chiefly genealogies that other, now legendary, figures may earlier have undergone the same identification. The narrative sequence of myth, and the interaction of its prototypical beings serves as a model, transposable to many different domains, of the correct relationships between things (Sahlins 1981, p. 13). However, contrary to Lévi-Strauss' view, myth did not merely swallow up historical events, since the colonial impact transformed the significance of many cultural practices (ibid., p. 43). Instead of reproducing itself, Hawaiian culture entered 'into a dialectic with practice' which resulted in radical change (ibid., p. 33). Gullick (1985, pp. 89–92) shows how some Carib Indian oral traditions concerning their wars with European colonists take on the structure of myth, but others retain valuable historical information (cf. Carrier 1987, Merlan 1978, Morphy & Morphy 1984). Goody (1977) and Ong (1982) would go further, arguing that history can only be kept lastingly distinct from myth in literate cultures, an assertion which will be considered later in this introduction, but which hinges in part on how the structure of historical analysis is defined.

Why is the past important?

The simple answer to this question is that, contrary to the implication of Functionalist and Structuralist models, social life takes place through time. Social interaction creates an accumulation of debt and credit, on the basis of which the current states of particular social relationships are evaluated. Beyond this, individual relationships are assessed within the framework of more generalized expectations and values embodied in a community's (more or less) shared culture, which comes into being and is transformed through usage. Were social life actually lived within an instantaneous slice out of time, then it would be without content or meaning. Recognition of this issue in theory has led to modifications in both the Functionalist and the Structuralist traditions. In social anthropology, static Functionalist accounts gave way to studies of the dynamics of exchange (for example, Kapferer 1976) and Marxist models of process (for example, Bloch 1975). In cultural anthropology, analysis of structure gave way to studies of performance (Bourdieu 1977, Ricoeur 1979). An accurate representation of the past, as it is perceived to bear on the present, is a critical element of all social life. It is its value which so often makes knowledge of the past a political resource. These developments in the theory of the social sciences have been synthesized by Giddens through the concept of structuration (for example, Giddens 1979, pp. 69–73). 'Every process of action is a production of something new, a fresh act; but at the same time all action exists in continuity with the past, which supplies the means of its initiation' (ibid., p. 70).

Among contributors to this book Chase (Ch. 14) directly addresses the relevance of Giddens' theory to his material. Raharijaona (Ch. 16) urges archaeologists not only to respect the validity of indigenous versions of history, but also to understand their role in the creation and affirmation of cultural identity. Williams & Manunggurr (Ch. 6) write similarly of time as a dimension in which social life is constituted. They criticize the assumption that, because Western society associates time with change, more stable social systems must somehow induce an unawareness of linear time. Such a view is found in Leach's (1961) essays on time. Leach drew attention to two forms in which the experience of events through time are perceived: as repetitive or as irreversible processes (ibid., p. 125). Although the view of time as something which repeats itself 'applies equally to Australian Aborigines, Ancient Greeks, and modern mathematical astronomers' (ibid., p. 126), certain modes for perceiving time, he argued, are characteristic of non-literate communities. 'Most primitive peoples', Leach contended, 'can have no feeling that the stars in their courses provide a fixed chronometer . . . on the contrary it is the year's round itself which provides the measure of time' (*ibid.*, p. 133). He concluded that ' "discontinuity of repeated contrasts" is probably the most elementary and primitive of all ways of regarding time' (*ibid.*, p. 134).

The danger here is that of setting up the kind of absolute dichotomy between 'us' and 'them' which Finnegan & Horton (1973, pp. 16–18) criticize. If 'we' possess certain traits, then 'they' – by definition – must lack them. If we are interested in history, other cultures must live in the present; if we pride our-selves on our objectivity, other cultures must be characterized by subjectivity (cf. *ibid.*, p. 30). Not only, as Finnegan & Horton point out, do such dichotomies obscure equally interesting differences between the diverse cultures in the 'other' category, such simplistic thinking tends to attribute opposed functions to oral art forms and written literature (Finnegan 1973, pp. 133–4). I will, however, indicate where I consider caution should be exercised in accepting indigenous historical accounts.

Undoubtedly one of the most interesting divisions within the diversity of non-Western societies is that between orality and literacy. Contributors to this book describe both types of culture, and consider the relevance of their tradi-tions to archaeological research. The distinction is one on which Goody (1977) and Ong (1982) have written in fascinating detail. However, both appear to under-estimate the significance of the past to members of oral cultures. Goody (1977, p. 91) argues that archives are a prerequisite for history, but goes on to suggest that their oral equivalent exists in the recitals of past events given by the spokesmen of Ashanti chiefs, which provide short summaries of the happenings in a certain reign (*ibid.*, p. 92). Ong is more dogmatic: 'literacy . . . is absolutely necessary for the development not only of science but also of history' (Ong 1982, p. 15). Oral culture exhibits 'lack of introspectivity, of analytic prowess . . . of a sense of difference between past and future' (*ibid.*, p. 30). Ong cites both Goody and Lévi-Strauss in support of his position (*ibid.*, pp. 46–9). It will be argued below that there are, indeed, differences between oral traditions and written histories, explicable in terms identified by Ong. However, this absolute distinction between historical consciousness and a timeless present overstates the case. Hobsbaum sees matters differently, arguing that since the Industrial Revolution, the past has in the West becomes increasingly *less* relevant as a model for human behaviour (Hobsbaum 1983, p. 11), a vacuum partly filled by the *largely new* phenomenon of 'inventing tradition' (*ibid.*, p. 4).

How is knowledge of the past structured?

The chapters of this book demonstrate that, contrary to Leach's inference, models of the structure of past events do not fit so easily into a simple contrast between 'primitive' and 'civilized', in which small-scale communities perceive the passage of events as repetitive while complex ones perceive a linear pro-gression. Correlations between the social order and knowledge of the past must be sought in other ways.

Phases of the past

Far from perceiving themselves as belonging to a changeless world people commonly distinguish between the recent past which lies within living memory and that more-distant past which preceded it. The Aboriginal communities of north Queensland described by Chase in Chapter 14 distinguish between *kuma* (the span of events witnessed by the speakers), *anthantnama* (a long time ago) and *yilamu* (the creation period). The Portuguese peasants studied by Pina-Cabral (Ch. 5) draw a line between *agora* (now), *antes* (before) and *antigamente* (ancient time). Analogous distinctions are recorded among the Hadza and Inuit in the contributions of Ndagala & Zengu (Ch. 3) and Anawak (Ch. 2).

Both complex and simple communities may be inclined to regard history as the decline from an initial order that those living in the present strive to replicate, or as a cumulative sequence of development. Hindu tradition, discussed by Pandey (Ch. 4) and Prasad (Ch. 12), depicts early mankind living without domesticated animals and plants, without towns or trade, and without the experience of pleasure or pain. After the onset of the seventh *manvaṇtara* conditions change; pleasure and pain are experienced, the landscape is ravaged and domestication becomes a necessity. As Ndagala & Zengu report in Chapter 3, the Hadza hunter–gatherers of East Africa similarly speak of the region's first inhabitants as giants who lacked fire and tools, but who killed animals without effort. In successive stages hunting became a necessity, tools and weapons were introduced, and the exchange of objects and marriage alliances were initiated. The concept of change as cumulative is therefore not the prerogative of literate cultures.

The Hadza paradigm is far removed from that of the Australian Aboriginal premise of a creation period, discussed by Williams & Mununggurr (Ch. 6), Chase (Ch. 14) and Clunies Ross (Ch. 13). *Yilamu* (see Chase) or *Wangarr* (Williams & Mununggurr) refers to the distant past, when the creator spirits established contemporary social customs, technology and the present landscape. Equally Sparkes (Ch. 10) describes how the heroic actions of the past provided a model against which current behaviour was judged in Ancient Greece: in the centuries that followed the collapse of Mycenaean culture, oral tradition looked back to a time when life was richer, and men were more courageous and possessed a taste for warfare and adventure. Even in classical times, heroes from the past provided prototypes for the evaluation of contemporary behaviour in the writing of Pindar, Aeschylus and others. However, while in Sparkes' words Greek epics 'were set in a timeless age with no connection with the present', the Australian Aboriginal creation period has both spiritual and material continuity with the present. Clunies Ross (Ch. 13) recounts discussion surrounding the production of a sand sculpture in ritual which makes these concepts clear. In Chapter 11 Baines deals with texts from the Old and Middle kingdoms of ancient Egypt. He presents a number of cases in which contemporary events are measured against the greater achievement of a prototypical past, and describes how later monuments were at times modelled so skilfully on earlier forms as to make their dating problematic.

Although the dominant framework for evaluating the past may take characteristic forms in one culture or another, this does not preclude variability among personal interpretations within a single cultural tradition; recognizing such variation is intrinsic to Giddens' theory of structuration. Variability is illustrated well by the Egyptian harpists' songs cited by Baines (Ch. 11), which 'display a private discourse about central values'. Both Emmott (Ch. 1) and Stone (Ch. 17) document a variety of interpretations of the past's significance in contemporary Britain, highlighted, as Stone points out, by conflicting ideas over the proper uses to which Stonehenge might be put in celebrating the past. It is important to recognize that personal interpretations are not the prerogative of complex societies. Ndagala & Zengu (Ch. 3) quote alternative accounts by Hadza men and women. Morphy has examined this phenomenon among the Yolngu, the subject of Chapter 6, by Williams & Mununggurr. Discussing how, out of a 'currency of meanings a multiplicity of more specific images can be constructed', Morphy (1984, p. 91) shows how individual Yolngu can construct their own metaphors, and experience private understandings of the re-enactment of ancestral songs, dances and paintings produced in the course of the funeral (see also Layton 1970, pp. 489–93).

Interpretations may change over time. Nwana (Ch. 15) refers to different assessments of traditional customs by young and old among the Bali-Nyonga. Is this the result of increasing Westernization, or a manifestation of the common attitude that the young show insufficient respect for traditional authority? Anawak (Ch. 2) notes that Inuit have come to value the remains of their past more intensely as outside pressure has been brought to bear on them by miners, drillers and archaeologists. Sparkes (Ch. 10) shows how Herodotus and Thucydides articulated a new attitude towards the past in classical Greek society. The last case is bound up with the effects of literacy discussed by Goody (1977, p. 28).

A number of the contributors also demonstrate that communities cannot be distinguished according to whether they perceive the passage of events through time as exclusively linear or cyclic. On the contrary, both of these models are found in early Hindu texts and coexist among the Páez Indians, the Yolngu, the Bali-Nyonga and the Portuguese peasants of Alto Minho. Rappaport (Ch. 7) writes of Páez historical narratives that, when integrated, they have a clear chronology and yet are also grouped in a different order according to the ritual calendar, in such a way that a number of events are said to have occurred at the winter or summer solstice. Williams & Mununggurr (Ch. 6) state that Yolngu frequently explain sequences of events in terms that express linear temporality, yet also relate events to a variety of cyclic timescales, including times of the day or night, and seasons. Nwana (Ch. 15) cites the traditional West African eight-day week. Pina-Cabral (Ch. 5) detects in the Alto-Minho model of past stages in society, a concept of the passing of linear time yet points to community rituals celebrated according to the annual cycle of saints' days, which restore moral order and deny the need for change. Probably the most impressive vision of grand cycles discussed here is that of Hindu chronology, through which Pandey (Ch. 4) and Prasad (Ch. 12) seek an independent record of the origins of domestication in India.

Hindu cosmology exemplifies the development of a literate philosophy. The *Rg Veda* are believed to have originated as unwritten hymns composed by priests in the second millenium BC, and to have been orally transmitted for over 3000 years. The *Purāṇas* and epics probably date to later Vedic times, from *c.* 900 BC onwards (Basham 1967, pp. 31–9). Belief in Prajapati, the primeval man sacrificed to create the universe, has probably persisted from the time of the *Rg Veda* (see texts cited by Prasad in Ch. 12). However, Basham is sceptical of the historical value of the epics and *purāṇas*, considering that they 'are so overlaid by the accretions of later centuries that no attempt at interpreting them historically has so far won general acceptance' (Basham 1967, p. 39). The brilliance of Indian mathematics, which included the invention of the concept of zero, was a later development (*ibid.*, p. 498). There is no good evidence that India had any regular system of recording the year of an event by dating in a definite era before the first century BC, and the earliest inscription recording the date by a system of nine digits and a zero, with place notations for the tens and hundreds, is dated to correspond to AD 595 (*ibid.*, pp. 495–7). The skills of dating thus systematized in literate form earlier oral traditions. Hindu philosophy developed a dazzling formulation of the duration of the cosmos. Its basic cycle is the *kalpa* or 'day of the Brahma', lasting 4320 million earthly years. Each 'night of Brahma' is equally long. Three hundred and sixty such days and nights constitute a 'year of Brahma', and his life spans a hundred such years, of which we are located in the 51st. Each *kalpa* is divided either into 14 secondary cycles called *manvantaras*, lasting 306 720 000 years, or 1000 *mahāyugas*. Basham (1967, p. 324) notes that these two modes of subdividing the *kalpa* are somewhat inconsistent, implying the literate synthesis of two distinct traditions. In each *manvantara* the world is recreated, while each *mahāyuga* is subdivided into four *yugas* (ages) which represent a progressive decline in morality, strength, stature, longevity and happiness. The *yuga* are named like the numbers on dice, and last as follows:

Kṛta	(1st) age :	4 800 years
Tretā	(2nd) age :	3 600 years
Dvāpara	(3rd) age :	2 400 years
Kali	(4th) age :	1 200 years

Basham (1967, pp. 40, 323) notes that the most recent *Kali Yuga* is traditionally held to have begun in either 3102 BC or 900 BC, although Prasad, in Chapter 12, prefers to equate the commencement of the *Kṛta Yuga* with 8508 BC.

Knowledge and the social order

Are there, then, ways in which concepts of the past, or the handling of knowledge about the past, correlate with the scale, type or complexity of a society's political organization?

The control of knowledge

One respect in which this may be so lies in the control over the transmission of knowledge about the past. Raharijaona (Ch. 16) describes how, among the Betsileo of Madagascar, it is the oldest males who have authority to speak about the past. However, they must speak in the presence of other knowledgeable people; inaccuracies might offend the ancestors and bring about social or physical harm. 'Oral traditions serve to define, preserve and valorize a group's identity and customs within a more englobing cultural context.' The archaeologist must respect local custom in his search for information. Among the Betsileo knowledge about the past is vested in the household, village or territory (cf. D'Azevedo 1982). In Classical Greece it was vested in the City State: dramatic performances took place before audiences numbering tens of thousands. Playwrights drew on shared traditions, but gave them a personal interpretation: 'slices from Homer's great banquets'.

The Betsileo forbid women from proclaiming knowledge about the past, on the grounds that marriage takes them from their natal village and thus fragments their local understanding. Among the Yolngu and Gidgingali of northern Australia this sexual and age-defined bias is more forcefully expressed. Ritual knowledge about the Creation Period is carefully monitored, but is vested in clans or individuals (see Clunies Ross in Ch. 13). Williams & Mununggurr write, in Chapter 6, that it would be impossible for one Yolngu individual, or the members of one clan, to be knowledgeable about all the Creation Heroes that crossed Yolngu country. The more important the Yolngu consider a category of knowledge to be, the more precisely they express rules of access to it. The most esoteric knowledge 'is held in the safest repository of all: inside the heads of the oldest clan leaders'. Such an approach to knowledge about the past imposes severe constraints on responsible anthropological research, for much of the data that the anthropologist might wish to publish, to advance the subject (and his or her career), is knowledge whose closed control is essential to Aboriginal politics. Publication would seriously threaten its status as a valued cultural commodity. The ancient Egyptian material reveals yet another permutation. Literacy was very restricted and the data discussed by Baines (Ch. 11) were the product of a limited élite.

Calibration of linear time

A second correlation between the form in which knowledge of the past is organized and a society's political structure is suggested by the mode of attaching concepts of linear time to shared experience.

A number of contributors record a distinction between the recent and the distant past. Clunies Ross (Ch. 13) draws out of the conversation with which her chapter opens, use of World War II as the dividing line between the long past and the recent past. She infers that other, more local, events could have played the same role in earlier periods. For the Aboriginal community studied by Clunies Ross, World War II had little local impact. A theme which runs through a number of the Third and Fourth World contributions, however, is the benchmark created by colonial impact. In north Queensland *kuma* (living memory) is separated from *anthantnama* (long time before) by the advent of White Australians. The Inuit for whom Anawak speaks (Ch. 2) distinguish the present from the recent past as the time since government-enforced settlement. For the Páez Indians the legendary *caciques* belong to colonial and pre-colonial times; recent political process to the Indians' struggle against the creole governments since independence from Spain. In such cases the distant past assumes particular significance as the source of a distinct cultural identity, whereas the recent past (or present) finds that identity encapsulated within a dominant society (cf. Collard 1987).

Further into the past, the degree of calibration is variable. Pina-Cabral found relatively little sense of history among the peasants of Alto Minho but, for the Otovalos, rebellions calibrate time from the Spanish conquest onwards (Ch. 5).

What particular needs lead people to record linear time? Pina-Cabral (Ch. 5) discovered a greater specifiable time-depth in the memories of land-owning householders (to whom genealogies were significant) than among the landless. Centralized political systems offer the reign of kings as the building blocks of a community's shared timescale. The Bali-Nyonga trace their history from the time they are said to have been driven south by the Fulani, through a royal genealogy. Ben-Amos, in her study of the art of Benin, notes a fundamental shift in modern Benin treatment of time from the founding of a Yoruba dynasty in about the 14th century. The earlier period 'is archaic and essentially mythological. Neither strict chronology nor the exact number of Kings is important. The second dynasty, in contrast, is founded on temporal duration and the activities, personalities, and innovations of nearly every oba (King) are remembered in lavish detail' (Ben-Amos 1980, p. 13). It is this dynasty which carries Benin through to the present. Ancient Egypt provided an exceptional example. Sparkes (Ch. 10) cites the incredulity of Egyptians when the Greek Hecataeus 'traced his genealogy and connected himself with a god sixteen generations back'. Egyptian priests declared, according to Herodotus, 'that three hundred and forty-one generations separate the first King of Egypt from the last I have mentioned'. They denied that anyone could have a divine ancestor.

Serial recording of years in Ancient Egypt was, writes Baines in Chapter 11, introduced for administrative purposes (cf. Goody 1977, p. 90). This should warn us against the facile assumption that non-literate or small-scale communities do not maintain a detailed chronology of the past because they lack the necessary cognitive skills. It is more likely that serial recording would serve no useful purpose. This point is elegantly discussed by Williams & Mununggurr (Ch. 6). Far from accurately reflecting the observation of celestial phenomena, attempts to subdivide the year into months and weeks are repeatedly confounded by their lack of correspondence with lunar cycles, etc. Strict divisions of the time in the Western world have social causes: the regularity of prayer in the medieval church, the control of the working day, and the synchronization of the movement of trains (cf. Leach 1961, p. 125). Aboriginal cultures have devised measurements of time that are appropriate to their tasks: the rhythm of ritual songs and the organization of ceremony. Yolngu have a numerical system based on multiples of five, which allows counting to 100: 'Of course, Yolngu can use these and other means to express time'.

The past and its material remains

Wherever the past is valued, this value imbues the past's material remains. Nwana (Ch. 15) refers to museums or culture houses which have been set up in the country of the Bali-Nyonga. He expresses the hope that artefacts found by local farmers will be stored there, and that school children will be taken to archaeological sites. Mbunwe-Samba (Ch. 9) writes that many chiefdoms in Cameroon have museums which predate the colonial period, and points out that the contents of such museums have been selected according to specifically African criteria. Anawak (Ch. 2) describes how valuable he found the experience of camping at old Inuit occupation sites, both to protect them and to explain their significance to his own children, and to local and foreign visitors. Sparkes (Ch. 10) suggests that during the Greek Dark Age ruined Mycenaean palaces upon hilltops provided a visible locus for the legends of princely society.

Yet what is considered a significant vestige of the past depends on indigenous concepts of human (or divine) agency. Archaeologists will be familiar with a progressively broadening conception of patterning in the archaeological record as the discipline has developed its understanding of stratification, of interaction between humans and the environment reflected in pollen frequencies, of pottery firing and thermoluminescence. The amateur with his metal-detector has a narrower concept of significant, or valuable, remains and, as Stone argues (Ch. 17), the fault for his narrow understanding lies in part with archaeology.

Members of other cultural traditions may consider features to be significant that conventional Western archaeology discounts. A marginal case is cited by Mbunwe-Samba (Ch. 9): a pile of stones standing by a river which records the flight of a defeated community. Although the sand sculpture discussed by Clunies Ross (Ch. 13) is reconstructed for each ceremonial performance, it is considered by the Gidjingali to be a legacy of the ancestral heroes.

There are particularly interesting parallels between the chapters by Pina-Cabral (Ch. 5) Rappaport (Ch. 7) and Williams & Mununggurr (Ch. 6) in their discussion of how the past is objectified in topography. The peasants of Alto Minho associate rock formations with the Moors who preceded Christians in the area. The Páez Indians articulate the history of their culture heroes through the association of personalities and events with mountains and lakes. Rappaport identifies three purposes which this serves: the creation of a mnemonic device which to some degree parallels the function of written records, the demarcation of political boundaries and 'a tangible link with the past, something that can be seen, touched and climbed, something that merges past with present'. The Yolngu landscape, write Williams & Mununggurr, 'is saturated with signs [of creator beings] that bear meanings that are still immensely important'.

The implications for archaeology are twofold. On the one hand, such instances illustrate the intrinsic importance, in any cultural tradition, of *signifiers*, tangible embodiments of shared values and ideas. As Durkheim wrote long ago, 'without symbols, social sentiments could have only a precarious existence' (Durkheim 1915, p. 231). A community's interest in the remains of the past is therefore unlikely to be casual. On the other hand, the particular values with which members of a culture imbue material evidence of the past may well predicate a different attitude from the archaeologist's. Williams & Mununggurr (Ch. 6) explain why it is that the Yolngu consider it 'inherently dangerous to disturb the earth or any of its features in a visible or lasting way'. This divergence has a vital impact on the conduct of archaeology with regard to human skeletons, an issue examined in another book in this *One World Archaeology* series, *Conflict in the archaeology of living traditions*.

Oral and literate transmission

Among the tangible remains of the past, written records occupy a special place. The transmission of both oral and written history relies on particular, culturally-acquired skills. Oral performances and written texts are therefore differently structured. Written lists, such as king lists, process information in a different way from spoken language (Goody 1977, p. 81, Ong 1982, p. 99). Attempts to learn such lists, or texts, word for word, result in characteristic patterns of recall (see Roediger & Crowder 1982, Rubin 1982). Whereas written history tends to be generalized and impersonal, orally communicated history is specific, intimate and personalized. It tends to crystallize around Great Men, even to the extent of displacing the original actors in favour of those who are more memorable (Allen & Montell 1981, pp. 18, 32, 37). Written history generally follows a rigorous serial chronology, oral history groups events around people, places and other key events (*ibid.*, p. 27). Although a narrative plot is a powerful mnemonic and necessarily concerned with a temporal sequence, it often has little to do with strict linear presentation (Ong 1982, pp. 141–7).

Oral memory is often not trained to achieve word-for-word recall of a putative original text. Rather, the narrative is actualized differently on each occasion with the aid of a store of elements the teller has learned. In their study of Yugoslavian oral epics, Parry and Lord identified two levels at which such repeated elements occurred. A *formula* is 'a group of words which is regularly employed under the same metrical conditions to express a given essential idea' (Lord 1960, p. 30); a *theme* is a type of event which occurs in many different songs. The particular formulae adopted, and the details with which themes are developed, can vary without affecting the 'story line' (Ong 1982, p. 59, cf. Mbiti 1966, pp. 26–7). Finnegan & Horton (1973, p. 55, cf. Goody 1977, p. 8) argue that even the profound structures Lévi-Strauss identified in myth may operate essentially as aids to recall. Dube (1982) and Colby & Cole (1973) showed that skill in retelling oral tales could be quantified, along the lines established by Parry and Lord, and measured.

Neither oral nor written traditions have a monopoly on objectivity. Oral tradition may show written records to be suspect, or vice versa (Henige 1982, pp. 71–2, Gullick 1985, Ch. 5). 'Orally communicated history is as subject to bias as written materials, such as newspaper editorials or accounts of military or economic conflicts penned by partisans' (Allen & Montell 1981, pp. 82–3). A striking example is cited by Males in Chapter 8. Contemporary documents may themselves be transcriptions of eye-witness accounts by a third party. Written texts may, like oral performances, be revised to suit current political exigencies (Goody 1977, p. 91). The crucial difference is that whereas oral performances are transient, written texts often survive to be reconsulted and reinterpreted (*ibid.*, pp. 76–8, Ong 1982, p. 67). Thus, transformations in a written historical tradition are, at least in theory, reversible, whereas discarded elements of an oral one are irrecoverable. The imperfect historical validity of orally-transmitted genealogies is the subject of extensive study (Bohannan 1958, Goody & Watt 1986, pp. 32–3, Henige 1982, p. 102). This criticism should be kept in mind when reading Nwana's Chapter 15. Kaberry noted that the origin legend of another Cameroon kingdom tended to telescope historical events (Kaberry 1957, p. 46) and this parallels the findings of research in Oceania reported by Henige (1982). However, it would be wrong to depict the oral transmission of knowledge as a game of Chinese Whispers – in other words a single, degenerating chain. Performances are generally public, and the tellers of oral narratives are likely to live in a milieu where many past performances can be recalled. The teller will construct his own mental field of variations, themes and elements within the given legend, from which selections are made to actualize any single performance, which is subject to public scrutiny and does not erase the memory of alternative realizations (Layton 1985, Morphy 1984, Street 1984). Goody's characterization of history should be considered with these points in mind: 'it is not only the existence of archives or the formalization of information that makes history possible, but the kind of critical attention that one can devote to the original documents and the comments of others, particularly when one can examine different versions side by side' (Goody 1977, p. 149). Although history is here defined as a product of literate cultures, the different strategies employed in transmitting an oral tradition do not necessarily imply a lack of concern for the character of the past. However, for archaeologists the practical difficulty remains that of distinguishing factual elements of the past from parables which serve equally to embody moral and political values. Henige comments 'there is an irony' in the use of genealogical material for dating historical events; 'When outside data show that oral records are accurate, they also render such oral records at least partly superfluous' (Henige 1982, p. 102).

Implications for archaeology

This introduction has argued against Malinowski's assertion that Third and Fourth World communities had no particular interest in their past. However, there remains a second proposition in Malinowski's argument: belief about the past is a tool wholly shaped to serve the political purposes of the present. Does this mean that indigenous histories cannot assist archaeological reconstruction?

The Malinowskian side of the coin is that knowledge about the past will only be transmitted if it retains significance in the present. Carr followed Collingwood in arguing that this was a feature of Western history (Carr 1961, pp. 21, 103). It is therefore not a trait specific to oral tradition, but Carr emphatically rejected the conclusion that there are no historical facts. Because a mountain appears to take on different shapes from different angles of vision, he argued, it does not follow that it has no shape at all, nor an infinity of shapes (ibid., p. 27).

A number of contributors to this book support this aspect of Malinowski's argument. Stone (Ch. 17) characterizes its extreme forms as the 'Flintstone' view of history. Chase (Ch. 14) writes that in north Queensland 'tradition' is flexible and interpretive, concerned with the authorization of contemporary routine. To this end 'quite recently created mythologies' may be as effective as those from a more distant past. Although Captain Cook's journal records that he passed this part of Australia outside the main Barrier Reef, Cook is emblematic of early White contact, and is therefore associated with its physical remains. Chase, Sutton and I, on a field-trip to the area south of that described in Chase's Chapter 14, were shown a cluster of large boulders on the coast identified as 'Captain Cook's bullets'. An archaeologist who failed to appreciate Cook's current role as a metonym of European discovery would be misled by such an attribution (cf. Allen & Montell 1981, pp. 38, 72–3, on 'migratory motifs'). Sparkes (Ch. 10) contrasts the attitude of classical Greek historians who set out to record 'what actually happened' with playwrights and lawyers who tailored accounts of the past to suit their present dramatic purposes: for them, 'slipshod detail counts for little provided that the points reach their target'. Mbunwe-Samba (Ch. 9) argues in favour of Malinowski's dictum that both the text and social context of folklore, as well as the time and circumstance of performance, are significant in assessing its content.

The other side of the coin is that if the past is of common concern as a validation of present behaviour, then there will be pressure within the community to ensure that knowledge is, by consensus, accurate. Raharijaona (Ch. 16) makes this point for the Betsileo, as do Williams & Mununggurr (Ch. 6) for the Yolngu.

The principal avenue to individual prestige among initiated men in Aboriginal Australia is the acquisition of a wider and deeper knowledge of religious traditions in one's region. To invent the location of sacred sites or associated knowledge would, in such a context, be comparable with forging banknotes in Western society. Elaborate checks and balances, which determine who may display knowledge and who must confirm its accuracy, make it virtually impossible to perpetuate a fraudulent claim to the significance of a site.

Durability of oral tradition

How durable may oral traditions be? There is no simple answer, both because it is difficult to obtain independent evidence of their age and because durability is likely to depend on context (cf. Henige 1982, pp. 102–5).

Firth was able to establish that oral traditions on Tikopia agreed 'very closely with the completely independent record of Dillon' made in 1825 (Firth 1961, p. 158). The Opies have shown, in a number of studies, that some European children's games have considerable antiquity (for example, Opie & Opie 1969, p. 122, 299) and that in some cases the accompanying songs or rhymes have remained similar for several centuries (for example, the discussion of counting-out rhymes – ibid., pp. 47–54).

Flood asserts unequivocally that knowledge of the distant past in Australia comes from two sources, 'archaeological evidence and Aboriginal oral traditions handed down from generation to generation' (Flood 1983, p. 15). As instances of the concordance between the two she cites the arrivals of ancestral populations from overseas (ibid., p. 29), the flooding of coastal areas after the last Ice Age (ibid., pp. 113, 133–4, 180), the hunting of giant marsupials (ibid., pp. 146–7) and the conversion of inland lakes to salt pans (ibid., p. 179).

When archaeological material is related, in tradition, to phases of a linear chronology there may be room for useful collaboration between archaeologist and local community. Raharijaona (Ch. 16) describes the concern of the Betsileo to correct spatial and orthographic mistakes on topographic maps, since Betsileo history is traced through site occupation and abandonment, as well as through a temporal sequence of events (cf. Allen & Montell 1981, p. 83). He notes that the relative importance attributed to sites by the archaeologist may be at variance with the local community's evaluation, and asks: what is it exactly that archaeologists have to offer to a cultural group already in possession of a sufficient and valid version of their own history? Chase (Ch. 14) writes that the contemporary Aboriginal knowledge of sites, group boundaries, seasonal and task-specific camp locations offer important insights toward the elucidation of pre-contact archaeological data. Nwana (Ch. 15) correlates the Bali-Nyonga oral historical account of their arrival and displacement of earlier inhabitants to changes in settlement pattern and the existence of abandoned hamlet sites. He further argues that only excavation can answer questions about the diet and technology of the previous inhabitants.

However, one stumbling block in the path of collaboration between the archaeologist and an indigenous community is likely to be that they have different interests in the events of the past. Hodder has discussed this problem with regard to African material culture. African indigenous history tends to focus on the role of small groups in the transformation of government. Such groups will not necessarily have much impact on aspects of past behaviour such as pottery decoration of interest to archaeology (Hodder 1978, pp. 5–7). However, Hodder is perhaps wrong to criticize oral or written tradition for its 'exaggeration' of the role played by the ancestors of ruling clans or lineages; from another perspective archaeologists might be accused of exaggerating the significance of pottery design! Hodder goes on to argue that the lack of success in correlating excavated artefacts with the records of contemporary non-material culture may arise because the archaeologist has been too simplistic in the analysis of variability and distribution, or that ethnographers have not asked the appropriate historical questions (*ibid.*, p. 24). These issues are addressed by contributors in Hodder (1978). There is a further problem, already mentioned. To the extent that history or archaeology imbues the past's remains with value, there may be conflict over the treatment of those remains where values differ. This issue is discussed more fully in another series book, *Conflict in the archaeology of living traditions* (see also Ucko 1983).

As Finnegan points out with regard to oral poetry, it would be as wrong to assume unthinkingly that oral traditions are necessarily long-lasting (Finnegan 1977, pp. 36–9) as it would be to assume they have no historical validity. Different genres of poetry are susceptible to the creation of new verses, ornamental embellishment, etc., to different degrees (*ibid.*, p. 57). Finnegan concludes that there is no universally valid theory of oral transmission: in some cases the performer may make no original contribution, in others the performer may be guilty of allowing gradual deterioration, in yet other traditions the performer actively strives to create a new version on each occasion (*ibid.*, p. 152). Clunies Ross has elsewhere analysed Aboriginal oral tradition as a distinctive genre (Clunies Ross 1983).

The *Iliad* is regarded as a good instance of oral poetry which allowed the performer to engage in creative reorganization (Finnegan, 1977, pp. 58–60), yet archaeological research has confirmed that some genuine records of Bronze Age warfare are contained in the *Iliad*, albeit interspersed with misunderstandings, for instance on the use of chariots, and the interpolation of later arms and techniques.

The same is clearly true of visual arts: some favour innovation, others favour adherence to strictly determined models (Layton 1981, Ch. 5). For instance, at a gross level Aboriginal totemic traditions lie at the opposite end of a continuum to Inuit shamanic art. Whereas Inuit valued masks depicting new, original shamanic visions, expressions of Aboriginal religion appear to be rigorously governed by set patterns laid down by the ancestral heroes. Yet, at a finer level of analysis it becomes clear that some aspects of Aboriginal religion are more open to creative interpretation than others, as Clunies Ross shows in Chapter 13. I have argued elsewhere that such creativity is necessitated by the structure of human culture: to narrate a myth, selections must be drawn from a pool of defined terms, and particular relationships must be highlighted (Layton 1985, cf. Hodder 1982, pp. 8, 10). Contrary to Clunies Ross (1983, pp. 17–18, 21), I do not regard the distinction between knowledge and performance as a trait distinctive of oral traditions. Written histories of the French Revolution or the Enclosure Acts are also performances peculiar to their authors.

Nwana (Ch. 15) shows that Bali-Nyonga chronology (with the proviso noted above) extends back to the early 19th century and has some independent confirmation in the records of European colonists. Benin king lists extend to the 14th century. Ancient Egyptian lists spanned three millenia. Flood (1983) is willing to accept Aboriginal oral tradition as a record of events extending back 7 000 years or more. However, here it is generally archaeology which elucidates oral tradition, rather than the other way round.

One of the greatest challenges to conventional Western thinking is presented by Pandey (Ch. 4) and Prasad (Ch. 12). Pandey cites an 11th century Indian king's treatise on the four divisions of human history in Hindu thought. He notes that details of prehistoric life are not always present in such works, but demonstrates a keen interest on the part of a King Bhoja in the use of stone tools. How Bhoja derived this information is problematic. Pandey emphasizes (pers. comm.) that it is 'not a record handed down from prehistoric times', but is rather likely to have been found in the Hindu sacred texts, the *Purāṇas*, which date from about 900 BC onwards. The *Purāṇas* almost certainly incorporate elements of an earlier oral tradition, but the content and age of that tradition are now irrecoverable. Prasad's thesis is more ambitious. Detailing the four stages of human history alluded to by Pandey, Prasad focuses on climatic fluctuations and their relationship to traditions concerning the origins of agriculture. Prasad presents detailed arguments for the view that the scale and direction of changes recorded in Hindu texts matches those established independently through archaeology. Such a claim must be critically considered in the light of the retrospective application of literate Hindu chronology to existing tradition. I have included this chapter in this book because, even if Prasad's hypothesis is proved wrong, the more substantial point remains, that medieval Hindu chronology was on a scale comparable with that now accepted in Western archaeology.

Symbolism and indigenous elucidation

The scope for collaboration between archaeology and indigenous communities goes well beyond issues of chronology and the identity of physical populations. The shift in archaeological theory represented by 'Symbolic Archaeology' renders information about indigenous culture central to archaeological explanation.

As long as culture was conceived to offer merely an extension of physiological adaptation, differences in local adaptations to similar environments might be considered mere 'noise'. Once it is accepted that cultural adaptations involve the construction of systems of meaning, the position changes. Systems of meaning are, to a large extent, a matter of social convention, not subject to environmental determinism. The distinctive historical trajectory of a community, and its internal dynamics, become critical to explaining its form at any moment. It should be added that this is, in a sense, equally true of physiological evolution, which frequently displays alternative pathways in adaptation to particular ecological niches. However, the more fundamental point with regard to cultural variability is that it is, to an important degree, produced by conventional ('arbitrary') encoding of information about the social and natural environment. Access to meaning may only be gained through ethnography. One example is provided in a recent public lecture on Australian prehistory by Mulvaney, who notes that the 'Nitchie' male buried in western New South Wales more than 6 000 years ago had lost his upper incisors during life. Mulvaney argues that: 'As a number of other burials in the Murray Valley dating from the last few thousand years also show a similar condition, it is reasonable to infer that it resulted from ritual tooth avulsion'. He adds, in support of his inference, 'This was the most widespread Australian initiation rite in 1788' (Mulvaney 1986, p. 54).

The Functionalist search for laws of cultural process, questioned by Evans-Pritchard in anthropology (Evans-Pritchard 1950 [1962]), is challenged again in archaeology by Hodder: 'there is more to culture than functions and activities. Behind functioning and doing there is a structure and content which has partly to be understood in its own terms' (Hodder 1982, p. 4). Similar social structures may be culturally coded in diverse ways (ibid., p. 10). For instance, respect for the deceased may be manifested in adornment of the body, as in the Nitchie case cited by Mulvaney, or in the dismemberment and crushing of the skeletal remains, a mortuary style eloquently portrayed in Waiting for Harry, a film of the ritual from which Clunies Ross' material (Ch. 13) is drawn. Raharijaona's (Ch. 16) observation that the Betsileo asked what non-locals could pretend to understand of their history, never mind contribute to it, is pertinent. Elsewhere Raharijaona further illustrates ways in which Betsileo knowledge aided the interpretation of, archaeological material:

> To each vestige, each household item, each object the Betsileo gave a name and details of its usage. . . . The temptation to attribute the same names to similar objects from different regions is likely to be mistaken since their context and symbolism may differ from one region to another (Raharijaona 1986, p. 6).

Yet, he warns, this method is limited by the extent of local 'collective memory'.

It may be that cyclic models of time encourage continuity in cultural symbolism, but no doubt the processes are more complex and have many causes.

Chase (Ch. 14) writes that Aboriginal knowledge of pre-colonial culture is greatest with regard to the conceptual system of sacred sites, the geographical boundaries of clan ritual responsibilities and linguistic divisions. Traditional artefacts are seen to belong to linguistic groups and, although many are no longer used for subsistence purposes, 'making a particular form of spear or spearthrower, or body decoration, is a current political statement' (cf. White & Modjeska in Hodder 1978). On the other hand, indigenous reconstructions of pre-colonial subsistence are less reliable because of greater European impact on this area of traditional life.

It would be tempting for the archaeologist to assume that he or she possesses privileged access into those periods of the past which appear to lie beyond local memory, but the contributions in this book should caution against that view. If the archaeologist suspects that the value of material remains for an indigenous community has changed over time, it should be recalled that much of the archaeologist's valued evidence of his or her own society's past was once deemed household refuse, and remains mere spoil for developers, to be removed before work can begin. The remains of the past on which archaeology relies are not, as a proponent of colonial expansion wrote of the natural resources in central Australia, 'dormant wealth lying about in almost criminal uselessness now' (Day 1916, cited in Layton 1986, p. 64). Just as the surface water and plant foods of central Australia were, in truth, essential subsistence resources for the Aboriginal people, so the remains of previous generations are frequently an essential cultural resource for living communities. Stone (Ch. 17) challenges archaeologists to beware of the assumption that their evaluation of the past is self-evident: 'The complacent attitude of archaeologists and their apparent disregard of the opinions of the rest of the population is a near-suicidal stance'. In Britain, of which Stone writes, the dilemma is a stark one, since the 'rest of the population' provide the funds on which archaeology depends. It would be sheer colonialism to assume that in the absence of such dependence indigenous values could be disregarded. Anawak (Ch. 2) writes of contemporary Inuit attitudes to archaeology, 'there is . . . a feeling of concern if Inuit organizations or elected Municipal Hamlet Councils are not consulted and see themselves to be directly involved or benefiting from such activity'.

Archaeologists are not the only people with a genuine interest in the past. Like others, the archaeologist's particular focus may be selective (pottery or kings?). As archaeological theories change, new aspects of variability assume significance. So, too, indigenous concepts of the past focus attention on particular aspects. Archaeologists are not alone in regarding knowledge of the past as a valuable commodity, nor are they immune to the politics which surround the control of any valued resource. However, Western archaeologists working in the Third and Fourth Worlds have a singular quality: they are members of a dominant political system. It should not surprise them that, where the aspirations of minority groups to retain a distinctive identity have been undermined by colonial encounters, such groups should attach particular significance to the remains of their pre-colonial heritage.

Acknowledgements

The advice of Charles Gullick, Elizabeth Nissan, Peter Ucko and Anthony Woodman, which helped me to prepare this introduction, is gratefully acknowledged.

References

Allen, B. and L. Montell 1981. *From memory to history: using oral sources in local historical research*. Nashville: American Association for State and Local History.
D'Azevedo, W. 1982. Tribal history in Liberia. In *Memory observed: remembering in natural concepts*, U. Neisser (ed.), 258–68. New York: Freeman.
Basham, A. L. 1967. *The Wonder that was India*. London: Fontana.
Ben-Amos, P. 1980. *The art of Benin*. London: Thames and Hudson.
Bohannan, L. 1958. Political aspects of Tiv social organization. In *Tribes without rulers*, J. Middleton and D. Tait (eds), 33–66. London: Routledge.
Bourdieu, P. 1977. *Outline of a theory of practice* (transl. R. Nice). Cambridge: Cambridge University Press.
Bloch, M. (ed.) 1975. *Marxist analyses and social anthropology*. London: Malaby.

Carr, E. H. 1961. *What is history?* Harmondsworth: Penguin.

Carrier, J. G. 1987. History and self-conception in Ponam society. *Man (new series)* 22, 111–31.

Clunies Ross, M. 1983. Modes of formal performance in societies without writing: the case of Aboriginal Australia. *Australian Aboriginal Studies* 1 (1), 16–26.

Colby, B. and M. Cole 1973. Culture, memory and narrative. In *Modes of thought: essays on thinking in Western and non-Western societies*, R. Finnegan and R. Horton (eds), 63–91. London: Faber.

Collard, A. 1987. Investigating 'social memory' in a Greek context. Paper presented at the Association of Social Anthropologists' Conference on History and Ethnicity, University of East Anglia, Easter.

Dube, E. F. 1982. Literacy, cultural familiarity, and 'intelligence' as determinants of story recall. In *Memory observed: remembering in natural concepts*, U. Neisser (ed.), 274–92. New York: Freeman.

Durkheim, E. 1915. *The elementary forms of the religious life* (transl. J. W. Swain). London: Allen & Unwin.

Evans-Pritchard, E. E. 1962. Social anthropology: past and present. In *Essays in social anthropology*, E. E. Evans-Pritchard (ed.), 13–28. London: Faber. (Reprint of 1950 Marrett Lecture.)

Finnegan, R. 1973. Literacy versus non-literacy: the great divide? Some comments on the significance of 'literature' in non-literate cultures. In *Modes of thought: essays on thinking in Western and non-Western societies*, R. Finnegan and R. Horton (eds), 112–44. London: Faber.

Finnegan, R. 1977. *Oral poetry*. Cambridge: Cambridge University Press.

Finnegan, R. and R. Horton 1973. Introduction. In *Modes of thought: essays on thinking in Western and non-Western societies*, R. Finnegan and R. Horton (eds), 13–62. London: Faber.

Firth, R. 1961. *History and traditions of Tikopia*. Wellington: Polynesian Society.

Flood, J. 1983. *Archaeology of the dreamtime*. London: Collins.

Giddens, A. 1979. *Central problems in social theory: action, structure and contradiction in social analysis*. London: Macmillan.

Goody, J. 1977. *The domestication of the savage mind*. Cambridge: Cambridge University Press.

Goody, J. 1987. *The interface between the written and the oral*. Cambridge: Cambridge University Press.

Goody, J. and I. Watt 1968. The consequences of literacy. In *Literacy in traditional societies*, J. Goody (ed.), 27–68. Cambridge: Cambridge University Press. (Paper first published 1963.)

Gullick, C.J.M.R. 1985. *Myths of a minority*. Assen: Van Gorcum.

Henige, D. 1982. *Oral historiography*. Harlow: Longman.

Hobsbaum, E. 1983. Introduction: inventing traditions. In *The invention of tradition*, E. Hobsbaum and T. Ranger (eds), 1–14. Cambridge: Cambridge University Press.

Hodder, I. 1978. Simple correlations between material culture and society: a review. In *The spatial organization of culture*, I. Hodder (ed.), 3–24. London: Duckworth.

Hodder, I. 1982. *Symbols in action*. Cambridge: Cambridge University Press.

Hugh-Jones, S. 1987. Varieties of history in a non-literate society. Paper presented to the Association of Social Anthropologists' Conference on History and Ethnicity, University of East Anglia, Easter.

Kaberry, P. K. 1957. Myth and ritual: some recent theories. *Bulletin of Institute of Classical Studies, University of London* 4, 42–54.

Kapferer, B. (ed.) 1976. *Transaction and meaning*. London: Tavistock.

Layton, R. 1970. Myth as language in Aboriginal Arnhem Land. *Man (new series)* **5**, 483–97.

Layton, R. 1981. *The anthropology of art*. St Albans: Granada.

Layton, R. 1985. The cultural context of hunter–gatherer rock art. *Man (new series)* **21**, 18–33.

Layton, R. 1986. *Uluru: an Aboriginal history of Ayers Rock*. Canberra: Australian Institute of Aboriginal Studies.

Leach, E. R. 1961. Two essays concerning the symbolic representation of time. In *Re-thinking anthropology*, E. R. Leach (ed.), 124–36. London: Athlone.

Lévi-Strauss, C. 1958. *Race and history*. Paris: Unesco.

Lévi-Strauss, C. 1973. *From honey to ashes* (transl. J. Weightman and D. Weightman). New York: Harper.

Lord, A. B. 1960. *The singer of tales*. Cambridge, Massachusetts: Harvard University Press.

Malinowski, B. 1954. Myth in primitive psychology. In *Magic, science and religion*, B. Malinowski (ed.), 93–148. New York: Doubleday.

Mbiti, J. S. 1966. *Akamba stories*. Oxford: Clarendon Press.

Merlan, F. 1978. 'Making people quiet' in the pastoral north: reminiscences of Elsey Station. *Aboriginal History* **2**, 70–106.

Morphy, H. 1984. *Journey to the crocodile's nest*. Canberra: Australian Institute of Aboriginal Studies.

Morphy, H. and F. Morphy 1984. The 'myths' of Ngalakan history: ideology and images of the past in northern Australia. *Man (new series)* **19**, 459–78.

Mulvaney, J. 1986. 'A sense of making history': Australian Aboriginal studies 1961–1986. *Australian Aboriginal Studies* **4(2)**, 48–56.

Ong, W. J. 1982. *Orality and literacy: the technologizing of the World*. London: Methuen.

Opie, I. and P. Opie 1969. *Children's games in street and playground*. Oxford: Oxford University Press.

Raharijaona, V. 1986. Archéologie et traditions orales dans la région de Mitongoa/ Andrainjato (pays Betsileo-Madagascar). In *Archaeological 'objectivity' in interpretation*. World Archaeological Congress, vol. 3 (mimeo).

Rappaport, J. 1987. Mythic images, historical thought, and printed texts: the Páez and the written word. *Journal of Anthropological Research* **43**, 43–61.

Ricoeur, P. 1979. The model of the text: meaningful action considered as a text. In *Interpretive social science, a reader*, P. Rabinow and W. M. Sullivan (eds), 73–101. Berkeley: University of California Press.

Roediger, H. L. and R. G. Crowder 1982. A serial position effect in recall of United States presidents. In *Memory observed: remembering in natural contexts*, U. Neisser (ed.), 230–7. New York: Freeman.

Rubin, D. C. 1982. Very long-term memory for prose and verse. In *Memory observed: remembering in natural contexts*, U. Neisser (ed.), 299–310. New York: Freeman.

Sahlins, M. 1981. *Historical metaphors and mythical realities: structure in the early history of the Sandwich Islands Kingdom*. Michigan: Michigan University Press.

Ucko, P. J. 1983. The politics of the indigenous minority. *Journal of the Biosocial Society Supplement* **8**, 25–40.

1 A child's perspective on the past: influences of home, media and school

KATHY EMMOTT

The past is what all people build their present and future on; without this they sit in a void waiting to reclaim their history, suspended in a bottomless pit

(Garrison 1986, p. 1).

Our image of the present, our consciousness of ourselves and other peoples is founded on our knowledge of the past. This knowledge reflects the history we are taught as children. As Ferro points out: 'This history marks us for life' (Ferro 1986, p. ix).

In the 1970s educationalists and politicians started to talk about education for 'this country's multicultural society'. Has the past decade seen a radical shift towards multicultural education? Have elements of multicultural education been introduced into teaching about the past? What do children learn about the past of other countries at school, and what do they and their parents think about multicultural education? Do children from other cultures feel cut off from their history and culture if it remains invalidated and undervalued by the host society? What are the factors which mould children's perceptions of prehistory, history and archaeology, and do their perceptions vary from culture to culture? These are just some of the questions to which this chapter is devoted.

Definition of multicultural education

Multicultural education is a term which is open to a variety of interpretations. To some, introducing multicultural education merely involves adding a few new lessons about Asia, Africa and the Caribbean to the old curriculum. Others have interpreted multicultural education as a means of providing a special curriculum for 'ethnic minority' children. A broader and more wide-ranging interpretation is that multicultural education recognizes and celebrates the cultural diversity of our modern society by including the study of both 'host' and 'minority' cultures in the school curriculum, and treating them with equal respect and seriousness. This last view was endorsed by the Home Affairs Committee (1981, p. xvi) and the Rampton Committee (1981, p. 34), and it is the definition adopted in this chapter. However, some educationalists have expressed reservations that equal treatment of all cultures is virtually impossible, due to the unequal power relations within society (Sarap 1986, pp. 17–18).

One of the aims of the survey reported here was to ascertain whether learning more about other cultures would be of benefit in the context of the Britain of today, where many people have unrealistic views of the past and present, and where racial attacks are happening increasingly. 'British' society has long cherished a tolerant, just and humane image which is contradicted by the facts of racial discrimination and attacks (Fryer 1984, p. 387).

If the education system gave 'British' people a more thorough understanding of the mixed nature of 'British' culture, the normality of human migration from the dawn of time, and the historical background to migration, then it could have a positive effect on racial attitudes.

Swann observes

> The diversity of British society today and the interdependence of the global community also has clear implications for the teaching of history. . . . A global perspective to the teaching of history can help to counter and over-come the negative stereotypes of ethnic groups which lie at the heart of racism
>
> (Swann 1985, p. 330).

Survey procedure

This survey is intended to enlarge on Suffield's (1986) work, which involved questioning 40 children in the 11 to 14 age-group and their parents from four religio-cultural groups: Hindus, Moslems, Chinese and 'English'. It involved 117 children from six schools. The schools were selected, from local knowledge, to include a range of social class and ethnic composition. The children were in the 10 to 12 age-group, and were interviewed individually for about 30 minutes. All of the interviews were conducted in an informal conversational manner, and they were taped to form an archive.

This chapter concentrates on the findings from the children's questionnaire, and includes some of their parents' comments (see key to abbreviations at the end of the chapter).

Terms relating to nationality

The selection of terms referring to race and nationality is fraught with problems. Here, children from white 'Anglo-Saxon' families are referred to as 'British', and children whose parents originated in other countries are referred to as 'ethnic minority' children. The term 'British' was chosen instead of 'English', as used by Suffield (1986), because the sample included small numbers of Scots (1), Irish (2) and Welsh (2). A few 'European' children (one each from Norway,

Hungary, Bulgaria and Poland) were included in this category because their numbers were too small for effective statistical comparison.

All of these terms are unsatisfactory, but have been used in the absence of other suitable 'umbrella' words. The distinction is drawn only for the sake of comparison, and is not meant to cast doubt on any person's right to British nationality.

The composition of the sample

Of the children, 91% were born in Britain: 66% were 'British' and 22% were 'Asian', which included children born in Bangladesh, India, Kenya, Pakistan and Mauritius, 3.4% (4) were Greek Cypriot and 2.5% (3) were classed as Afro-Caribbean, consisting of one each from Nigeria, St Vincent and Ghana, 2.5% were Arab (1 Lebanese, 1 Saudi-Arabian and 1 Iraqi), 1 child was Iranian and 4% (5) were of mixed race.

For statistical purposes, ethnic origins were classified as:

Group 1	'Asian'
Group 2	Afro-Caribbean
Group 3	'British'
Group 4	Arab
Group 5	Greek-Cypriot
Group 6	Iranian
Group 7	Mixed race

The ethnic minority composition of the school classes varied quite significantly (from 83.3% in a class to 23.4% in a class), which made it possible to examine whether this affected the teaching content. All of the classes had some proportion of 'ethnic minority' children. The religions of the sample included Anglican, Roman Catholic, Greek Orthodox, Sikh, Hindu and Moslem, with one-third professing to have no religion. Social class was determined by assessing the school's location, based on a multidimensional scaling analysis of the City of Southampton (Mar Molinero & Leyland 1986). As this was not assessed for each individual, it can only be taken as a broad generalization.

Findings of the survey

Definitions

The terms 'prehistory', 'history' and 'archaeology' are used throughout this chapter and require some definition. The conventional division between history and prehistory on the basis of the widespread introduction of writing has been used. 'Archaeology' is defined as the study of the material remains of the past.

In order to ascertain whether their personal definitions of these terms were similar to those given above, both the children and the parents were asked to explain what prehistory, history and archaeology were. Of the children, 47% stated that they did not know the meaning of these terms. This question, involving such a series of long words, may have proved rather intimidating for some who may have plumped for the 'Don't know' alternative rather than struggle with the words. History did not feature as a subject heading in the curricula of any of the classes surveyed; instead the children were given projects on such themes as 'clothes' or 'transport', in which history played some part. 'Correct' responses to this question were taken as those which most closely approximated to the definitions given above. Other responses were encouraged and noted. After this question the above definitions were explained to ensure that the children understood what we meant by these terms.

History (53.8%) and then archaeology (47%) were the most familiar terms to the whole sample. Many children associated archaeology with digging for and finding ancient bones – usually dinosaur bones – and treasure.

According to one child, archaeologists reflected their subject, for, he remarked,

'All archaeologists are 60 years old' (57.B.*3).

Another believed that

'Archaeologists are "poshish" ' (84.B.*3).

'British' children were more confident about these terms, for 49.4% gave the 'correct' definition of history, as opposed to 30% of the other ethnic groups; 44% to archaeology, in contrast with 35%; and 16.85% to prehistory, as opposed to 10%. Archaeology was most familiar as a term to the 'ethnic minority' children (35%). One class, consisting of a large number of 'ethnic minority' children, had visited York Buildings excavation with the City Museums Education Officer, and many of the recent digs in Southampton have been located in the inner city area of St Mary's, where there is a large concentration of 'ethnic minorities'. It was the distinction between prehistory and history which caused the most confusion to the whole sample. Having decided that history was the past, some found it difficult to conceive of the place of prehistory, to the extent that one even thought it must be the future. Others expressed the belief that prehistory was a very, very long time ago.

The parents generally thought of history as a school subject, and expressed reservations about their ability to answer the questions because they could not remember any dates. Dates and history seemed to be synonymous for some parents, who felt unsure of the validity of their comments without them. This probably reflects the emphasis on dates in their schooling. In contrast, the children did not mention dates at all.

History was often conceived of as remote in time and significance:

'When you said "history" I thought you meant 600, 700, 800 years ago sort of time' (84.B.*3).

Of the children, 93% chose the 'Long time ago' alternative from a checklist on history, while 59% thought it involved '10 years ago' and 32% 'what is happening now' (see Table 1.1, below). A few children pointed out that the past had little relevance to them:

'I don't see how it could help you nowadays. Nowadays is so different' (90.B.*3).

'You're in this world now. The past is gone' (39.B.*3).

Whose history did they think it was? Nearly 80% selected 'the lives of kings, queens and powerful people', while 64% felt it involved ordinary men and women. Responses showed that history is often seen as the preserve of the élite,

'It seems to be in books. It's more about politics, kings and queens and battles' (P. 122).

While analysing the choice of alternatives from the checklist (see Table 1.1, below) it should be noted that these categories were not treated separately, i.e. kings, queens and powerful people were not differentiated and, although men and women were given subsections, the children always gave the same response to both. The part of the question about women was regarded as an afterthought by the children. A subsequent question revealed that few children could name more than two women in history (see Table 1.2), and the ones most frequently mentioned were Joan of Arc, various queens and Florence Nightingale. Most of the children from one particular school mentioned Mary Seacole, a black nurse in the Crimean War, whose life formed part of their curriculum. When asked this question one boy shook his head thoughtfully and replied:

'No, there were only men' (23.B.*1).

Girls recorded far more 'Don't know' answers in the questionnaire than boys did, which could be due to a sense of lack of involvement in history. Such hesitance or ignorance may be a consequence of the virtual invisibility of women in most school textbooks and curricula. Reading many history books one could be forgiven for thinking that women had no role to play in the past, apart from cooking or raising children.
Scott comments:

Even among highly qualified history scholars the centrality of women in history is not yet accepted. Since school texts so frequently seem to depend on the received knowledge of at least one intellectual generation

Table 1.1 Responses to the question: What does history include? (Choose any number of alternatives from a checklist.)

Items specified	Percentage of positive answers	Percentage of all boys	Percentage of all girls	Percentage of all ethnic groups 1, 2 and 4	Percentage of all 'British'	Percentage of all middle class	Percentage of all working class	Percentage of all mixed class
a long time ago	93.2	93.5	92.7	96	93.5	97.4	93.3	84.2
ten years ago	59	56.4	61.8	65	62.3	57.9	58.3	63.2
the present	32.5	37	27.2	36	36.4	39.5	28.3	31.6
the lives of ordinary men	64.9	66.1	63.6	74.6	57.1	63.2	66.7	63.2
the lives of ordinary women	64.1	67.7	60	75.9	54.5	63.2	66.7	57.9
the lives of kings, queens and powerful people	79.5	83.8	74.5	96	72.7	84.2	76.7	78.9
wars	76.1	80.6	70.9	84	72.7	73.7	80	68.4
Total number questioned	117	62	55	40	77	38	60	19

before them, children will be condemned for some time to reading about the exploits of men. . . . More social history is being taught but examination syllabuses still focus on political and economic history which conventionally excludes women. I looked at several texts directed at the upper half of secondary schools. . . . Typical was a view of the past which left women invisible. A book on the first world war made no mention of women's contribution to the war effort at home or abroad (Hoare 1973) . . . There are modern history books which ostensibly focus on periods of great social change but the reader could have been forgiven for reaching the conclusion that there have been no social changes which have involved/ affected women

(in Spender & Sarah 1980, p. 112).

And she concludes that:

What is required in history, if girls are to have equal opportunity with boys in school, is both a full investigation and exposure of women's past – plus an integration of women and their contribution to history within existing accounts. The two sexes are not experiencing equal educational opportunity while the only version of the past they are presented with looks almost exclusively at males and has been recorded almost exclusively by males

(in Spender & Sarah 1980, p. 113).

A dichotomy emerged between what was thought of as 'history' and 'the past', for the former was often perceived as an academic subject and the latter as 'our roots and background'. The term 'the past' was used in many of the questions for simplicity and in order to express the concept in its widest sense. Respondents were asked, in separate questions, to attribute values to 'learning about the past' in order to ascertain the level of significance placed on it. 'Interesting', 'important' and 'useful' were classed as positive responses and 'useless', 'boring' and 'don't know' were considered negative. Some gave it a mixed set of values and these were classed as negative in the overall total. Ninety-three per cent thought it 'interesting', although some pointed out it could also be 'boring', depending on the content and the way in which it was communicated: 83% described it as 'useful' and 77% as 'important', although quite a few found it hard to supply any reasons. The explanations given for the positive values overlapped to a certain extent but 'functional' reasons were more often attributed to 'important' and 'useful'. Vocationally it was often given a low priority:

'The sciences are more important, like computer sciences. In the modern world people use computers more. You need maths for that' (58.G.*3).

Although 17% felt it could lead to success in examinations and career opportunities, one child commented:

'I used to want to be an archaeologist but now I know they don't get paid very much' (11.G.*3).

Others thought it contributed to their general knowledge:

'It makes you more brainier' (17.B.*3).

'It gives you more of an education – to learn – makes you feel like you're part of it' (40.B.*3).

This sense of personal involvement, the past as our 'roots', was quite commonly expressed by both parents and children:

'I like roots. Plants don't grow well without them. People are the same' (P.120.*3).

'You should know about it. It's part of your family a long time ago' (56.G.*4).

'It helps you to understand yourself better – your surroundings and to understand the present' (83.G.*3).

It was learning about the past as a contribution to a sense of background and identity that was felt to be its greatest relevance to the contemporary world:

'It has a lot of bearing on our lives. "History repeats itself" is true, it's not just a glib phrase. Now things change so rapidly' (P.124.*3).

Slightly more 'ethnic minority' children thought learning about the past was 'interesting' and 'important', and more 'British' children described it as 'boring'.

Conceptions of the past

What conceptions do children have of the past? How much does their view of the present determine these images, and vice versa?

In order to explore these conceptions the questionnaire included a section on 'Your ideas of the past'. The children were asked whether dinosaurs and people lived at the same time, if early people were as clever as people today, which countries are powerful now, and those that were in the past; and what makes a country powerful.

Only 20% believed that dinosaurs and people coexisted, including one who stated confidently:

'In the Iron Age they killed dinosaurs for food. My teacher told me that' (35.B.*3).

The fact that his teacher gave him this idea may or may not be accurate, but it became clear during the course of the survey that many children have a hazy and confused picture of the past. It appears from the survey that mental conceptions of the past are often formed by impressions rather than by clear details, unless an individual is particularly interested in a specific era. Films like 'One Million Years BC' – which features Raquel Welch dressed in skimpy skins, pursued by pterodactyls – and TV cartoons such as 'The Flintstones' and 'Journey to the Centre of the Earth' give the impression that dinosaurs and humans lived side by side. Considering the popularity of dinosaurs and cartoons with children, this type of film is one probable source of this idea. Twice as many boys (29%) as girls (14.5%) subscribed to this belief, suggesting that those kind of programmes are more popular with boys.

Opinion was divided over the question of early people's intelligence. No guidance or prompting was given about the definition of 'cleverness', and generally the children interpreted 'clever' as denoting the possession of knowledge and technology.

Nearly 19% thought that early people were cleverer than their modern equivalents, and their comments showed an appreciation of the skills and inventiveness displayed by early human society:

'These days we learn things from books. We don't learn how to do things ourselves like they did' (89.G.*3).

'Some people say that they weren't civilized – well they were, but in a different way. They were cleverer because they didn't have machines to help them' (10.G.*1).

One child illustrated the difficulties of looking at the past through modern eyes:

'It was hard for them. They had to learn how to live without electricity' (34.B.*1).

However, 41% believed that early people were less clever or stupid, due to lack of knowledge, technology or education:

'They had no-one to teach them or help them to find out' (83.G.*3).

'They didn't know much – they only knew how to keep themselves alive' (117.B.*7).

This educational deficiency was viewed somewhat differently by another child, who said, enviously:

'They didn't have school in the Iron Age. I think they were lucky' (57.B.*3).

Responses revealed that most children viewed history as a linear progression from a cold, bleak, disadvantaged past to a comfortable, technologically sophisticated present,

'They were less clever because they used stone axes and today we use chain saws' (91.B.*3).

Some thought it important to learn about the past precisely because

'You realize how lucky you are' (95.G.*3).

The influence of such values has also led to a sense of complacency about the 'superiority' of Western life in the present. This emerged in some of the comments about Third World countries, which were viewed disparagingly because of a lack of material luxuries:

'I'm very proud to be British – other countries have so much problems. England has more' [i.e. a better standard of living] 'it's a lovely country' (76.G.*3).

The prevalence of this attitude may have affected some 'ethnic minority' children's views of their own cultures and countries of origin. An 'Asian' child who was born in Britain talked about his visit to India:

'It is so poor there. They don't have televisions. I wouldn't like to live there' (21.B.*1).

However, one 'British' child was concerned that no progress has been made at all:

'They were the same 'cos we haven't got any further. . . . They were just as stupid as we are . . . but we've come on more about knowing more, but we're not really getting anywhere. I mean like we still hit each other with things, even though we're hitting each other with harder things, we're still hitting each other. We haven't done anything really' (38.B.*3).

The theme of warfare recurred many times in the interviews. Seventy-six per cent believed that wars played an important part in history (Table 1.1), and some commented:

'It is history, you can't get history without wars' (25.G.*1).

'Wars – that's the worst part of history' (58.G.*3).

Bombs and weapons were cited by 59.8% as the instruments of power, and their comments revealed that many feel that the world's future is precarious:

Table 1.2 Responses to the question: Can you tell me the names of any important women in the past?

No. known	Percentage of total	Percentage of all boys	Percentage of all girls	Percentage of all ethnic group 1	Percentage of all ethnic group 2	Percentage of all ethnic group 3	Percentage of all ethnic groups 4, 5, 6 and 7
0	29.1	29.0	29.0	26.9	0	32.4	22.2
1	29.9	27.4	32.7	42.3	0	25.9	44.4
2	20.5	20.9	20.0	7.6	33.3	22.0	44.4
3	15.4	17.7	12.7	23.0	33.3	12.9	11
4+	5.1	4.8	5.4		33.3	6.4	0
Total number questioned	117	62	55	26	3	77	9

'Today they think it's weapons – Reagan and Gorbachov – they think the more weapons the better chance of survival – but they'll just blow everyone up one day' (91.B.*3).

'They – the US – think that just because they've got nuclear weapons they are powerful. In fact they're just as weak as the rest of us' (89.G.*3).

The children chose these categories without any suggestions from the interviewers. It emerged that twice as many boys as girls thought that weapons made countries powerful, and 10% more boys than girls chose the 'history includes war' alternative, possibly reflecting their greater exposure to war toys, cartoons and films. The other power bases mentioned were good leaders, money and size. A very few cited knowledge and wisdom. One spoke with relish of colonial power:

'[If we had] a good Prime Minister, a good king and queen and a big empire, that makes us just right, then we'd be really powerful' (39.B.*3).

Another said that love was important:

'The army thinks it's weapons . . . but it's probably love for each other. If we didn't have love people would be hitting each other all the time' (40.B.*3).

If children's views of the past and present are dominated by images of warfare, do they also believe that the countries that are powerful now were powerful in the past? Do they still see Britain as a world power? While most children identified the USA (75%) and the USSR (58%), more than one-fifth (22.2%) still saw Britain as a powerful country. Britain was the country mentioned most as being powerful in the past, with the USA and Europe (Germany and France) predominating in the other responses. A very few children, mainly those from 'ethnic minorities', cited countries or continents such as India, Egypt and Africa. As Crispin Jones points out:

'although the sun has set on the Empire, the attitudes and emotions that sustained it in Britain have continued to shape many thoughts and actions'
(in Gundara et al. 1986, p. 32).

Ethnocentrism emerged in a few children's views on language and history:

'All language comes from England. English is easier to say. I don't think people should speak different languages' (76.G.*3).

'Britain's more interesting. The other countries don't have so much history' (21.B.*1).

A parent criticized the behaviour of people from other cultures:

'They shouldn't make it obvious that they want to be different in someone else's country. It's like at school – you see them wearing those funny
clothes. They should only wear those clothes with their own people – not
at school' (P.119.*7).

It is interesting to note that this parent had an Indian father. This type of attitude
may explain the fact that 'ethnic minority' children were often hesitant about
discussing their culture in the interviews unless actively encouraged so to do.
A Hindu parent said:

'I've always lived surrounded by English people in England. My wife
used to wear a sari but my son hated it. It upset him, so now she doesn't
wear it any more' (P. 125.*1).

The past in the public eye

Television and books

All the children watch television and two-thirds see more than three hours daily.
Working-class children appear to watch more daily, but these figures do not
vary significantly according to cultural group. How far does television influence
attitudes, and what is the nature of that influence?

The Swann Report concluded that television had an important role to play in
shaping opinions:

Hartmann and Husband (1974) found that for the children and adolescents
they interviewed, television was undoubtedly the most important source
of information about the world. They argue that the important effect of
the mass media is not that watching television makes us more violent or
permissive or racist, but that the media throw some features into sharp
relief, obliterate others, select and limit the issues which are worthy of
consideration and recall. The mass media do not determine attitudes, but
they do structure and select information we may use on which to base
decisions on what attitude is appropriate. Attitudes themselves are ill-
formed and may be focused by the images and attitudes of the mass media
(Swann 1985, p. 43).

How is the past represented to viewers? There are relatively few
documentaries about the past, and only half of the sample watched them.
Among those about the past, programmes on history were most popular (66%).
Some children mentioned watching 'How We Used to Live' (BBC for Schools)
at school, and one child, who had seen it at home when ill, expressed a desire to
have it included in their class activities. This programme appealed to them

because they could relate to the lives of ordinary people depicted in it. Programmes about prehistory and archaeology were slightly less popular (both 54%), although this may be due to the lack of programmes on these subjects remarked on by Frost (1983, p. 2). However, the programmes mentioned, such as the BBC 'Blue Peter' coverage of the raising of the Tudor warship *Mary Rose*, 'The Body in the Bog' (Q.E.D., BBC) and the local news about the children of Itchen Abbas, who are helping to excavate a Saxon graveyard in their playground, were often discussed with enthusiasm.

Fictional films about the past were more popular (84%), so it is probable that such programmes influence perceptions about the past most. The children frequently mentioned films about World War II, and most had seen 'Raiders of the Lost Ark', which also features Nazis as the enemy. This type of film may have led to the impression described by one child:

> 'Germany – you say the name and they sound like people who go round bombing things up' (89.G.*3).

Another child was convinced that

> 'Colonel Gadafi's taken over everything' (92.G.*3).

The Swann Report makes the observation that

> Both B.B.C. and I.T.V. continue to show a variety of old films, which portray Africans and American Indians as untrustworthy savages, fit peoples for subjugation and civilisation by the white man
>
> (Swann 1985, p. 43).

As a form of leisure activity, reading books proved to be substantially less popular than TV, for only two-thirds claimed to have read books about the past outside school. 'British' and 'middle class' children read more, which may reflect these groups' greater identification with the subject matter, and perhaps indicates that they have more access to books.

Are children able to distinguish historical 'fact' from 'fiction'? 44 per cent believed in the whole or partial veracity of books about the past, and about the same number (43.6%) recorded a 'don't know' answer. Three-quarters thought that fictional films about the past gave a true or partially true picture. One child summarized many people's attitudes to films on TV:

> 'I think they do [give an accurate picture of the past] but people don't really take it seriously. They don't watch it properly. They just watch it for what's happening' (77.G.*1).

'British' children are less critical of these fictional films, for 95% believed them to be partially or wholly true, as opposed to 62% of 'ethnic minority' children. This may be explained by the fact that these children are exposed to alternative views of the world through videos from their country of origin (which the majority mentioned watching), their religion and listening to adults from their community. Although there have been more factual and fictional programmes and films recently about India and Africa, they have still often concentrated on British or European colonialism ('Passage to India', 'The Far Pavilions', 'The Jewel in the Crown', 'Out of Africa'), and so have done little to contradict monocultural views.

This lack of critical appraisal may be traced to the education system and children's books about the past. At school pupils are not taught to examine the information contained in books critically, to detect bias and prejudice. Instead, books are treated almost as 'Bibles' on which everything is based, whereas the fact is that many textbooks which purport to be definitive authorities are often misleading and inaccurate.

History books exhibit a strong tendency to recreate the past from an ethnocentric perspective. Ferro points out that

> 'This way of writing was, though tacitly, narrowly Eurocentric, since other peoples only "entered" the history books with their "discovery" by the Europeans'
>
> (Ferro 1981, p. x).

In a chapter entitled 'White History' he continues:

> Selecting systematically the school textbooks of several European nations, Roy Preiswerk and Dominique Perrot have made up a record of the stereotypes underlying this "White" history, the principles behind its periodization, the principal values stressed by the whites in comparison with the rest of the world – respect for law and order, national unity, sense of organisation, monotheism, democracy, settlement, industrialization, the march of progress, etc.
>
> (ibid., p. 1).

Frank Whitehead and his team researched into children's responses to fiction as part of the Schools Council project. He states:

> Consider the role of print in shaping children's attitudes towards the world and relate it to the multicultural society in which they are growing up. The population of Britain has changed radically in the past forty years: books have changed little. . . . Many children see cultural diversity all around them but find little confirmation of it in what they read. Children from ethnic minorities in Britain need to see their culture accurately portrayed and their existence acknowledged in the books they encounter. Children in areas still predominantly white and monocultural are likely to accept without question exclusively monocentric portrayals of other lands and racial stereotypes in books
>
> (Whitehead et al. 1977, p. 7).

Some children's books on archaeology and prehistory use out-of-date archaeological theories, are racist and sexist, and often distort or misrepresent the evidence. Very few are written by archaeologists; most writers are also white and male. This has clear implications for our image of the past. A recent book on the history of Britain, for example, confidently depicts 'A Neolithic Funeral', showing a group placing a body in a long barrow. However, all of the evidence indicates that Neolithic peoples practised excarnation – i.e. corpses were left outside to rot and then the bones were placed in long barrows. The picture conveys the impression that Neolithic burials are merely less sophisticated versions of modern funerals (Sauvain 1982, p. 17). Prehistory is generally written in terms of building, hunting, fighting and farming. All of these activities are designated as male, and women are rarely featured, except in the background, holding a child or cooking. Many of the books believe implicitly in technological evolution, thus damning present-day societies who are still in stages of so-called 'savagery' and 'barbarism'.

Books on archaeology and (pre)history should present evidence for theories about the past and allow the reader to evaluate it. Most children enjoy 'detective' work, and this would involve their minds more actively than just passively absorbing so-called facts. Archaeological techniques are particularly appropriate for the current methodological emphasis on child-centred learning and active enquiry.

Visits

Visits to sites of historical and archaeological interest can help to bring the past to life. Seventy-four per cent felt they had learnt a lot from these visits, and one child explained:

> 'It helps you to understand. You find much more satisfaction from going to a castle and knowing what you're looking at' (47.G.*3).

Ninety-seven per cent of children visited these places with school and 62% with parents, which illustrates the importance of the allocation of school funds for this purpose. One school head explained that educational cuts forced schools to rely on parental resources for trips, and that this contribution was often impossible for working-class families, which resulted in a widening gap between the resources available to schools in different areas.

More 'British' parents (67.5%) than 'ethnic minority' parents (45%) took children on visits to historical sites. This could be explained by the fact that 92% of 'ethnic minority' parents in the sample were working class, with many husbands and wives working split shifts. Another contributory factor may be the failure of most museums to adopt a policy which reflects the existence of 'ethnic minorities' in the community (Hastead & Jones forthcoming, p. 1). Although Southampton City Museums have held one exhibition 'The Caribbean Connection', there still remains a great deal to be done to attract more 'ethnic minority' visitors. It is surprising that a cosmopolitan port like Southampton should have so little information, either on display or in books, about the many different peoples who have settled there.

The figures for visits made with parents were higher for the middle class (60.5%) compared with 40.2% of the working class, and this may again be a reflection of the fact that many museum policies do not cater for the experiences of the working class (Hodder *et al.* 1980, p. 60). One local example is that, despite recent oral history work on the working class of Chapel and Northam, an exhibition on the Edwardians in Tudor House Museum, Southampton, featured only one small display board on the working class.

The collecting policies of museums should be widened to cover the contribution of the working class, women and 'ethnic minorities' to our past. If this were done in a concerted fashion, rather than as a token gesture, it would hopefully kindle interest in a broader section of the community.

Of the sample, 71.8% knew what an archaeological dig was, when shown a photograph, although one child asked

'Are they growing things?' (42.G.*3).

A higher number of 'ethnic minority' children (82.5% as opposed to British 66.2%) were familiar with what an excavation is which may be explained by the fact that most of the recent excavations have taken place in the vicinity of their neighbourhood. Only 19.5% of the 'British' children had visited an excavation compared with 42.5% of the 'ethnic minority' children.

Education about the past

The Swann Report recommended that, 'Britain is a multi-racial and multicultural society and all pupils must be enabled to understand what this means'. It further recommended that 'Multicultural understanding has also to permeate all aspects of a school's work. It is not a separate topic that can be welded on to existing practices' (Swann 1986, pp. 363–4). Although this report was commissioned by the government, the Secretary of State for Education declared that no additional funds would be made available for its implementation. In an era of stringent cuts in education spending, have schools been able to implement a multicultural curriculum? How much do children learn about the history of other countries? Which countries form part of the syllabus? What is the children's opinion on the subject?

Our findings revealed that 67.5% were taught about the history of other countries, but half of the countries mentioned were in Europe. Looking at the picture school by school, it emerged that schools with a higher percentage of 'ethnic minority' children included more work on other countries in the curriculum. These schools also featured more displays on other cultures and religions, and provided mother-tongue teaching of 'Asian' languages in school and facilities for learning 'Asian' music. This concentration of a multicultural emphasis in certain schools seems to be fairly typical all over Britain, for multicultural education has often been seen as the preserve of 'ethnic minorities'. Suffield quoted a history teacher from a predominantly white area of Southampton: 'We don't need it here, we've only got two of "those" girls' (Suffield 1986, p. 38). This state of affairs is only possible due to the concentration of 'ethnic minotirites' in certain schools. Fuller observes:

> Racial discrimination in and exclusion from employment and housing restrict black people to certain parts of Britain. This means that multi-racial schools are rarely to be found outside certain areas. Even in towns and cities with sizeable black populations, only a minority of schools have any black pupils. Thus the low number of multi-racial schools reflects racial differentiation outside the education system
>
> (Fuller 1984, p. 19).

The Swann Report argued that 'The fundamental change that is necessary is the recognition that the problem facing the education system is not how to educate children of ethnic minorities, but how to educate all children' (Swann 1986, p. 363).

Our survey showed that 87% of 'ethnic minority' children wished to learn about their country of origin at school. Learning about these things outside the home can help to reinforce a child's sense of identity and validation. However, the way in which these subjects are taught is a vital factor, as a young Asian schoolboy illustrates:

> I remember thinking when I was younger that maybe, somehow, my language – the language of my parents – isn't a real language. . . . All history is from a British point of view. We're taught that Robert Clive was a hero and how the British introduced the railway and democracy to India . . . but we're never told how Indian industry was smashed and replaced by British industry. What we are saying all the time is that white is right. So we grow up with English nicknames and no self-respect
>
> (Gundara et al. 1986, p. 54).

A purely ethnocentric view of history can perpetuate racism through ignorance. A Greek-Cypriot child told us:

> 'We should learn about little countries as well as big ones, including islands, because if you come from that country, if people don't know about it, they might make fun of it' (115.G.*5).

Indeed, the interviewers themselves noticed that 'ethnic minority' children exhibited a degree of hesitancy over discussing their culture, giving the impression that they felt 'British' people would not be interested in, or value, such information. During the course of our survey a teacher told us a story which illustrates the damaging consequences of ignorance. He reported that he had found

an 'Asian' boy crying because some of the other children had called him a
'Paki'. The teacher said that his reply to the child had been 'I'm sorry, but children often call each other names. Anyway, you are a "Paki" and people will
always call you that'. He then related the dismay he had felt when the child told
him that he was not from Pakistan at all, but was a Hindu from Mauritius.
While the teacher was obviously sympathetic and concerned, his ignorance of
other countries had led him to make racist assumptions. He also failed to recognize that 'Paki' is a term with derogatory connotations.

One parent felt that multicultural education could be detrimental to the education of 'British' children:

> 'I don't think it's a good thing – to get schools run by Hindus, etc. When
> in Rome you should do as the Romans do. You can bend over too far.
> British people have lost some of their rights' (P.121.*3).

One head told me of the adverse reaction from a few parents over school visits
to mosques and Sikh temples.

Multiculturalism would seem to have the support of almost all of the children in the survey, as 93% declared that they would like to learn more about
the past of other countries, and the figures did not vary much between the cultural groups. One child gave a surprising answer:

> 'I'd like to learn about Transylvania. I'd just like to know what's there, is
> it lies about Dracula?' (37.G.*1).

Some of the children volunteered the following reasons:

> 'They're different kinds of people and they do things differently'
> (97.B.*3).

> 'Then you know about others and not just yourselves' (15.G.*3).

> 'I think it helps you understand other people's problems because at the
> moment there's racial fighting and things' (51.B.*3).

> 'All humans are the same, but they live in different countries. We should
> learn more about Africa and places like that. All European countries are
> the same – it's better to do countries we've never heard about in our
> lives' (111.B.*7).

> 'Asian countries – they have an old history. Through these countries you
> can get to the bottom of how man came on the Earth' (58.G.*3).

> 'Because then we would know what they'd been doing, and they'd know
> what we'd been doing, and maybe we'd be able to get on better'
> (88.G.*3).

Contact with a classmate from an 'ethnic minority' inspired interest in one child:

'Chrystella's learnt me the Greek alphabet. That's why I want to learn about Greece' (54.G.*3).

At the same time 63.6% of the children wanted to learn more about the past of Britain than of other countries. The figures for 'British' and 'ethnic minority' children were about equal on this question (see Table 1.3). This may show that the majority of 'ethnic minority' children were born here and regard themselves as 'British' to a certain extent.

The influence of home, community and culture

Children's perceptions of the past must be shaped to a great extent through the influence of parents, the community and culture. Our survey concentrated on ascertaining whether certain aspects of culture were passed on from parent to child, and on exploring the maintenance of cultural links in the community.

The 'British' parents' responses to questions on cultural identity displayed a degree of hesitancy about the nature of British culture. When asked if the sense of cultural identity was disappearing, a 'British' parent said:

'It's more so with British people, foreigners keep it more' (P.119.*7).

Another commented:

'You know, I've often wondered about things like the fact that everybody else has a national costume and we don't. Perhaps it could be the smock?' (P.120.*3).

This uncertainty may be explained by the fact that the British culture is dominant and is taken for granted, whereas minority cultures are thrown into sharp relief by the mere fact of being in the minority. One 'British' parent gave the following reply when asked if it was important to keep one's cultural identity:

'Well, yes and no. It definitely is if you're expatriate – it's nice to know where you belong' (P.118*3).

Many of the 'British' parents attributed this loss of cultural identity to greater social mobility leading to communities breaking up:

'It was kept up before because communities were small. Now people come from other cities – it's dying out all over England' (P.119*7).

Table 1.3   Responses to the question: Do you think you should learn more about the past of Britain than the past of other countries?

Should learn more about GB?	Percentage of total	Percentage of total ethnic groups 1, 2, 4, etc.	Percentage of total 'British'
yes	63.3	62.5	63.6
no	14.5	17.5	13
same	18.8	17.5	20.8
don't know	3.4	2.5	2.6

'It's inevitable with people travelling around' (P.124.*3).

Another felt that the British cultural identity had been eroded by economic problems:

'There's no pride because of unemployment' (P.121.*3).

Two 'British' parents believed that excessive adherence to one's culture could create problems:

'Taken to the extreme that's why we have wars. It's necessary to recognize the importance of other people's culture and identity' (P.124.*3).

'It's not so important today because of multiracial problems' (P.118.*3).

One Hindu parent expressed the opinion that it was vitally important for his children to retain their culture:

'You are not "Paki" I say to him. You are a Hindu and stay a Hindu. If they learn more about Hindus they go further because they know where they are standing. The culture they hold very tight. They should know their connections, their background, what he is' (P. 126.*1).

At the same time he thought that his children should learn about other religions:

'God is the same. If you do good things and pray nicely – that's alright'.

Another Hindu parent felt that whereas cultural identity was important for one's individuality, it was necessary to transcend this in order to foster greater tolerance and co-operation:

'The world really is one country, maybe that seems far-fetched, but it's what we should be working towards – everyone working together' (P.125.*1).

'Culture' is a wide-ranging term that is unlikely to be comprehensible to children of this age, so one section of the questionnaire focused on whether certain aspects of culture – myths, legends and stories, music, art, religion and language – had been passed on to them by their parents. Another part of the same section sought to discover whether the children would pass the same aspects on to their children. The children's responses show that, for the 'ethnic minorities', religion is the primary medium through which children are made aware of their cultural heritage: 72.5% go to extra schools run by temples, mosques or churches, where they learn primarily about religion, and to a lesser extent about history and language. In contrast, less than one-third (28.5%) of 'British' children go to a religious school or club.

It emerged that 'British' parents place the greatest emphasis on language (68.8%), in the form of correction of ungrammatical speech. Art (48%), music (46.7%) and myth (39%) were seen as less important, with comparatively few (27.2%) passing on religion. While assessing these responses, it should be remembered that 'British' children are exposed to all aspects of their culture at school. This may explain the fact that significantly fewer 'British' parents passed on these aspects of culture.

The 'ethnic minority' parents also gave language a high priority, for 95% taught their mother-tongue to their children. Myths were considered important (75%), possibly because of their religious nature (most Asian children mentioned the stories from the Ramayana), followed by religion (67.5%), music (60%) and art (35%).

The responses revealed that most children claimed that they would pass on proportionally more about all aspects of culture than their parents had. They placed the greatest emphasis on language, myths, religion, music and art (in that order). Some said that one reason for learning history was to pass it on to their children.

Family history was of paramount importance to most of the sample, although they did not seem to make a connection between this and history. History again seems to be regarded as something remote from ordinary people's lives – the preserve of academics and school teachers. As 89% found family history interesting, this could be exploited at school to create a sense of the personal meaning of the past and its effect on ordinary people's lives. Projects could be designed in which the children interviewed their grandparents or pensioners. This would be mutually beneficial, for the children would be involved in active enquiry and the old people may gain a greater sense of the worth and meaning of their lives to others.

With regard to multicultural education, all of the parents felt that it would be desirable for their children to learn about other cultures and religions. The following are some of the reasons given:

'It helps them to understand other people's ideas, and prevents them from being bigoted' (P.118*3).

'It's narrow not to do so . . . like my view. I didn't do much about other countries. . . . We had Empire Day then, you know! It's a good idea so that he [his son] can respect other people's customs. . . . If there's no respect, that's when the trouble starts – what is important to one culture isn't nearly so important as to another' (P.124.*3).

Acknowledgements

The help and assistance of the following has been invaluable: Research Assistants: Herdeep Jassal and Genevieve Wheatley; J. D. Hill and Phil Vine for help with Data Base 3; the staff and pupils of Highfield, Mount Pleasant, Portswood, St Mark's, St Mary's and Swaythling Middle Schools; the parents who agreed to be interviewed; Fyona Suffield; Peter Ucko; Simon Hays; Cecilio Mar Molinero; Clare Mar Molinero; and Roy Jones.

Note

The survey was undertaken by three members of the Archaeology and Education Community Programme Team, based at Southampton University (and see Ch. 17, for details of the Archaeology and Education Project and its aims).

Key to abbreviations

The numbers in parentheses after each quote are the record numbers for the child or parent from whom the quote is taken:

P	indicates a quote from a parent;
G	indicates a quote from a girl;
B	indicates a quote from a boy;
*	followed by a number indicates ethnic origin. The numbers used follow the numerical system outlined in 'The composition of the sample' (p.23).

References

Ferro, M. 1981. *The use and abuse of history or how the past is taught.* London: Routledge.
Frost, J. 1983. Archaeology and the media. Undergraduate dissertation, University of Southampton (unpublished).

Fryer, P. 1984. *Staying power. The history of black people in Britain*. London: Pluto Press.

Fuller, M. (ed.) 1984. Block 6, Unit 27, *Inequality, gender, race, and class*. Milton Keynes: Open University.

Garrison, L. 1986. Leaflet on *First Black cultural archives museum in Britain*, c/o ACER Centre, Wyvil Road, London.

Gundara, J., C. Jones and K. Kimberley (eds) 1986. *Racism, diversity and education*. London: Hodder and Stoughton.

Hastead, R. and S. Jones (eds) forthcoming. *Combating racism: papers from the WHAM Conference*. Available from Bruce Castle Museum, Haringay, London.

Hodder, P. P., N. Peck and P. Stone. 1980. *Archaeological surveys in Britain*. Unpublished material available from the authors, University of Cambridge.

Home Affairs Committee 1981. *Racial disadvantage*. Vol. 1: *Report with minutes of proceedings*. London: HMSO.

Mar Molinero, C. and A. Leyland 1986. *A multi-dimensional scaling analysis of the City of Southampton*. Research paper, Department of Accounting, University of Southampton.

Rampton, A. 1981. Committee of Inquiry into the Education of Children from Ethnic Minority Groups: *West Indian Children in Our Schools*. London: HMSO.

Sarap, M. 1986. *The politics of multiracial education*. London: Routledge.

Sauvain, P. 1982. *Before 1066*. London: Macmillan.

Spender, D. and E. Sarah (eds) 1980. *Learning to lose: sexism and education*. London: Women's Press.

Stone, P. G. 1988. Interpretations and uses of the past in modern Britain and Europe. In *Who needs the past?*, R. Layton (ed.), ch. 17. London: Unwin Hyman.

Suffield, F. 1986. Multi-cultural perceptions of the past by children and their parents in relation to teaching within schools. In *Archaeological 'objectivity' in interpretation*. World Archaeological Congress, vol. 3 (mimeo).

Swann, Lord 1985. *Education for all*. The Report of the Committee of Inquiry into the Education of Children from Ethnic Minority Groups. London: HMSO.

Whitehead, F., A. C. Capey and W. Madden 1977. *Children and their books*. A report from the Schools Council Research Project into children's reading habits, 10–15. London: Macmillan.

2 *Inuit perceptions of the past*

JACK ANAWAK

My people the Inuit (Arctic Eskimo) have a continuing high regard for the past, and throughout our life we are taught by example and observation that it is through the knowledge gained over time that our people have managed to survive.

From the earliest possible time an Inuit child is given an Inuktitut name by which he or she will be known. This name is bestowed and 'twins' him or her with someone else much older, who may be living or deceased, and who is of importance to the child's family or group and was also known by that name. This name may have come to the child's parents or close relative in a dream or a penetrating thought. In any event the child is thenceforth dealt with by all as bearing that name. All members of the family and extended group then respond to the child according to the relationship they had with the previous bearers of that name.

Hence, Illuitok, a respected, elderly woman from the community of Pelly Bay near the Arctic Circle has a son who, later in his life, when she is old and ill, names his own son Illuitok. This child is now the old lady's namesake. The passing on of his mother's name to the man's son signifies the importance of this system in preserving the past on an intimate daily level. It also carries with it the necessity of repeating an oral history, and causes our people to relate to the figures who throughout time have held this name.

Great reverence is shown by those who most closely relate to a bearer of a name. In this case the man who gave his son his mother's name at birth relates to the baby by addressing it as 'my mother'. As the baby grows up and becomes aware of the name he carries, he will in turn address his parent as 'my child'. Others who were related to old Illuitok will also address this small male child in the exact manner and with the same degree of intimacy as they would have displayed to the old lady, with no distinction by gender. Thus, we as Inuit are taught that all things stem from and continue to be tied to the past, and that it must continue to be respected and preserved.

In a harsh environment such as our home in the Canadian Arctic, it is necessary to hand down from generation to generation the knowledge and skills to ensure survival. Learning these skills is not optional. The recent arrival of the 'White men', or *Kabloona* as we call them, has brought with it the introduction of clothing, vehicles, implements and adornments. Many are now being utilized, but they prove to be of limited use compared with time-honoured ways of creating shelter and providing transport on the land. We continue to rely on caribou and seal-skin clothing for hunting, and erect snowhouses, called igloos, in which to sleep. Our tools, although often made from metal, still reflect the designs that have proved most suitable since our people first came to be a part of our land.

From birth, through stories and legends about survival, endurance and respect for nature and all mankind, children are taught. Toys and playthings are fashioned for them, including tools and traditional dress so that they may learn early about the roles they will assume. Girls are provided with packing parkas, called *amoutis*, and carry their dolls on their back as they will carry their children in the future, and they are taught the traditional styles and methods for sewing and designing clothing. Boys are dealt with from an early age as budding hunters, and are introduced to traditional games, group play and exercises to learn agility, improvisation and endurance.

Children quickly come to understand in my culture that time-honoured skills and attitudes can never be relegated solely to the past; that they ensure a way of life and survival in the present and for the future.

A great amount of time is spent by the child in listening to the elders as they recount tales of their past, and in hearing through individual songs, called *Ai-yai-yahs*, the experiences of the singers who are the owners of each specific song. These songs usually speak of events that occurred in the singer's past, and detail their reaction to them.

The school system in the Eastern Arctic reflects this same emphasis and the budget of the Government's Department of Education places importance upon this respect for the past, ensuring that Cultural Inclusion funds are provided to enable elderly people to function as Land Instructors to acquaint students with survival skills, legends, hunting techniques and terminology, traditional food and skin-clothing preparation, production of implements and shared on-the-land living experiences.

The ties to the past have essentially been passed down verbally through legends, anecdotes and song. Information is now being set down on paper for dissemination and for preservation by the Inuit Cultural Institute. One of their main activities has been to standardize the Inuit syllabic writing system, which until recently had been taught differently by Roman Catholic and Protestant missionaries and government educators. Another goal has been to develop a Roman orthography. Audio-visual techniques have recently been employed to tape elders' stories, which are then played over the local community radio. A project for creating a tape library and making film and musical recordings, for the enjoyment of old and young alike, is now under way.

In winter, while the majority of women and children now remain in the settlements which have sprung up over the past 25 years, the hunters actively hunt on the land, practising the same hunting methods as their fathers in pursuing game. In spring, summer and autumn families relocate from the settlements to live on the land. Although canvas has replaced the skin tent, the anchoring is still achieved by placing large stones around the tent. Stone fishing traps called weirs, are rebuilt annually in which fish are trapped and speared. Fish and caribou meat are hung to dry or stored in stone caches using the same method our ancestors used. When families vacate these camping areas the sites often resemble, at a glance, those archaeological sites which have been found to be hundreds of years old.

The necessity of facing what is considered to be such a harsh environment makes it imperative to learn that the traditional methods for coping must always be practised. This means not only acquiring the skills associated with procuring food and shelter, but actively practising the traditional skills and attitudes and coping mechanisms that allow for adaptation and survival as a distinct people. These skills are only attained through incorporating the past into the present.

I am Illuitok. As my namesake was taught, there will be many bearers of this name in the future, as there was in the past. I am part of something that time has not erased. As an Inuk I have learned first-hand that the knowledge handed down by my people on survival in our land is not to be disregarded, and failure to practise and uphold this wisdom can only result in tragedy or disharmony to an individual or a group. We, as Inuit, have a strong sense of self – of who we are, and why we are as we are. Although our north is changing, and at times we select those things that are of use to us that stem from other cultures, we maintain to ourselves that which is passed on to us and will be passed on by us.

The past as I refer to it is measured in three distinct ways. I have a *recent* past, and I refer here to the years in which I pursued a more outwardly traditional style of life – that of being a small child of less than 10 years of age, living a nomadic life with members of my family group before the creation of permanent settlements. We lived in igloos and travelled by dog-team before contact with White men. These are the years in which the skills were taught to me through legends, stories and observation, and by example.

Most Inuit adults make the same delineation with regard to a recent past, and describe it as being associated with the years in their life which were before settlement living and the impact of settlement living, permanent housing, school system–wage economy and the presence of a non-Inuit government bureaucracy in our land. We are aware of the tales and stories associated with the earliest contact with non-Inuit – in the form of traders, missionaries, geographers and whalers – that occurred from the period AD 1700 to 1900, and our older people speak of their parents meeting the early visitors and sharing our food and shelter with them. Remains of the early whalers' look-outs, stone winter houses and shipwrecks dot our landscape. Beyond that period there is no precise measuring stick when it comes to time. The past stretches back over the years, and stories and legends are handed down which do not contain within them any specific references in the manner of other societies which had developed and utilized a writing system which set down their history on paper and measured time in terms of other happenings. Although the timespan that we refer to is general, the information handed down is very specific and detailed.

Through our legends we Inuit speak of our close ties with the spiritual world, and of our reverence for and understanding of wildlife. Stories handed down through time depict our interrelationship with the animal world, and tell of animals and humans exchanging roles, acquiring supernatural powers, and teaching and providing for one another. Our artwork also reflects these relationships, and we have rituals that show our respect for and acceptance of this oneness and this harmony, which are displayed in our world-famous Inuit soapstone carvings and silk-screen prints.

As a people we are aware that others have come before us to our land. Elders pass on stories of a people who were known to us as the Tunnit, described as being much taller and possessing great strength, and who preceded the Inuit.

Because we lived a nomadic life until 25 years ago, there is evidence of our camp-sites, graves, fox traps, storage caches, stone weirs, stone kayak rests and semi-subterranean houses throughout the north. As there was no written system before the coming of the missionaries, there have only been recent initiatives to document these sites. However, as stated earlier, great emphasis is placed on transmitting oral history, and most adults can readily identify the old structures and many of the tools and implements found around them.

Most of the sites, while known, have been of limited historical interest to the Inuit, as they have simply accepted their existence as a part of their life. At times they utilize portions of them while out camping on the land. However, this attitude may be changing as outside pressures intrude which have resulted in a new awareness of these sites as the key to preserving the past. As the population grows in the Canadian North and my people become increasingly concerned about the threat to the environment and way of life that oil, gas and mining exploration coupled with an increasing outside population poses, there are initiatives being taken by the Inuit through our organizations to press for additional legislation to protect various sites.

As we are now conducting Land Claims negotiations with the Government of Canada, we are developing key agreements, including an archaeological sub-agreement which awaits ratification. Various Land Use and Occupancy Studies have been carried out by Inuit organizations to bolster our Land Claim negotiating positions. Funding has been received to conduct Unmarked Graves projects, utilizing a military grid system for mapping. These studies are carried out by elders in each of our settlements, who also interview other old people about their knowledge of the locations and information surrounding these sites.

As Canada's North becomes a growing tourist destination, there is also an awareness that these sites can be utilized to acquaint and educate visitors regarding the Inuit way of life, and many settlements are exploring ways to cater to this market, while also serving to increase their own awareness and that of their children by developing historical sites and trails, signage and information brochures. This new interest in these old sites sometimes gives way to concern as the Inuit survey the large quantity of artefacts that have been removed over the years by non-Inuit, and which are presently housed in private collections, universities and museums throughout the world. Our people want to find ways to house and preserve these artefacts within our homeland.

Whereas there was minimal response to archaeological teams conducting digs many years ago, recently a feeling of concern has arisen if Inuit organizations or elected Municipal Hamlet Councils are not consulted and see themselves to

be directly involved or benefiting from such activity. This heightened awareness on the part of our people to protect, preserve and retain control of our past
is now supported by Northwest Territories legislation which prohibits excavation
or investigation of any site unless a permit has been obtained. No land-use
operation can now be conducted within 30 metres of a known or suspected
archaeological site or burial area unless authorized by an inspector, and if any
such site is unearthed such land-use activity must be suspended and the location
and unearthed materials, structures or artefacts must be reported.

It is necessary for the archaeologists and the Inuit to share their understanding and knowledge of the past. At times archaeological teams have spent a
mimimal time in communities in discussion with Inuit and our organizations,
developing a common approach to sites or enlisting their assistance in identifying artefacts. More time and attention will have to be paid to the strong concerns we have regarding the removal of artefacts to distant museum locations,
where we question whether we shall ever get an opportunity to view them
again and utilize them to educate our own children.

There is also a continuing need to train more of our people to be involved in
the investigation and interpretation of these sites. Few Inuit have gained a
secondary education, and almost none have gone to university. However, the
pressures upon us and the times we live in demand quicker and more innovative
training methods than the standard secondary school and university route to
obtain a grasp of archaeological principles and procedures if we are to work
hand-in-hand with people in this profession.

Although archaeologists working in our homeland have been able to identify
a wide variety of artefacts through seasoned practice, it remains to be seen how
much more could have been known or how much more refined their studies
could have been if they had enlisted our elders to work side-by-side with them
to challenge and share each other's perceptions. Both of us can only gain from
this process, and I hope that, in the future, innovative programmes will be
developed within the archaeological community to meet the needs of the Inuit
and other aboriginal peoples of the world in preserving, interpreting and pro-
tecting yesterday for tomorrow.

As we view with such concern the newcomers to our land, some of us feel
that we cannot wait for additional legislation and increased Northwest Territories
Government funding and programmes to begin to protect some of the sites.
People such as myself and my family have gone ahead and spent time at the sites
to monitor, mark and protect them from being disturbed. Last summer we set up
our tent camp as close as we thought necessary to a Thule site, thought to be
several hundred years old, on the banks of the Meliadine River. Throughout the
next two and a half months we cleaned and maintained the area, while showing
visitors through it along designated walking paths so as to prevent damage and
disruption to it.

We realize that it will take many more of us actively doing our part to preserve areas such as this if we are to move sufficiently quickly in the next few
years to locate and protect them while they are still relatively intact. Already I

can see how valuable an experience caring for this site has been to me and to my children. As we spend time there, we look at our way of life.

Often visitors come by in the form of families or local groups, and sometimes tourists from southern Canada and the USA. We spend time touring the tent rings, meat caches, kayak stands, graves and semi-subterranean winter houses. From time to time we are joined by a friendly sik-sik and birds, who watch our progress as we walk through the site. I am aware, as they may be, that their ancestors probably watched mine in the same manner and in this same place hundreds of years ago. Here, at this site, nothing has changed through time. I – Illuitok – and the land and the animals are all still here. This is my past, and this has become a special place. Even though I am young, I too am the past as much as I am the future.

The formal education I received has made me aware that my country – Canada – and other cultures, for the most part through their long written history, have developed reference points and time-frames through which they view their history. My people have developed and passed on the wisdom and stories of the generations without the assistance of a written history spanning hundreds of years.

Our unique way of passing on this knowledge which allows our young to know who they are, and to see how they belong to time immemorial, has allowed us to survive.

3 From the raw to the cooked: Hadzabe perceptions of their past

D. K. NDAGALA and N. ZENGU

Introduction

The Hadzabe, who are sometimes referred to as Hadza, Hadzapi, Tindiga or Kindiga, are a small, relatively isolated hunting–gathering society living near Lake Eyasi in northern Tanzania. Although the Hadzabe have never been effectively counted, they are estimated to number between 1 200 and 3 000. They are said to belong to the earliest inhabitants of East Africa. According to Were & Wilson (1972, p. 6) these ancient inhabitants ' . . . were late Stone Age peoples, skilled in the making and use of stone and bone tools. They lived by hunting and gathering wild plants. They lived near water and most of them occupied the Kenya and northern Tanzania Highlands, the Rift Valley and shores of Lake Victoria. . . . The Hadzapi and the Sandawi of Tanzania are probably the last remnants of these people in East Africa'.

Since the anthropological research by Woodburn (1966, 1980) and others in the late 1950s there has been so much research carried out on the Hadzabe that these hunter–gatherers have been claimed to be relatively over-researched (Ndagala & Waane 1982, p. 101). One aspect which has not received sufficient attention is the Hadzabe past. This chapter discusses the way in which the Hadzabe perceive their past. The presentation is based on the oral traditions collected in the western part of Hadzabe country. In collecting this information we had to differentiate between the recent past and the distant past. The recent past is that time which has been experienced by the present generations and those just before them. The distant past, on the other hand, is that time which is so distant that its experiences are only known through oral traditions. We realized that unless this distinction was made in our requests for information, we were likely to get accounts of the recent past based on our informants' own experiences, and therefore to lose sight of the time depth of the distant past. We therefore asked about what the Hadzabe knew of the original people, what the Earth was like in the past, and so on. This was part of an enquiry which is still going on in respect of Hadzabe oral traditions.

The Hadzabe past constitutes four successive epochs. Each epoch is known by the characteristics of the people who lived in it. Four peoples are mentioned in the oral tradition. The description of the way they lived throws light on the environment, the types of skills, and so on. Starting from the distant past, these peoples are known as *Akakaanebe* or *Gelanebe*, *Tlaatlaanebe*, *Hamakwabe*, and *Hamaishonebe*. Let us now look at each people and its epoch.

Akakaanebe/Gelanebe

These are said to be the very first people who lived at the beginning of the world. They were gigantic, with very strongly built, hairy bodies. They never used fire, although they could produce fire sparks by knocking stones together. Game animals were quite abundant, and the people did not have to go far in search of them. Moreover, they are said not to have used tools in killing animals. They simply had to stare at an animal and it fell dead. Although the types of animals are not mentioned, it is generally believed that there were as many varieties as there are today. However, it is noted that game animals were rather stupid and were not afraid of people. Meat was eaten raw because the people did not make fire. In this epoch of raw meat the people never built houses: they sheltered themselves under canopies of trees. Furthermore, they made no tools and had no instruments of self-defence.

There are variations on the reasons for not using fire. Some informants say that in this epoch the earth was wet and soft, and therefore could not support fire. Other informants say that the then new Earth was afraid of fire. The younger informants, especially those who have been to school, say that *Akakaanebe* ate meat raw simply because they did not know how to make fire. Nevertheless, the common version of the oral tradition attributes the non-use of fire to the physical condition of the Earth immediately after its creation.

Tlaatlaanebe

These people were equally gigantic, but their bodies, unlike those of the *Akakaanebe*, were not hairy. The earth was no longer wet in this epoch. There are variations in the accounts as to why wetness had disappeared. This is illustrated by the following extracts from three accounts recorded in 1981:

> *Tlaatlaanebe* prayed for better earth which was not afraid of fire. Their prayers were answered and the wet earth was replaced by earth which was tolerant to fire (by Balosha Yaeda of Mang'ola).

> The wet earth went up and was replaced by dry earth (by Gimbi Malapa of Yaeda Chini).

> By this time the earth had matured and hardened and could accept fire (by Matina Majui of Yaeda Chini).

In the first account the wet earth is replaced by the dry earth due to the prayers of *Tlaatlaanebe*. In the second account the wet earth goes up by unknown forces to give way to the dry earth. According to the third account the earth is not replaced, but matures. In this case hardness and dryness seem to be elements of maturity acquired through time. These variations in the individual accounts may be due to some omissions of detail, or some factors which are yet to be identified.

With the dry earth the people of this epoch could produce fire from stones and preserve it. Despite the abundance of game, it was no longer possible for the people to cause animals to die by staring at them. The animals are said to have become wiser, and to have learnt to flee from the people. To get the animals the people had to give them a hard chase. Possibly to make this task simpler, the people of this epoch kept dogs and used them in pursuing the animals. Meat was roasted before it was eaten. Dancing to a powerful sacred being, *epeme* (cf. Woodburn 1982b), was started by these people. Subsequently, *epeme* became a regular feature in the life of these people. Unlike the people of the previous epochs, these hunters were able to protect themselves from their enemies by way of medicines and charms. For accommodation they used caves and rock shelters. Parents married their daughters to skilful hunters. Bride wealth was composed of a breast of a large animal such as an eland.

Hamakwabe

Unlike the preceding peoples, *Hamakwabe* had a relatively smaller physique and their bodies were not hairy. They made and used bows and arrows in hunting. Dogs were also kept, and were used in hunting. These people were able to make fire with firesticks, one stick twirled between the palms of the hands, its point turning in a notch made in another (usually softer) stick. In addition to roasting meat they could also boil it. Boiling was done in wooden containers which they made and coated with soil. Instead of living in caves, *Hamakwabe* built themselves houses, using sticks and grass in a way similar to that of the present Hadzabe. The people in this epoch travelled longer distances than people of the previous epochs. It is during this time that exchange relations developed between the hunter–gatherers and other societies. Forest products were exchanged for knives, arrowheads and other utility items. With the passing of time, but within this epoch, the people were able to forge iron and make their own tools such as knives and arrowheads. The gambling game *lukuchweko* (cf. Woodburn 1982a, pp. 442–3) was started by these people.

Hamaishonebe

Though this group includes the present Hadzabe, it emerged in the distant past. It has elements of the distant past, the recent past and the present. The physique of these people is said to be relatively small compared with that of the previous epoch. In addition to having the skills of the previous peoples, *Hamaishonebe* evolved more skills to cope with the changed circumstances. Intermarriage with other societies started with these people, and so did the payment of bride-wealth in the form of cash and beads.

When talking about this epoch the informants tend to dwell on personal experiences and those of the generations just before them – things which in this respect are more definite both in space and in time. The elders can give the names of places where such-and-such took place, the people with whom they associated and the approximate time when the respective events took place. The details and specificity in the versions increase as one moves to the recent past. Hadzabe perceptions of their recent past are discussed in greater detail elsewhere (McDowell 1981a, b, Ndagala 1985).

Discussion

The Hadzabe oral traditions reveal many elements of continuity and change, not only in recent decades, but also from the very beginning of human existence. The Hadzabe do not make any fuss about the past, especially the distant past. They retell their oral traditions with a high degree of self-confidence. They regard the change from the distant past to the present as relatively positive. They pity their predecessors for having had to eat raw meat due to the problems of making fire at the material time. The cooking of meat and the general utilization of fire are seen as achievements. Apart from the relative diminution in bodily size and absence of bodily hair, the people of each subsequent epoch possessed new skills in addition to those held by people of the previous epochs. A number of our elderly informants indicated that they had no regrets in respect of the past, because they had more skills than the hunters who lived in the distant past. Game meat is still available, but rather than eating it raw they eat it cooked. There are no implications of a 'golden age' in the Hadzabe perception of the past. To them the past is the medium through which hunter–gatherers developed to their present stage. The past, to use Mbiti's words, '. . . is not extinct, but a period full of activities and happenings' (Mbiti 1969, p. 24).

The change from what the Hadzabe occasionally refer to as 'animal people' – with massive, strongly built bodies, but who cannot make a fire and, therefore, cannot cook – to a people with relatively smaller bodies, but who can take better care of themselves, is seen as progress. These Hadzabe perceptions of the past, as contained in their oral traditions, put to question Mbiti's generalization that African peoples have neither the belief in progress nor the idea that development activities and achievements move from a low to a higher degree (Mbiti 1969, p. 23).

In the course of moving from the 'animal people' to the present Hadzabe, neither heroes nor villains are made. This is because matters relating to the distant past are not individualized, but are seen to embrace the entire people, who did only what they could at the material time. Each people presented in the oral tradition is different from the previous one. There is continuous change and development. The present Hadzabe are thus not a replica of their ancestors many millenia ago (compare Schrire 1980 on the San). They see themselves as different from the hunter–gatherers of the distant past. They are able to cope with the demands and strains of modern society. We similarly agree with Woodburn (1980, p. 96) that the Hadzabe are not '. . . survivors miraculously preserving palaeolithic or mesolithic traits into the present, but as the living and efficient practitioners of a mode of subsistence which if understood, may allow us to make some limited generalizations about others with similar modes of subsistence both in the present and the past'.

Conclusion

According to the Hadzabe oral traditions, hunting has always been their only subsistence strategy until recently, when they came into contact with non-hunting societies. Again, we learn that hunting was a more immediate return system (Woodburn 1980, 1982a) than it is today. No tools were needed to kill animals, because they fell dead from the stare of the people. Meat was immediately consumed without having to be cooked or roasted first. Although we cannot link any of the epochs in the Hadzabe perceptions with any specific archaeological period, the oral tradition throws light on a number of aspects of the hunter–gatherers. For instance, many of the caves and rock shelters in the present Hadzabe country are full of paintings which, according to Woodburn (1966), were not made by the Hadzabe. In the light of the oral tradition, is there no possibility that these rock paintings were made in the distant past by the *Tlaatlaanebe* who lived in the caves and rock shelters?

The Hadzabe perceptions of the past, as enshrined in their oral traditions, offer points of comparison to the archaeological theories on the ancestry of man. Moreover, the important archaeological finds in Tanzania in respect of early man are near present Hadzabe country, and within the area believed to have been occupied by hunter–gatherers in the past. We agree with Schmidt (1978, p. 287) that the view advanced by Vansina (1965, p. 174) that it is often impossible to link the information obtained from oral traditions with any definite archaeological finds is a result of the limited methodologies at the time of his writing. Having successfully used the archaeological method to verify oral traditions in Buhaya, Schmidt (1978, p. 297) observes that ' . . . it should be possible for historians and archaeologists to formulate hypotheses that seek to explain cultural change caused by the exploitation of the environment as well as the interaction with the social environment'. Archaeological objectivity and interpretation could be greatly improved if the researchers started from what the people in and around the research areas know of the past. Rather than starting our archaeological investigations with abstract propositions alone, why not incorporate propositions based on oral traditions of the respective areas? Oral traditions and indigenous perceptions of the past are a still under-utilized resource in archaeological investigation and interpretation.

References

McDowell, W. 1981a. Hadza traditional economy and its prospects for development. Paper written for the Rift Valley Project, Ministry of Information and Culture, Dar es Salaam.

McDowell, W. 1981b. A brief history of Mang'ola Hadza. Paper written for the Rift Valley Project, Ministry of Information and Culture, Dar es Salaam.

Mbiti, J. S. 1969. *African religions and philosophy*. London: Heinemann.

Ndagala, D. K. 1985. Attempts to develop the Hadzabe of Tanzania. *Nomadic Peoples* **18**, 17–26.

Ndagala, D. K. and S. A. C. Waane. 1982. Effects of research on the Hadzabe, a hunting and gathering group of Tanzania. *Review of Ethnology* **8** (11–19), 94–105.

Schmidt, P. 1978. *Historical archaeology*. Westport: Greenwood Press.

Schrire, C. 1980. An inquiry into the evolutionary status and apparent identity of San hunter–gatherers. *Human Ecology* **8**, 9–32.

Vansina, J. 1965. *Oral tradition: a study of historical methodology*. Chicago: Aldine.

Were, G. S. and D. A. Wilson. 1972. *East Africa through a thousand years*. Nairobi: Evans.

Woodburn, J. C. 1966. The Hadza: the food quest of a hunting and gathering tribe of Tanzania (16 mm film). London School of Economics.

Woodburn, J. C. 1980. Hunters and gatherers and the reconstruction of the past. In *Soviet and Western anthropology*, E. Gellner (ed.), 95–117. London: Duckworth.

Woodburn, J. C. 1982a. Egalitarian societies. *Man (new series)* **17**, 431–51.

Woodburn, J. C. 1982b. Social dimensions of death in four African hunting and gathering societies. In *Death and the regeneration of life*, M. Bloch and J. Parry (eds), 187–210. Cambridge: Cambridge University Press.

4 An 11th century literary reference to prehistoric times in India

DEENA BANDHU PANDEY

The study of prehistoric times in India is taken to have started with the works of Robert Bruce Foote, who collected and studied prehistoric stone tools in India as early as 1863 (Sen & Ghost 1966, iii, iv). However, ancient scholars in India definitely had knowledge of prehistoric times. It has long been a tradition in India to divide the period of human culture from its origin to present times into four quarters (see the Introduction). The earliest quarter is termed the *Kṛta Yuga* or *Sata Yuga* – the Age of Truth. In literary descriptions of the Age of Truth we are told how people lived in India in early times. Not every such description contains clear reference to prehistoric times. Fortunately, however, a very clear literary reference is found in an 11th century work composed by King Bhoja of the Paramara dynasty (*c.* AD1000 to 1055), who was a famous patron of learning, and himself an erudite scholar.

In his work on the science of architecture (*Vastusastra*) entitled *Samarāṅgaṇasūtradhāra*, Bhoja describes the early stage of human culture, the life of primitive man and its development. It is interesting to note his reference to a stone tool used to cut down trees.

In the beginning of the sixth chapter of the *Samarāṅgaṇasūtradhāra*, Bhoja wrote that in the *Kṛta Yuga* men used to live in groves, hills, forests and near rivers and lakes, together with the gods. The *Kalpa* or 'Wishing' Tree existed to fulfil their needs. When men lost the Wishing Tree, they had to subsist upon other trees and nature produced rice (*sali*) grains which later they cultivated (Bhoja 1966, p. 1). Bhoja relates that men were gradually disgusted with trees, and began to cut pieces from them with a stone tool, and started to build houses:

> Ajātapritayovṛikshaiḥ kuṭṭimāṇi gṛihāṇi cha.
> Vyadhuśchhitvāśmabhirvṛikshānanyan dukkhārtachetasaḥ.

In the beginning they constructed huts and, later, buildings of one, two, three, seven or ten rooms (Bhoja 1966, p. 37).

The description which Bhoja presents is concerned with the first quarter of human civilization according to Hindu tradition, and the description under reference closely corresponds to the state of men in prehistoric times, when they lived in forests or hills near rivers or lakes. The dependence referred to by Bhoja of people's use of trees hints at the stage when prehistoric man had advanced from his hunting stage and was depending increasingly on the vegetative productions of nature and agriculture. By this time people had started a settled life in houses. From archaeological finds we have found that it was in the Neolithic age in India that prehistoric people started to dwell in constructed houses. The dwelling houses of prehistoric people known from different sites in India (Kili Ghulmohammad, Brahmagiri, Maski, Piklihal and Burzhom) may well be taken in reference (Sankalia 1963, pp. 177, 250, 296).

It is particularly interesting to note the form of the stone tool to which Bhoja refers, which was used in cutting trees (*Vyadhuśchhitvāśmabhirvṛikshān*). The stone tool is called *Aśma*. This word is a technical term. It is specially used for 'any instrument made of stone'. The word with this meaning has been used in Indian literature since the Rigvedic period (Williams n.d., p. 114). The reference given by Ghoja is of a stone tool used for cutting (*Chhetṛi-aśma*), as one can see in the phrase *Chhitvāśmabhiḥ*. The *Uṇādisūtra* (Ch. 4, v. 120) refers to a cutting tool as *Chhidi*, an axe. Taking all these into consideration shows that Bhoja probably refers to a 'stone axe' with which the trees were cut, apparently the Neolithic celt or axe. One of the purposes of the Neolithic axe was felling of trees (Sankalia 1964, p. 84). Sankalia states that such an axe can split, with speed and ease, a casuarina log more than a foot or so in diameter without the blade suffering any injury, even if it is forcefully used. The expression *Vyadhuśchhitvāśmabhirvṛikshān* of Bhoja clearly refers to the cutting of the trees by striking with the stone tool (i.e. axe).

Bhoja was a widely read scholar who was acquainted with several branches of learning. He must have received knowledge about prehistoric life through a tradition, either verbal or literary – probably the latter. The Puranic literature contains references to the habitations of early Man. The *Vāyu*, *Mārkandeya* and *Brahmāṇḍa Purāṇas* (chs 8, 49 and 8, respectively) contain corresponding references to early dwellings, stating that early people depended on shelter from trees, but later constructed houses. Whatever his source, we may conclude that the life of prehistoric people and their artefacts were known to Indian scholars since the 11th century.

References

Bhoja 1966. *Samarāṅganasūtradhāra*, T. Gaṇapati Śāstrī (ed.), (revised and edited by V.S. Agrawala). Gaekwad's Oriental Series 25. Baroda: Oriental Institute.

Sankalia, H. D. 1963. *Prehistory and protohistory in India and Pakistan*. Bombay: Registrar of the University of Bombay.

Sankalia, H. D. 1964. *Stone-age tools: their techniques, names and probable functions*. Poona: Centenary and Silver Jubilee Series I, Deccan College Postgraduate and Research Institute.

Sen, D. and A. K. Ghost (eds) 1966. *Studies in prehistory, Robert Bruce Foote memorial volume*. Calcutta: Firma K. L. Mukhopadhyay.

Williams, M. M. n.d. *A Sanskrit–English dictionary*, New edn, E. Leumann, C. Cappeller *et al.* (eds). 1st edn published Oxford: Clarendon, 1899; reprinted Delhi: Oriental Publishers.

5 *The valuation of time among the peasant population of the Alto Minho, northwestern Portugal*

JOÃO DE PINA-CABRAL

In all cultures, time is experienced as a multi-faceted phenomenon. The French sociologist Gervitch has argued, 'social life takes place within times which are *multiple, always divergent* and frequently *contradictory*. Their unification . . . represents a problem for any society' (1958, p. 1). This temporal complexity carries within itself potential contradictions, yet the relative unification of times is an essential aspect of all cultural life. In this paper, I will summarize three instances from rural northern Portugal: popular opposition to the building of modern paved roads, the division of the past into distinct phases and belief in the existence of an autochthonous population. By this means I hope to illuminate the processes to which the peasant society of Alto Minho resorts in its struggle to unify the experience of time.

The Alto Minho is a region of green hills, with V-shaped valleys at the bottom of which run small rivers making their way westward, among big boulders, towards the sea. In the lower reaches the hills are worked into terraces where an intensive form of mixed farming is practised, which is based on stabled cattle, irrigated maize, and wine grapes grown on pergolas – the famous *vinho verde*. Rural residence is typically dispersed, with small hamlets loosely scattered on the hillsides. However, as we move uphill the terraces become smaller, the pergolas which surround the maize plots are less abundant and pine forests predominate. Further up still, on the mountains which border Spain to the east, the forests give way to bushes of broom and furze, which cover the rocky hill-tops. Here goats and free-roaming cattle are kept by the inhabitants of the small, tightly clustered villages where, until very recently, they lived a very isolated life.

Continuity and change

The two parishes where I went to live in 1978, and which I have repeatedly visited since – Paço and Couto[1] – lie in the middle ranges. They face the river on its south bank, and thus have been open to river and road traffic since the Roman armies arrived in 137 BC. Notwithstanding, *minhoto* peasant life has to this day preserved an element of independence – this is a cherished prerogative which even economic interest is not always sufficient to counter: witness the opposition to the building of paved roads into the parishes.

All of this must not be interpreted to mean that these villages for centuries remained untouched by the momentum of history. As far as the goat-herding villages of the mountains on the Spanish border are concerned, physical isolation, and consequently socio-economic isolation, was indeed a fact until the 1980s. However, in the riverside area where Paço and Couto lie, the distinct impression of autarky and social independence that we observe did not at all imply a lack of contact with the wider world. Paço and Couto have been as deeply involved in Portuguese political history as any other region of the country. Some aspects of local society, which are indeed very old, lead one on occasion to feel the presence of a closer link with the past than is found in urban areas. The division of the rural plots, of hamlets and of parishes, their names and boundaries, some aspects of family and community organization, and some religious attitudes are aspects of local life which often date back to the 6th century, when the conquering Visigoths converted to Christianity. This is a region of the Iberian Peninsula where the Islamic presence in the 9th century had the lightest of effects. However, continuity is perfectly compatible with change. What both the casual observer and the local inhabitant seldom know is that profound changes have characterized rural life at all stages of its history.

To take a significant example, consider the agricultural system. Farmers today find it difficult to believe that there was a time when maize was not dominant in the area, that the omnipresent olive trees arrived in the 19th century, and many already forget that the pine forests on the hill-tops were planted in the mid-20th century. Stabled cattle also date only from the early 19th century, and vine growing on pergolas (rather than trees) results from the chestnut tree epidemic which took place earlier this century. Today chestnuts are not an important part of the diet. They have been replaced by another recent import, potatoes. Previously chestnuts had been a staple food.

Moreover, isolation from urban centres and from contact with foreign lands is by no means a characteristic feature of this society – quite the contrary. The Portuguese discoveries of the 14th and 15th centuries were staffed mostly by *minhotos*; Brazil owes much of its population to local men who, in the 18th century, emigrated in such large numbers that complaints were being made that only the old men and the women were left behind; in the 19th century emigration to Brazil and America was again important, and always growing. Therefore, in the 1960s, when rural areas were nearly emptied by the run for well-paid jobs in industry in France, Germany, the USA, Canada and Australia, this was by no means an unprecedented way of reacting to rural poverty in local society.[2] Finally, emigration to Spain for men, and to the towns and cities for women, has always been common for those who could find in local society no means of earning a living. Many of these people stayed behind in the countries to which they escaped, but the desire to return was strong in most, and a large number of them have always succeeded in re-establishing themselves in their parishes of origin. Witness the houses and churches they built, repaired and furnished, which are visible everywhere in Minho.

In the light of this tradition, popular opposition to the building of modern paved roads, which is documented in 19th century reports and continued until recently, seems to require some explanation. Rural Minho is characterized by a profound association between social units and specific stretches of land (cf. Pina-Cabral 1986, pp. 3–4). In this sense, boroughs, parishes, hamlets and households correspond not only to different levels of socio-geographic classification but also to different levels at which a sense of community is experienced.

In such a context, the building of modern paved roads alters the relation between the social group and the land it occupies and thus it comes to represent a change in community relations. Through these roads, motorized transport can take place, which escapes community control because it is fast and private. This new privacy is certainly welcomed by individual neighbours in their competitive struggles with each other. The taxi and the private automobile become important parts of daily life, for they afford transport with privacy. However, the privacy which is welcomed by the individual is also an open attack on the community. The main difference between *caminhos* (old paths) and the modern paved roads is that the earlier were fully controlled by the local community. They were eagerly watched, and this effectively prevented the entrance of undesirable strangers. Conversely, main thoroughfares and modern paved roads are open, public and national spaces where everyone is entitled to move unobserved and unchecked.

While jeopardizing local autarky, paved roads also bring 'progress', 'modern ideas' and modern facilities. Spatial isolation is translated into, and associated with, a time factor. Peasant life is seen as backward (*atrasada*, literally 'retarded') and more basic or primitive. Peasants are thought to be nearer to nature and further away from the seats of civilization, the towns. I have undertaken a fuller discussion of this set of ideas elsewhere (Pina-Cabral 1986, pp. 100–4), and will limit myself here to pointing out that this interpretation of the differences between the bourgeoisie and the peasantry in terms of a linear evolution from backwardness to increasingly greater civilization is shared by both peasants and urban élites alike.

The penetration of urban society into rural areas, which is facilitated by paved roads, is thus interpreted by all involved in temporal terms. 'Progress' is entering a society which perceived itself as unchanging. The peasant past is perceived as one of uniform isolation – both by the town-dwellers, who accuse peasant life-styles of being 'anachronistic', 'archaic', 'backward' and 'medieval'; and by the peasants, who see their life as more traditional and only recently diverging from age-old custom. In historical terms, of course, both are wrong, as was argued above. However, in symbolic terms this merging of the spatial and temporal dimensions is central to the understanding of why road building and so many other forms of penetration of the State into local society are perceived as sources of danger by peasant communities. The lynchpin which permits this merging is the feeling of community itself. On the one hand, community is essentially defined spatially, in sociogeographic terms; on the other hand, however, it depends for its reproduction on a specific manipulation of temporality which is achieved by means of a set of rituals, as will be argued below.

Time present and time past

In talking to local residents about their society, one soon encounters and learns to operate with the loose classification of their past into *agora* (literally 'now, the time present'), *antes* (literally 'before, the time past') and *antigamente* ('in the old days'). This is accompanied by a classification of people into *a gente* (literally 'the people'), *os velhos* (literally 'the old ones') and *os antigos* (literally 'the ancient ones'). I am by no means the first to note this fact. Similar classifications have become commonplace in European ethnography (e.g. Zonabend 1980: *autrefois* and *aujourd'hui*, Bestard 1985: *antes* and *ahora*).

It is furthermore evident that a distinct measure of agreement can be observed concerning the actual chronological referents of these loose classifications of the recent past. Zonabend, whose fieldwork experience antedates mine by approximately 10 years, places the break between the *aujourd'hui* and the *avant* in the decade that followed World War II (Zonabend 1980, pp. 13, 145). In the Alto Minho there is also no doubt about the timing of the break: it occurred in the wake of the surge in emigration of the 1960s. This difference between our dates can be interpreted to concur with Bestard's comment that the break between the 'now' (time present) and the 'before' (time past) is deeply related to genealogical time (Bestard 1985, p. 6). Time past would then be the time of the *velhos*: the time when the parents of the present householders and the grandparents of the present marriageable set were in charge. This is a period that is remembered well, but one which is already imbued with tradition, with custom and with righteous timelessness by its association with the prestige of the retired parents and grandparents – who are also usually godparents of many of the members of the younger generation. Their authority is no longer present, and therefore no longer oppressive or visibly misused, but it is still sufficiently remembered for it to be imbued with prestige. Genealogical time and domestic time are, in this sense, intricately associated.

However, this explanation is not sufficient. In the same way as Zonabend argues that the 1950s was, indeed, a period of radical alteration in northeastern France – the period of 'une sorte d'éclatement de la communauté' (Zonabend 1980, p. 145) – in northwestern Portugal the 1960s was a period when community life suffered a radical alteration. To give just one example, a farmer who, between 1958 and 1964, used an annual average of 372 days of extra-household labour, in the period between 1971 and 1974, on the same farm and with a significantly similar household labour force, used only 105 days of extra-household labour (Pina-Cabral n.d.). His dependence on the co-operation and support of his neighbours, and their dependence on him for wages and mutual help, was drastically reduced. Similar indices of change can be detected when we look at change in family patterns (e.g. in the average age of marriage, Pina-Cabral 1986, p. 70, or the rate of illegitimate births, *ibid*, pp. 55-9).

We may therefore conclude that, in their everyday classification of social time, local inhabitants are merging genealogical and household considerations with considerations concerning the alteration in socio-economic conditions. In this way they derive a form of classification of time which has a fuller existential and practical significance.

My observations in the Alto Minho differ from those of Zonabend and Bestard only in that, in Paço and Couto, 'time past' is not perceived as uniform. *Antes* is an intermediary stage between *agora* and *antigamente*. This distinction too has a strong genealogical component: *antes* is roughly the period of the headship of the last ancestors whose memory is still alive. Although the depth of memory varied, at most these were the great-grandparents of present householders. *Antigamente* is a legendary period when peasant society was at its most typical or traditional – as no specific events are remembered concerning it, local inhabitants see this period as stretching back to the society's origins in undivided continuity.

The *minhotos* of today do not have at their disposal any of those means by which past events are recorded and preserved in societies where knowledge is orally transmitted: viz. epic poetry, formal genealogies and formulaic expressions. Knowledge of actual historical events rarely survives recounting. In my experience no actual events were remembered which antedated the informant's great-grandparents. At times people still remembered things which their parents and grandparents had been told, but this information was usually too vague to be passed on. This became evident to me when I attempted to collect information from local inhabitants concerning events which took place in the mid-19th century.

For instance, I became interested in the Maria da Fonte Revolution (which took place in 1846, and led to a civil war in the years that followed it) as a result of my study of burial practices in the region (see Pina-Cabral & Feijó, 1983). The revolution was started by peasant women in the Alto Minho when the government attempted to impose a set of laws, the ultimate aim of which was to open rural areas to capitalist development. These involved a bureaucratic reorganization, road building, new fiscal policies and, in particular, a set of laws designed to reform Public Health. What ultimately caused the peasants to revolt was the imposition of a tax on burials, the forbidding of burials inside churches and in churchyards, and the attempt to enforce construction of cemeteries. Paço and Couto were well within the area where the uprising was at its most fierce. Furthermore, the effects of the revolution are still felt today for, as far as burials are concerned, the peasants did win the day. It was only well into the 20th century that rural cemeteries were built in the region. Only since the 1970s, for example, has Couto had a cemetery away from the church-yard.

It was therefore with surprise that I discovered that no positive information survived about a movement of such tremendous local importance, and which had occurred well within the lives of the great-grandmothers of the older informants with whom I worked.[3] The only thing which was remembered was the name of Maria da Fonte, the legendary peasant leader of the revolution. A tale was told of her exceptional cunning and heroic bravery in a battle against the Spaniards! No memory survived of the causes of the uprising or the events to which it led.

This kind of amnesia is not as extensive in all fields. Poor people, I found, who had inherited little or no land or buildings, were bound to be very vague about the history of those of their ancestors whom they had not known personally.

Conversely, people who belonged to wealthy households had a much deeper genealogical knowledge. For instance, the first member of the Gomes family in Paço (cf. Pina-Cabral 1986, pp. 75–6) was reported to have come from Amarante as a *feitor* (foreman) of an absentee landlord whose lands he eventually bought. His wife came from Couto, where some of the lands she brought with her are still in the ownership of their descendants. As this man was the great-grandfather of people who are presently aged in their 60s, his arrival at the parish is likely to have occurred only 10 to 20 years at most after the Maria de Fonte revolution. Yet his presence is well remembered because of the land he left. Moreover, this land functions as a reminder of the unity of the four wealthy households in the parish who own land which belonged to him.

Irreversible time

Rural society fails to construct an image of history – of a synchronized, sequential, historical past. Rather, the past is measured backwards from the present, and time itself is, as Zonabend puts it, 'diversifié, rompu en des séries discontinues' (Zonabend 1980, p. 9). Furthermore, this diversification seems to be accompanied by a refusal to impose a systematic valuation on the passing of time. A singularly interesting feature of the difference between 'time present' (*agora*) and 'time past' (both *antes* and *antigamente*) as they are encountered in the everyday discourse of Paço and Couto is that the valuation which is imposed on this essentially linear change is not uniform. When I put together the notes I had taken during fieldwork which bore relation to this topic, I found that two distinct types of valuation existed.

On the one hand, I was told that *antes* milk was healthier because it had more cream; wine was stronger because it had more body; people had not been weakened and polluted by fertilizers and insecticides; they were tougher and less prone to sickness; doctors were needed less and the natural remedies they used were less prone to cause other diseases; life was far more joyous; people were more fertile; households were far more tightly knit; relatives were far more co-operative; priests were more religious and knowledgeable; parish rituals were far more gay; and local festivities were much more impressive.

On the other hand, *antes* was also a time of hunger; when beggars and vaga-bonds abounded; when no-one could spare a crust for a starving man; it was a time of slaving in the fields till you stopped feeling the pain; when less fuss was made of children, who were born and died in greater numbers; a time of illegit-imacy and sexual abuse of poor women; a time of greater brutality; of fights between hamlets and parishes; and a time when travelling was hazardous.

This ambiguous valuation should not come to us as a surprise, for it is fully consistent with peasant attitudes towards nature and towards themselves. If, on the one hand, the peasant was more fertile and imbued with bodily vigour when, in the 'time past', he lived closer to nature, on the other hand, his life was also more chaotic, more hazardous and harder, and less imbued with knowl-edge and civilization.

This assessment of the relationship between 'time past' and 'time present' finds a reflection in the notions which *minhoto* society has of its origins. Above all, *minhotos* are Christians. Christianity is for them the bedrock of human society as they experience it. The break between disordered, dangerous space and ordered, social space is marked by means of crosses and other Christian symbols (see Pina-Cabral 1986, pp. 184–6). These protect the Christian against the anti-social forces of disorder. The arrival of Christianity is seen as the point of origin of society. Interestingly, although this is a precisely formulated notion, in Paço and Couto I did not encounter any generally accepted account of how the coming of Christianity occurred. One thing, according to local lore, is certain: before the Christians there were the Moors, and these were a very different sort of people.

Moors are believed to be autochthonous, literally to have sprung out of the Earth. In a hillside forest, near a parish boundary in Paço, there is a natural granite formation – a small and unimpressive rock with some spherical indentations which look somewhat like broken eggshells. It is here that the *Mãe-Moura* (Moor Mother) is said to have emerged from the ground, giving rise to the Moors who lived in the region before the Christians. The autochthonous nature of the Moors and their association with rocks is further stressed by the fact that there are at least four other large rock formations in these two parishes where Enchanted Mooresses are supposed to be hidden together with immeasurable treasures. Only magic, and frightening magic at that, will allow humans to gain access to these treasures. Stories are reported of a man who, just as he managed to get the rock to open with the aid of the Book of St Cyprian, was attacked by gigantic reptiles and hideous monsters. Had he been courageous, they would not have harmed him; however, he ran for his life and the treasure was lost.

Legends such as these are legion in the region. In their fascination with Moors the people of these parishes are no exception. In some parishes of the region age-old popular plays which deal with the struggle between Moors and Christians are still staged every year. In this region this fascination is all the more interesting since we know that Moors played practically no actual historical role. Moors are also sometimes confused with Romans, but on the whole the distinction is kept since the Romans, having left churches, are suspected of having been Christians – an interpretation which reverses historical truth, making the Moors antedate the Romans.

I did not succeed in eliciting from my informants a consistent account of what Moor society was like. However, common reference to Moors attributes them with the following characteristics: they were exceptionally hard-working; they had tremendous physical strength; they had many children; their women were very beautiful; they were extremely rich; they had incredible magical powers of a dangerous sort; and they had a superb knowledge of nature, drugs and poisons. Finally, they were associated with the Devil, with dangerous powers in general, and with failure to be Christian (though they were not necessarily reputed to be malicious or personally evil). Unbaptized children are said to be Moors – or, alternatively, they are said to be 'like an animal'.

Although they are clearly kept distinct, there does seem to be a distinct overlap in the characteristics which are attributed by the peasant worldview to the following three states: peasants (as opposed to urban people); peasant society in 'time past' (as opposed to 'time present'); and Moors (as opposed to Christians). They all participate in a greater proximity to the Earth and its values, to the animal nature in man and to the power of magic by opposition to the power of reason. Thus, even though no image of history as synchronized and unidirectional is constructed, there is a symbolic consistency in the way in which the *minhotos* approach phenomena related to the passing of linear time.

Repetitive time

As central to peasant life as this irreversible way of perceiving time is another way which emphasizes repetitive phenomena. Here the past and the present are constantly renewed with each other. Social life in the Alto Minho is characterized by a series of rituals of community, all of which participate in this cyclical nature and which utilize symbols of circularity, the right hand, straightness, correct motion, equality and reciprocity. Thus, for instance, breadmaking, processions (especially the Easter procession), the Mass, annual festivities (e.g. St John's Eve, Christmas and Easter), funeral practices and self-help systems share these features. Again, I have undertaken a detailed study of these elsewhere (Pina-Cabral 1986, pp. 134–50), and will limit myself here to observing how they affect peasant perceptions of time.

Why these rituals have become rituals of community is explained by the way in which they are all closely associated with sociogeographic units: the household, the parish and the borough. They all play a central role in helping to reproduce the feelings of identity which bind these units. Furthermore, symbolically they perform the function of counteracting the forces of evil and chaos which besiege human society: pain, toil, envy, inequality, sex and the Devil.

In this way rituals such as that of breadmaking, the Mass or the Easter celebration are rituals of cosmogony, of Eternal Return – to use Éliade's term. At each re-celebration they counter irreversible time and they deny the need for change. It is in this sense that we may follow Zonabend when she claims that 'community time' is a 'temps circulaire, marqué par le perpétuel recommencement, par l'éternel retour vers le "même", donc vers un temps statique, sans fin, sans heurt' (Zonabend 1980, p. 222).

This view of time as static duration, a social condition fully controlled by a cyclical return to the origins of social order, is best applied to the *minhotos'* assessment of the 'time past' (*antes*) and especially the *antigamente*. 'Time present' is too visibly marked by failure to comply to the rule of community. People's involvement in their present and its struggles weakens the power of mediation of these rituals of community – that is, their power to counteract people's unavoidable perception of present life as one of strife and error. I am by no means claiming that the rituals of community completely fail to impose a cyclical rhythm and cosmological stability to everyday life. Anyone who observes the joy and genuine friendliness of neighbours towards each other at Easter time, their sympathy and co-operation at times of bereavement, or their profound belief in the redeeming powers of the Mass, cannot doubt that these rituals do have a positive effect. Rather, I maintain that the distinction between 'time present' and 'time past' functions precisely as a validation of this effectiveness – 'time past' is idealized as a condition in which the community succeeded more fully in capturing and keeping under control the disorderly effects of linear time.[4]

The ambiguous valuation of the irreversible passage of time is, in itself, not a distinct feature of peasant society. Both the myth of the Golden Age – when people were closer to nature and were thus healthier, happier and stronger – and the myth of Progress – claiming that human society is being purified by the civilizing virtue of the human effort towards perfection – have been part of European civilization for a very long time. What has distinguished peasant society from its urban counterpart in the recent past has been: first, as I have shown, its failure to construct a unified and synchronized view of history,[5] largely due to lack of literacy; and, secondly, its stronger reliance on rituals of community which function as means of imposing cosmological *and* social order on everyday life. Since the 1960s in northwestern Portugal (and since the 1950s in northeastern France), these two conditions have started to disappear – literacy is slowly becoming commonplace, and community feeling is starting to fade and with it the rituals upon which it relied for survival. We are therefore led to believe that the polarization between 'time present' and 'time past', even if it is an age-old feature of peasant life, has come to assume a new significance.

At this point it is worth casting a backward glance at the question of the building of paved roads. Until these were built, a strong distinction was maintained between *caminhos* and *carreiros* (tracks). Motion along the former was seen as being *a direito* (straight), whereas along the latter motion was roundabout and erratic (for a more detailed study of these concepts see Pina-Cabral 1986, pp. 146–9). Suffice it to point out that *caminhos* were privileged by being prescribed as the only correct paths for all ritual occasions – both life-cycle and household rituals (baptismal, and wedding and funeral processions) and rituals of parish and hamlet unity (church processions, pilgrimages to chapels, the path of the Cross at Easter from household to household, the passing of the images of the Holy Family, collection of money for parish and hamlet festivities, etc.). Strong supernatural sanctions were imposed on those who attempted to shorten the way or to vary it by using *carreiros* on these occasions. Even the 'procession of the dead' – that ghostly cortège which only some had the power to see, when the recently dead left the parish cemetery to summon the souls of their next companions – even these followed the *caminhos*.

When paved roads were built, they tended to follow the general outline of the *caminhos*, but only rarely was strict superimposition feasible. The result was that the *caminhos*, being so much more impractical for everyday use than paved roads, came into disuse. Some attempts were made to continue to use the old paths for ceremonial purposes, I was told, but laziness and the prestige value of including automobiles in life-cycle ceremonies soon won the day for the paved roads. The *caminhos* were abandoned, and with them the previous close interrelationship between community, cyclical time and spatial movement within the parish was weakened.

The use of new paved roads is therefore consistent with a change in peasant attitudes, not only towards the space of community but also towards time. The perception of community is profoundly attached to an association between social groups and specific stretches of land – for this reason I call them sociogeographic units. The significance of the *caminhos* lay in the fact that they linked the rituals of community with an ordering of physical space. They were community engraved onto the land.

The building of paved roads, by itself, would not have seriously hindered this relationship. However, it was accompanied by a reduction in the significance of community relations and in the exclusiveness of the reliance of neighbours on local social relations. The new roads permit privacy and isolation for the local resident from his neighbours while, concomitantly, breaking the exclusiveness of the association between the community[6] and its land by granting full rights of entry to all. In this way paved roads are a symbol of the opening of peasant society to the future – that is, to a cosmological condition which is characterized by permanent instability, linearity, and movement.

Notes

1   The parish names are pseudonyms, as well as the family names referred below. Both parishes are in the borough of Ponte da Barca, district of Viana do Castelo.
2   See Cailler-Boisvert (1966). She is writing about a parish in this region which, at the time she carried out fieldwork, was nearly emptied of male inhabitants.
3   This is particularly the case since, in the second half of the 19th century, the average female age of marriage each decade in Paço and Couto oscillated between 27 and 32 years.
4   The rituals of community did not deny time, nor did they create timelessness. As Barnes (1984, p. 201) put it: 'The claim that a representation of stability through time is the same thing as a denial of time is an entirely arbitrary interpretation'.
5   What Zonabend (1980, p. 9) calls 'le temps éclaté, feuilleté'.
6   This generic reference to community must be understood as a means of facilitating expression. Community is a layered phenomenon: households participate in it, as much as hamlets, parishes and boroughs.

References

Barnes, R. H. 1984. *Two crows denies it: a history of controversy in Omaha sociology*. Lincoln and London: University of Nebraska Press.
Bestard Camps, J. 1985. ¿*Que hay en un pariente? Una explicacion cultural del parentesco en Formentera*. Doctoral Thesis, University of Barcelona.
Cailler-Boisvert, C. 1966. Une communauté féminine rural de l'Alto Minho. *Bulletin des études portuguaises* **27**, 237–84.
Gervitch, G. 1958. *La multiplicité des temps sociaux*. Paris: Centre de Documentation Universitaire.
Pina-Cabral, J. de 1986. *Sons of Adam, daughters of Eve: the peasant worldview of the Alto Minho*. Oxford: Clarendon Press.
Pina-Cabral, J. de, in press. Acting out change: popular theatre within a context of

altering work conditions. In *Change and continuity in twentieth century Portugal*, D. Goldey and H. Martins (eds). London: Macmillan.

Pina-Cabral, J. de and R. Feijó 1983. Conflicting attitudes to death in modern Portugal: the question of cemeteries. In *Death in Portugal: studies in Portuguese anthropology and modern history*, R. Feijó, H. Martins and J. de Pina-Cabral (eds). Oxford: JASO.

Zonabend, F. 1980. *La mémoire longue: temps et histoires au village*. Paris: PUF, Croissées.

6 Understanding Yolngu signs of the past

NANCY M. WILLIAMS and
DAYMBALIPU MUNUNGGURR

For the purpose of this chapter we assume that the past is an aspect of real time, universally experienced by all human beings, although perceived and structured by people of different cultures in different ways. Our geographic focus is Yirrkala, in the Northern Territory of Australia. Some 3000 Yolngu-speaking people are the traditional owners of lands in northeastern Arnhem Land consisting of an area of approximately 8 500 km²; since passage of the 1976 Land Rights Act, they are also owners in Australian law. Yirrkala, on the Gove Peninsula, is situated approximately 650 km east of Darwin. Here, on a site overlooking the Arafura Sea and near a permanent source of fresh water, Daymbalipu Mununggurr's father, father's brothers and other Yolngu leaders helped to establish a mission station in the 1930s. During the first years of the mission's existence, between 50 and 100 Yolngu people were regularly staying there. For the most part they were members of the clans on whose land the mission station was located, the clans with nearby lands and those with close marriage ties. Some 900 Yolngu now live at Yirrkala or on homeland centres (outstations) affiliated with Yirrkala.

The northeastern Arnhem Land Aborigines were called 'Murngin' by Warner (1937) and members of the 'Wulamba [cultural] bloc' by Berndt (1951), and are now generally known as 'Yolngu', after the word for Aboriginal human being in the mutually intelligible dialects they speak. The named patrimoieties, Dhuwa and Yirritja, provide labels and categories for the pervasive dualism that structures the Yolngu social and natural universe. In addition, every person is born into a patrilineal land-owning group we may call a clan, and the clans are divided by moiety, so that each clan, as well as each individual, is either Dhuwa or Yirritja. Each person acquires certain interests, including rights to use certain tracts of land, through their father's clan, which is also their own clan, and through their mother's clan.

Time: past time

For Yolngu, as for other people, notions about the past and perception of the past are related to present and future uses of time. It is impossible to discuss the past in any meaningful way without implying present and future. These aspects of time appear to be universal human perceptions, regardless of how they may be culturally moulded, including by means such as the use of tense and other linguistic forms. Yolngu people recognize and explain events of the distant past by the record that they see those events left in their environment. In analogous ways they read signs such as the footprints of known people, and interpret very recent activity. The value that Yolngu place on these past events, both positive and negative, underlies their interpretation of the present and expectations about the future. However, first we point out some presuppositions in 'Western' or 'European' notions of time, because that is the cultural background of one of the authors of this chapter, and because many (if not most) readers will either share or be most familiar with that background. That should allow us to bring to a conscious level and to assess taken-for-granted assumptions about time, and thereby guard against using them as a kind of accurate or value-free yardstick for Yolngu concepts of time.

Europeans generally perceive time as natural, real, moving, based on the ordered movement of the heavenly bodies, and therefore both precise and accurate. Yet a glance at the history of calendars and clocks renders that perception problematic. Calendars have generally been based on celestial phenomena, but the length of the different units used to calculate and express the passage of time has been arbitrary. The length of units may vary, depending on whether they are measured by stars, Sun or Moon. European calendars have attempted to correlate days and months with a seasonal year, as well as imposing a seven-day week, although celestially based phenomena have not turned out to be well-suited either for exact definition or for the interrelation, since it is not possible to create cycles of small units, such as months, which fill the larger periods, like the year, exactly. It is hardest of all to relate months to years. Since the year contains more than 12 but less than 13 lunar months, a consistent cycle of lunar months will either get ahead of or behind the seasonal year. Keeping the seasonal year as primary means that months will be very approximate lunar months, and will not follow the phases of the moon (Dunlop 1984, p. 27). People who have devised calendars have always had to devise ways of readjusting them, because of the inherent variability of the phenomena on which their units are based, and the history of change in calendars (and clocks) is enormous. Nor has readjustment of calendars always been accomplished without incident, as one example will show. Pope Gregory XIII promulgated a new calendar to replace the Julian calendar in 1582. When the English adopted it by an Act of Parliament in 1752, the difference between the Julian and the Gregorian calendars was 11 days. To rectify the difference, Parliament declared that 3 September 1752 should be called 14 September. People were so exercised by the fear that their lives had been shortened by 11 days that they rioted. They were apparently less concerned by the change that Parliament enacted at the same time to move the beginning of the year from 25 March to 1 January (Ronan 1963, p. 619).

One of the most common metaphors for the passage of time, or for time itself, is 'flow'. Indeed, it has been suggested that even though only material fluids flow, the experience of time, like the experience of other psychic phenomena, can only be expressed in terms of material phenomena. Mellor

(1981, p. 10) reasons that the flow of time is the accumulation of successive memories. Since memories can only accumulate at successively later times, our sense of the flow of time has the direction it has. Mellor (1981, p. 18) argues persuasively that it is causal order that fixes temporal order, and thereby distinguishes it from spatial order. Yet the European model of temporal duration ignores the possibility of variability in flow. In his history of clocks, Landes (1983, p. 4) notes that before mechanical clocks were developed, as increasingly smaller units were measured and the users of these duration-measuring devices wanted even more reliable performance, no available substance such as water, sand or mercury could be kept moving at a suitably continuous and even pace. Landes remarks in an endnote:

> I originally thought the notion that time is continuous was intuitively obvious and generally accepted. I have since learned that physicists have come to see time as part of a space–time continuum, and that some of them have hypothesized that time, like other apparently continuous phenomena such as light, is composed of quanta, that is, a stream of very fine particles. . . . In our present state of technique we have no way of marking and counting such small units of time, so that all of this is still in the realm of speculation; but even if the hypothesis were true, it would in no way effect the validity of the time measurement *as we know it* (Landes 1983, p. 391, note 7; emphasis added).

Landes (1983, p. 66) shares with other historians the view that by the middle ages, 'time-consciousness and discipline' had been internalized to a remarkable degree. However, after the development of the mechanical clock, the Church which had sponsored its development for the regulation of prayer, was not the sole market. First courts, then the growing bourgeoisie desired clocks. In tracing the development of clocks from their mechanical beginnings to their present quartz form (and the market domination by the Chinese in Hong Kong), Landes argues that the development of clocks and ever more 'precise' timekeeping, 'the peculiar and revolutionary sense of time', as Hobsbawm (1983, p. 35) puts it, was the crucial link in the development of modern capitalism.

If we accept that duration – that is, the passage of time – is universally experienced in a single direction, regardless of the ideational or verbal forms the expression of such experience may take (*contra* Dubinskas & Traweek 1984), and if context plays a determinative (although not the only) role in the form of its expression, then we can see that the association of change with time is a concomitant of the values associated with the development and spread of capitalism. Yet time and change are not identical. As Europeans came to value change in itself, and for its association with the idea of progress in their own societies, they attributed to non-Western, non-capitalist societies the opposite: that is, those societies were not only unchanging, they resisted change. Yet Bourdieu (1977) and others have argued what must surely now be the generally accepted proposition that 'time is a constitutive dimension of social reality' (Fabian 1983, p. 24). Colson (1984, p. 1) remarks that it is anthropologists' long-term involvement with the people whose ways of life they have tried to understand that has led to an understanding of the constitutive nature of time, as well as to an appreciation that 'the societies we study are a stream of time, rather than a stable environment whose dimensions can be securely plotted . . . once and for all'.

Interpretations of culturally different systems of time and time use that are based on dichotomies, binary oppositions or continua obscure the fact that all cultural systems have or use aspects of what are often presented as opposing or mutually exclusive features. The most common features in such interpretations are:

> timeless – time based
> cyclic – linear
> changeless – changing
> concrete – abstract

Each of these features is present in the culturally patterned time perception of the Yolngu, and probably in that of people in all societies. The most useful distinctions to be made are therefore those of degree or in the specific ways in which one feature may be emphasized or another played down. Comparative analysis of the temporal aspects of cultures that relies on these features as mutually exclusive oppositions is simplistic. Moreover, it is based on the implicit contrast between 'primitive' and 'civilized' , and the features on the right above which European users of this dichotomy assert characterize 'civilized' peoples are valued positively by Western societies. The features on the left they value negatively.

A number of historians have become interested in time and changes in perception of time, and in relating the changing perceptions to larger social and economic changes. Hobsbawm notes among the issues they have raised are

> debates on the roles of "church time"; the Western Church had a strange obsession with strict chronometric regularity of prayer, especially at night; and of medieval merchants' and employers' time, in the development of the clock . . . the struggles of craftsmen and laborers during industrialization against the imperatives of regularity and the clock, or, at least for the control of hourly or work time
>
> (Hobsbawn 1983, p. 36).

Landes (1983, p. 25) reflects the values of his own society in assessing the economic significance of the development of clocks, when he writes, 'That the mechanical clock did appear in the West, and with it a civilization organized around the measurement and knowledge of time, is a critical factor in the differentiation of the West from the Rest and the rise of Europe to technological and economic hegemony'. Landes and others have written of the internalization of time (they mean changing European notions about the measurement and value of time) as 'time discipline'. They contrast time discipline with a simple kind of 'time obedience', and characterize the development of time discipline as the result of a combination of changes in technology and economic organization. Landes believes that this development has profound implications, which he explains thus: once clocks could be miniaturized and thereby made portable, they could be carried about by individuals:

> It was this widespread private use that laid the basis for *time* discipline, as against *time obedience*. One can . . . use public clocks to summon people for one purpose or another; but that is not punctuality. Punctuality comes from within, not from without. It is the mechanical clock that made possible, for better or worse, a civilization attentive to the passage of time, hence of productivity and performance
>
> (Landes 1983, p. 7).

As Landes interprets it, the change in time perception is parallel with the development of European ideas about property. These ideas reached their full flower in the 18th century, and were expressed, for example, by Blackstone in his *Commentaries* (1765–9). These ideas continue to provide the legal and popular underpinnings for European assumptions about property (Williams 1986). In the context of explaining the failure of the Chinese to invent the mechanical clock, Landes writes ' . . . the whole system rested on the assumption that an official's time – all his time – belonged to the emperor, who could do with it (and waste it) as he pleased. The only way to correct this waste, which the Chinese could not even perceive as such, would have been to recognize time as *private* property' (Landes 1983, p. 52, emphasis added). In Landes' polarities (public–private, waste–save) the values of European bourgeois society of the 19th century as well as those of 20th-century North America can be seen. Attributing the development of these values to a shift from time obedience to time discipline assumes only one dimension of response to the ordering of duration, and further that its internalization produces a particular kind of motivation. Yolngu, to the contrary, do not regard themselves as being obedient to time, in the sense of having no conscious control over their ordering of duration. A striking example of such control, drawn not from Yolngu but from Pitjantjatjara people, is contained in a recent study by a musicologist.

Ellis (1984, p. 149) found that Pitjantjatjara performance of ritual reveals a phenomenon she calls 'perfect time', analogous to 'perfect pitch'. Perfect time 'enables accurate manipulation of time elements in musical structure. The patterns used appear to be learned as a set of formulae, each applicable to changing demands of duration . . .' Comparable study of Yolngu music would probably reveal that the Yolngu also make use of 'perfect time' in their ritual performances.

Yolngu time as 'task oriented'

One of the characteristics that some writers have used to distinguish the time-concepts of non-Western peoples from those of industrialized societies is 'task orientation'. (Presumably the logical converse is 'work orientation' – that is, tasks oriented to specific duration.) Yolngu refer to many of their activities, both in the realm of everyday life and in the specialized realms of ritual, in terms that express task orientation. Thus, a woman may refer to all of the activities necessary to weave a dilly bag, from gathering the pandanus leaves to the final finishing stitches, as *batji-djama* (*batji* = basket woven from strips of pandanus leaves; *djama* = work, that is all the tasks necessary to completion). A man may refer similarly to his occupation with *manikay-djama* (*manikay* = cycle of ritual song or chant). To a finished task the verb *buma* may be suffixed to convey the meaning that all of the appropriate work has been completed. Yet it would be a distortion if the impression were given that Yolngu time is solely perceived in terms of tasks and not also in terms of arbitrary measures of duration. The person in charge of a *manikay* performance may announce, for example, that a *manikay* must be concluded before the coming morning. A *manikay* performance is, in fact, frequently organized in terms of the days or nights (or both) or weekends that the people planning it expect to elapse until everybody is satisfied that it has been properly done. (See Philips 1974, on Warm Springs Indian time.) It is a matter of emphasis and context whether time is structured to focus on a task or on an anticipated lapse of time – or with appropriate verbal change, on *past* time. That is surely the experience of people in most if not all societies, including those of the industrialized West as well as the Yolngu.

Cyclic time: European versus Yolngu?

Europeans commonly characterize their notions of time as linear, even though major studies by European historians have been based on a concept of cycle (and at the popular level the notion of cycle is expressed for example in the adage 'history repeats itself'). Historians of such stature as Spengler and Toynbee, and the anthropologist Kroeber, as well as others drawing directly on Marx, have used cyclic temporality as their explanatory basis. Friedman, for example, says that

> . . . it is possible to conceive of social process in terms of social repro-
> duction, a complex of cycles that self-organize. . . . Business cycles,
> longer term cycles of accumulation (of prestige or capital), cycles of
> expansion and contraction, shifts in centers of accumulation, civilizational
> cycles, i.e. significant areas of historical reality, those where attempts
> have been made to show the transformational relations underlying specific
> changes . . . are those whose temporal properties are objective, external
> to the social organization, and the consciousness, of the societies that are
> dependent on them
>
> (Friedman 1985, p. 173).

Despite the claim that these historical transformations occur in cycles, the changes to which they refer are, in fact, repetitive phenomena or related series of events that occur (or have occurred) in a flow of time. Some social phenomena may, at a certain level of confidence, be predicted to precede or to cause others (or to succeed or post-dict them), and there may be striking parallels in their appearance. However, that is not the same thing as perceiving time flowing in circles or demonstrating precisely the same events continuously following each other in endless cycles. If time is indeed constitutive of social reality, how could they?

The notion of cycle has been used by Europeans to try to understand or to explain the manifestations of the Yolngu past, especially signs from the distant past. In that case the use of cycle should be seen as a metaphor to convey to other Europeans how Yolngu perceive their past, whether in the present or in terms of the future. Also, they should not be misled by such things as the recursive nature of kinship terms.

Yolngu concepts of recent past

Yolngu people have many ways of expressing duration and of locating events, whether unique or in series. They may specify detail in both location and duration in ways that would be familiar in terms of their 'precision', if not their idiom, to people in clock-dominated societies. In referring to the past (as well as to the present and future) Yolngu can call on terms from the conceptually detailed lexicon of seasons (cf. Thomson 1939, 1948), as well as those of other recurrent or cyclic phenomena, such as developmental terms (both physical and social) for stages in the life cycle, times of the day (in terms of the position of the Sun and the relative lengths of shadows cast), and times of the night (by characteristics of the Moon and positions of the stars).

The round of seasons, or a year (*dhunggarra*), is marked at its beginning by the build-up of thunder clouds that herald the coming of the first rains. The seasonal round may also be referred to as *waltjan*, the generic term for rain. Nowadays the beginning of a year may be expressed as Christmas, and Christmases may be counted in the same way as *dhunggarra* and *waltjan*. Yolngu numbers, to a base five, are symbolized by the distribution of turtle eggs, customarily arranged in lots of five, with four of the eggs placed in a 'square' and the fifth resting on the centre atop the four. For the Yirrkala school's literacy programme in the Yolngu dialects, Daymbalipu Mununggurr has illustrated the use of this base-five system up to 100. Of course, Yolngu can use these and other means to express time, and to refer to past events in units of duration that reflect linear time. They can, and frequently do, explain sequences of events in terms that express linear temporality.

A quick scanning of the Australian Aboriginal literature on 'message sticks' indicates that it has been fashionable since at least the 1880s (for example, Howitt 1889) to interpret them as mnemonic devices for their bearers, who delivered the message verbally, plus perhaps some totemic symbol to vouch for the *bona fides* of the bearer or the sender. Conversely, Yolngu assert that message sticks (*balarm*) themselves did (and still can) convey information about the precise time that, say, a ceremony is planned, as well as how many people were invited and expected to attend. The devices used include representations of the Moon in specific phases, and lines and circles that conveyed number.

Yolngu may locate events as sequences within, or as the defining aspects of, measured duration. Thus, they locate certain events in time by using a method of description which relies on synchronicity: when certain features are simultaneously present, or when all or sufficient conditions are met, then the event is placed in time. 'Season', for example, refers to the time when a particular set of features coexist – wind direction, ambient temperature, cloud formation, pattern of rainfall and stage of specific floral or faunal maturity. The temporal concatenation of features may also be extended to include a spatial referent. In fact, one of the most common ways that Yolngu signal the appropriate time for gathering a particular resource at a particular place is by naming the concatenation of events. Thus, when a certain flower blooms in one place, it is the time that a particular food may be harvested at another; for example, the flowering of a certain tree occurs when yams are fully mature at a particular place, or when there is most honey at another (gathered from a predominant species, therefore of a particular flavour), or when a certain fish has most fat, or when turtle eggs are freshly deposited in a turtle breeding area.

Yolngu cosmology and signs of the past in the present

For Yolngu there is a far-distant past about which no living person can have direct, therefore sure, knowledge. In Yolngu epistemology an individual's direct experience, seeing with one's own eyes or hearing with one's own ears, is the only basis for knowing, and hence for understanding, something that cannot be questioned. There is therefore a past (and a future) about which individual Yolngu will say they know nothing or can only speculate on the basis of accounts on which they do not place much reliance, because they have not experienced, cannot experience, it during their lifetime. However, there are for Yolngu means of understanding the past and the significance of the past in the present. These means exist in the tangible manifestations of the spirit-beings who travelled through Yolngu lands and waters and by their words and deeds, bestowed land on the Yolngu (Williams 1986, pp. 37–46). From the narrative accounts of their behaviour, Yolngu also find the rationale for proper behaviour in relation to their land and to each other. The ritual songs the spirit-beings chanted, and thus the ritual songs that present-day Yolngu men sing, are the reliable means for understanding and knowing the most-ancient past, for they recite in detail the journeys of those spirit-beings. Closer to the present, Yolngu place their trust in the accounts of past events that their parents, grandparents, and other known relatives and ancestors told them. The older an account is and the greater the number of more known people who are linked in its transmission, the greater its authority. (These are aspects that become critical in cases of disputed or contradictory accounts of past events.)

Ngurrunanggal signifies 'in the beginning' and marks the absoluteness of

Wangarr. *Wangarr* refers to the distant past, in which the spirit-beings travelled through the land doing many of the things that Yolngu on whom they bestowed land would continue to do. Also in doing them today, Yolngu claim the greatest authority is that of continuity: it has always been thus. They say, 'Our fathers taught us, as their fathers taught them'.

Wangarr is also the name for the spirit-beings and all their appurtenances – anything attributable to that time, whether object or event, is *Wangarr*. The *Wangarr* spirit-beings performed rituals, as well as manufacturing the beautiful objects used and celebrated in ritual. They also engaged in everyday activities, and Yolngu learned from *Wangarr* the details of the complicated technology required in the gathering and preparation of foods that need special treatment; for example, the way to remove a toxic substance from the cycad palm nut – a long and complex series of operations (as is the removal of another toxic substance from a certain yam). Use of these foods is marked by ritual in both their preparation and consumption.

Means of referring to the very distant past include placing prosodic emphasis on terms that can also be used to refer to shorter orders of past time. The context supplies the information necessary to understand what order of past time is meant. Thus, in ordinary conversation *baman* may mean long ago, or a long time, and it may also refer to a relatively recent event or short interval. For example, the question 'How long have you been chewing that mouthful of food?' may be appropriately answered by '*Baman*'. The time of the *Wangarr* is also *baman*, but additional terms may be used to emphasize the great length of time involved. *Baman* with a suffixing intensifier *birr* may itself be intensified, hence lengthened, by prolonging the trill of the final 'rr', thus *baman-birr-rr-rr-rr*!

Transformation and essential qualities

The essential qualities of a *Wangarr* being or species remain constant and undiminished, despite the differing external appearance or behaviour of a particular manifestation at a particular time. One essential feature is association with particular people. For example, the Djapu Shark retains the essence of Shark and also of human-ness through transformations that include fish, rocks, trees and human beings. In fact, an essential quality is the ability to transform, and by transforming to relate; thus the essence is relational. In a study of Yolngu conceptualization, Rudder (1984, p. 134) demonstrates how a series of objects has an essential nature that transcends their transformations, and relates them to a contemporary human group: the manifestations of a *Wangarr* snake include a particular grey-white clay at a certain place; it is used in painting after it is transformed into a red-coloured pigment by firing; Yolngu whom Rudder questioned identified the respective forms as the faeces and blood of the *Wangarr* snake.

Daymbalipu Mununggurr gives this as one account of *Wangarr* (in a very abbreviated form): Balana is a Djapu *Wangarr*. He performed his tasks in the very distant past (*ngathil baman*). He left the place Balana for Djapu people. He also left his canoe, which was named Gurndarriwuy. He left Djapu names for the Djapu owners of that place: names for people, places, canoes, the rope for harpooning turtle and for his home, Balana. Our first Djapu people told us that story. Now we stay there, control that place, use the resources of that place. Sometimes we go to another place visiting; we stay there with another group of people, then return to the same place, the same home. In another example, Daymbalipu Mununggurr gives an outline of Shark, the most important Djapu *Wangarr*: I am thinking about long ago (*ngathilmirr baman*), about Marna (Shark). My *Wangarr* is Marna. Before that he was Guyamiyana, Fish. You don't know about that; I don't know about that. That *Wangarr* Marna went into a human being, one human being, one human being whose name was Mununggurr. I know that myself. We follow that *manikay* all the way: Shark's water, his home place, and the path of his journey. We sing that *manikay* all the way. ('All the way' has both a spatial and a temporal referent.)

Djapu people, as they grow older, assimilate more and more of the essence of the *Wangarr* Shark. By the time they die they have only a short way to go before they are one with their *Wangarr*. The final resting place for Djapu bones is also imbued with meanings derived from the *Wangarr* Shark, although Djapu spirits may go to any of a number of Djapu places.

During their travels through Yolngu country, *Wangarr* spirit-beings left signs of their activities, both everyday events and those of religious import. They also left their appurtenances (such as digging sticks, dilly bags and spears), and marks or impressions at the places where they sat or ate or slept. Most sacred of all, they left parts of their very beings in the sites that are most important to Yolngu. Even though the appearance of all these sites and their particular features – rocks that are transformations of ritual dilly bags, mounds created by the thrust of a *Wangarr* spear into the ground, a waterhole formed by *Wangarr* fish swimming around to make a 'nest', their essence remains unchanged. Thus, in answer to the hypothetical question of what would happen if a pool of water made by the *Wangarr* Shark swimming around dried up, Daymbalipu Mununggurr says the mark or impression (*dharapul*) would remain, and someday there will again be water in the place where Shark swam around.

It is because the Yolngu landscape is saturated with signs that bear meanings that are still immensely important to Yolngu that they regard it as potentially dangerous to disturb the features of the landscape. Furthermore, Yolngu perceive the land as themselves in some respects, and their most sacred religious objects are the bones of the land. As a person's bones, especially the backbone, provide the physical structure of a person, so the sacred land bones provide the structure for the land. Therefore, the Yolngu say that they must exercise care and respect in looking after both. It would be impossible for one Yolngu person, or even one clan, to be absolutely knowledgeable about the locations of all the sites or paths followed by all the *Wangarr*, since each clan and each lineage within a clan has at least two or three major *Wangarr* and other lesser spirit-beings who left signs significant to Yolngu. This is why, in conjunction with the symbolic equivalences of bodies and land, it is inherently dangerous to disturb the earth or any of its features in a visible or lasting way. Thus, in answer to a query directed to learning more about the people who lived long ago and left the freshwater shells now seen eroding out of the bank of a billabong, Daymbalipu Mununggurr says, 'that was a very long time ago. And that place, where we see the evidence of people living there, we are not allowed to dig up. We must leave it like that'. He goes on to name the possible ill-effects of disturbing other places. Some places are dangerous because being there can cause sickness. Disturbing certain other places, like old Yolngu homes or places formed by the *Wangarr*, may result in floods occurring, or in cyclones. Disturbing still other places may result in searing heat that will dry up all the water. Disturbing yet other kinds of places will be followed by people becoming seriously or incurably ill. Daymbalipu Mununggurr adds that there are also places in the sea and in freshwater sites consecrated by the *Wangarr*. Yolngu know the places; they are dangerous and must be avoided.

In the absence of specific local knowledge, a Yolngu person makes a kind of uniformitarian assumption: signs exist, and they have meaning for somebody, even if unknown to a stranger or uninitiated person; they have meaning because of their association with and persistence from the past. A Yolngu person is loath to travel through unknown parts of Australia, even where European occupation has virtually obliterated signs of Aboriginal use or presence, and where no obviously Aboriginal person is to be seen. Without prior knowledge (which implies an Aboriginally appropriate introduction to the land) or a proper guide, one may unwittingly enter an area inherently dangerous and suffer some illness as a consequence, or may wrongly enter a site restricted to persons of specific religious status or gender. At the most generalized level, Yolngu feel sadness for the people and the lands of Australia where the Aboriginal owners are no longer alive or present. Thus, a young man from Yirrkala went for what his white companion styled a recreational walk in a suburban Sydney park, where he saw shells of freshwater molluscs eroding from a stream bank. He paused, touched the toe of his shoe to the disintegrating shells, and said, '*Gumurrdjarrark Yolngu-olngu* . . .' ('Poor Aboriginal people . . .').

Standing accounts: Yolngu protocol in managing the past

In a small-scale society in which most people are just now in the process of acquiring writing (that crutch of record-keeping), the forms developed in the past which use the memory of individuals for storage and retrieval of information continue to have the greatest authority. The types of information stored range from the obligations that individual kin owe each other, including betrothal contracts, use rights in land, to the outcomes of disputes and attendant sanctions, to suggest but a few. In fact, all the information that is necessary or important for individuals to carry on the business of everyday life as well as the most sacred religious knowledge and performance of the rich body of ceremony, is stored in Yolngu memory. The form in which it is stored, in terms of the approved or generally acceptable versions, must also be agreed upon, and the creation of a consensus concerning the acceptable version may itself require considerable negotiation. All these are aspects of the keeping of standing accounts. Because Yolngu decision-making is a continuous process, as people are expected to recalculate their options continuously, it is customary to have witnesses to the form of any completed decision (Williams 1985). People in certain relationships to the parties should be available to fill the role of witness. The expectation that people will be continuously, or at least regularly, calculating the costs and benefits of any particular decision is the basis for checking from time to time to see if the other party to a decision is 'still saying the same word', or 'still thinking the same way'.

The more important that Yolngu regard a category of knowledge to be, the more precisely they express rules of access. Thus, knowledge concerning the religious myth narratives of land bestowal at their most esoteric level, the objects that symbolize the bestowal and the ritual performances that enact them, is held in the safest repository of all: inside the heads of the oldest clan leaders. What is hidden in an apparently physically safe and secret place may be discovered and stolen, but nobody can force the revelation of what is inside another's head. Of course, that is a critical factor in the ability that leaders have in maintaining authority in their community. As long as the knowledge is valued, and as long as the leaders control access to it they have effective means of maintaining their authority. The more ancient the knowledge is reputed to be, if its pedigree is acknowledged as valid (usually in the form of a chain of agnatic antecedents), the greater its authority is. When the focus of a discussion is on clan or lineage forbears, whether for the purpose of constructing a genealogy or for instructing in clan tradition, at a remove of four or five generations from the most senior living generation, people may speculate that their actual ancestors interacted with the spirit-beings of the long-ago past, perhaps even with *Wangarr*. Significant to the present discussion is that access to knowledge, to information stored in any form, is governed by rules that are detailed and can be made very precise. The existence of rights does not, of course, imply that the rules of access operate automatically or universally without disagreement. Nevertheless, the existence of such access-governing rules is the moral basis on which competing claims may be made and judged.

Yolngu concepts of past time provide the means for appropriate precision. Of course, precision is not uniquely conveyed by measurement expressed numerically, although Europeans tend to perceive it that way. Near events of the past are more likely to be described in temporal detail than past ones where sequence may be more pertinent than difference in arbitrary units of duration. Thus, at *Ngurrunanggal*, the time of the *Wangarr* may be thought of as analogous to the time of creation of the world in Judeo-Christian cosmogonies.

It has been common for European scholars to refer to manifestations of 'the past in the present' in attempting to understand Aboriginal concepts of time. Yolngu concepts of time suggest that such explanations should imply neither conflation of perceptions nor dichotomous barriers of time, but simply the existence of a means of making the past available for the experience of people in the present. In that context, for individuals it constitutes an experiential potential for the expression of continuity of a shared and valued past. Seen in that way, the experience of Christians who ritually consume the body and blood of their deity is parallel to the experience of Djapu people in ritually enacting some part of the Shark's journey.

In comparative analysis, it may be that European notions of the past are culturally skewed toward the attribution of great value and expenditure of resources in discovering (or inventing) ever smaller and more discrete units for expressing the duration of time, including past time. At least the majority of Europeans appear willing to support the specialists who engage in that kind of activity while remaining relatively content with concepts of the past expressed in 'learning history' in forms such as 'Captain Cook discovered Australia in 1770'.

Perhaps the most useful guides to understanding Yolngu signs of the past are found in Yolngu procedures governing the keeping of standing accounts, including the protocol of access – the assignment of rights to know and to reveal knowledge that Yolngu value highly. Such knowledge includes the events and beings of the *Wangarr* and the rights and duties, privileges and obligations which they entail in the more recent past, for they provide a charter for the form of the accounts on which Yolngu at any present time may call in furthering the affairs of their private and public lives.

Acknowledgements

Nancy Williams thanks Raymatja Marika-Mununggiritj for comments on an earlier draft of the chapter, which added a significant dimension to the explanation of past time. She also thanks Tamsin Donaldson for a critical reading of an early draft.

References

Berndt, R. M. 1951. *Kunapipi*. Melbourne: F. W. Cheshire.
Blackstone, Sir W. 1765–69. *Commentaries on the laws of England* (4 Vols). Oxford: Clarendon Press.
Bourdieu, P. 1977. *Outline of a theory of practice*. Cambridge: Cambridge University Press.
Colson, E. 1984. The reordering of experience: anthropological involvement with time. *Journal of Anthropological Research* **40**, 1–13.
Dunlop, S. 1984. *Timeless? An examination of temporal concepts in primitive and Western societies*. Unpublished BA (Hons) Thesis, University of Sydney.
Dubinskas, F. A. and S. Traweek 1984. Closer to the ground: a reinterpretation of Walbiri iconography. *Man (new series)* **19**, 15–30.
Ellis, J. 1984. Time consciousness of Aboriginal performers. In *Problems & solutions: occasional essays in musicology presented to Alice M. Moyle*, J. Kassler and J. Stubington (eds), 149–85. Sydney: Hale and Iremonger.
Fabian, J. 1983. *Time and the other: how anthropology makes its objects*. New York: Columbia University Press.

Friedman, J. 1985. Our time, their time, world time: the transformation of temporal modes. *Ethnos* **50**, 168–83.

Hobsbawm, E. J. 1983. On the watch [review of Revolution in time by D. S. Landes]. *New York Review of Books* **30** (19), 35–6.

Howitt, A. W. 1889. Notes on message sticks and messengers. *Journal of the Anthropological Institute* **18**, 314–32.

Landes, D. S. 1983. *Revolution in time: clocks and the making of the modern world*. Cambridge, Massachusetts: Harvard University Press.

Mellor, D. H. 1981. *Real time*. Cambridge: Cambridge University Press.

Philips, S. U. 1974. Warm Springs 'Indian time': how the regulation of participation affects the progression of events. In *Explorations in the ethnography of speaking*, R. Bauman and J. Sherzer (eds), 92–109. Cambridge: Cambridge University Press.

Ronan, C. A. 1963. Calendar. *Encyclopaedia Britannica*, Vol. 4, 611–19.

Rudder, J. 1983. *Qualitative thinking: an examination of the classificatory systems, evaluative systems and cognitive structures of the Yolngu people of north-east Arnhem Land*. Unpublished MA Thesis, Australian National University, Canberra.

Thomson, D. F. 1939. The seasonal factor in human culture, illustrated from the life of a contemporary nomadic group. *Prehistoric Society Proceedings (new series)* **5** (2): 209–21.

Thomson, D. F. 1948. Arnhem Land: explorations among an unknown people. *Geographical Journal* **112**: 1–8.

Warner, W. L. 1937. *A black civilization: a study of an Australian tribe*. New York: Harper and Row.

Williams, N. M. 1985. On Aboriginal decision-making. In *Metaphors of interpretation: essays in honour of W.E.H. Stanner*, D. Barwick, J. Beckett and M. Reay (eds), 240–69. Canberra: Australian National University Press.

Williams, N. M. 1986. *The Yolngu and their land: a system of land tenure and the fight for its recognition*. Palo Alto: Stanford University Press and Canberra: the Australian Institute of Aboriginal Studies.

7 Geography and historical understanding in indigenous Colombia

JOANNE RAPPAPORT

Introduction

The Páez of southwestern highland Colombia maintain a historical memory of their passage from an independent nation to a tribe subjugated by Spaniards and Colombians. This history, which is based in part on written documents available to the Indians, traces the trajectory of conquest but, more importantly, outlines the means by which the community has resisted outside encroachment over the centuries through the adoption of novel political strategies. This chapter examines Páez historical consciousness with an eye to understanding its structure and its utility.

The approximately 60 000 Páez live in the northeastern corner of the department of Cauca, in southern highland Colombia. Cultivators of potatoes, maize, coffee and sugar cane, they inhabit the slopes of Colombia's Central Cordillera. The best-known Páez population is based in Tierradentro, on the eastern slopes of the mountain range. Their first contacts with Europeans were in the mid-16th century, when the *conquistador* Sebastián de Benalcázar invaded Tierradentro. The Páez were able to hold off the invaders for almost a century, and it was only in the 17th century that the *encomienda* or royal labour-grant was established in the area. By the 18th century, indigenous political leaders, or *caciques*, consolidated power in Tierradentro and expanded onto the western slopes of the cordillera, establishing *resguardos* – indigenous communities defined by clear boundaries within which title was vested in the community, individual members claiming usufruct rights. The *resguardo* was an early colonial means of penetration of indigenous communities in the Sabana de Bogotá (see González 1979), an institution which the Páez turned to their own uses. Through the *resguardo*, they were able to consolidate political power, legitimize pre-colonial boundaries and even expand their land-holdings to include terrain colonized since the time of the Spanish invasion.[1] The strength of *caciques* and the *resguardo* system diminished after independence from Spain, when the new creole overlords sought to liquidate *resguardos* and free indigenous lands for commercial exploitation. The 19th century marks further integration of the Páez into the Colombian politican system. The Indians participated in the numerous civil wars that took place in this era, joined nascent political parties and opened their territory to the exploitation of cinchona bark or quinine. The contemporary Páez still live on *resguardos*, and still enjoy some degree of political autonomy through *resguardo* councils, or *cabildos*, but the institution has been weakened through Colombian legislation, both in terms of the political power of indigenous authorities and the size of communal land-holdings.

The Páez' own account of their history follows these general lines, but focuses on a type of supernatural culture hero, the *cacique*, tracing his rise to power and his subsequent decline. Páez historical narrative concentrates more on political institutions and social relations than on events *per se*, and often events taking place over a broad span of time are condensed into single, cata-strophic occurrences. These historical referents are subtly changed so that, in effect, Páez historical thought concentrates more on 'what should have hap-pened' than on what really occurred. Most importantly, the Páez locate their historical record in sacred sites dispersed throughout the area, which serve both as mnemonic devices for remembering history[2] and as clear-cut boundary markers for *resguardos*. Because they are keyed to dispersed topographical refer-ents, Páez historical narrations are fragmentary, composed of episodes which can stand on their own or can be related to other episodes through visual obser-vation and movement through space. In this Chapter I analyse the various means by which these episodes can be grouped into a chronology.

Chronology and narrative

Páez oral history is an elaboration upon colonial written sources, *resguardo* titles in which we can hear the voices of colonial *caciques* (Archivo Central del Cauca, Popayán [ACC/P] 1881, 1883) who tell of how they achieved power and how they maintained it. The oral history parallels colonial documents, recounting the birth of *caciques* in mountain streams.[3] Colonial titles speak of the *cacique* Don Juan Tama y Calambás as the 'son of the stars of the Tama Stream' (ACC/P 1883: 2182v). According to contemporary stories, the colonial *resguardo* titles were born with the mythological culture-heroes, serving as their pillows as they floated down the stream. The *cacique* goes on to save the Páez people from invaders, including the neighbouring Pijao and the Guambiano; the second of these groups is also mentioned in colonial titles as a major adversary of the Páez (*ibid.*). Very similar to the encounters that the Páez have with other indigenous groups are their encounters with the Spaniards, who are described as violent historical actors, as opposed to the more civilized Páez. In order to repel European advances into their territory, the *caciques* climb high mountains and establish *resguardo* boundaries. Then they disappear into highland lakes from whence they can be summoned in an hour of need.

Páez historians go on to interpret post-independence events in light of the colonial experiences of these culture heroes or historical figures. Merging inde-pendence and 19th century civil wars into one large confrontation which they call the War of the Thousand Days,[4] oral histories highlight Páez collaboration with Colombian military leaders, and the loss of Páez lands resulting from this meeting of two distinct cultures and two distinct political programmes. Accord-ing to the Páez, the usurpers were not as successful as they would have liked to have been, because the Indians hid the original titles that had been born with the *caciques*, documents which validated territorial claims. However, without these titles, which were safely hidden in highland lakes, the Páez were without defences, and could not protect their land-holdings. Thus, we can see that, in the Páez vision of history, the *caciques* lost power during the Republican era.

Although the titles are missing and the *caciques* weak, the Páez are able to call upon their culture heroes for assistance in their hours of need. For example, they cite instances in which non-Indian visitors to sacred shrines and sites of buried treasure were turned away by supernatural apparitions sent by the *caciques*. In other cases military attackers were physically punished by the supernatural culture heroes.

All of these histories are told in an informal manner in the absence of any type of stylized performance. Although some take the form of narratives with coherent story-lines, others are simply short references to historical occurrences, information offered in a sentence or two (cf. Cohen 1980, Price 1983). They can be told by anyone: although there are some individuals known as skilled story-tellers, they are not thought of as the sole performers of these narrations. Many of the best narrators are political activists who link the events of Páez history to present concerns for the defence of the modern *resguardo*. This diffuse nature of historical tradition stems from the lack of a single, clear-cut authority since independence. The post-independence era has been marked by multiple indigenous authorities who have acquired transient power through military strength or through elections. These leaders have not been autonomous in any sense of the word, working primarily as intermediaries between reservation members and the State. Without an autonomous and overarching authority, a single official history is impossible; in contrast, multiple histories are created in an attempt to regain the autonomy that the Indians have lost. This is a clear example of the importance of understanding the relationship between indigenous communities and the State if we are truly to understand the nature of Indian visions of history.

It is possible to divide Páez accounts into two broad groupings: those that treat the mythological *caciques* in the pre-colonial and colonial eras, and those that outline historical process from the independence wars to the present. The Páez do draw a contrast between these two periods: Colombian independence is described as a 'second conquest' of the Indians by such founding fathers as Simón Bolívar. Interestingly, the Páez perceive independence as having come much earlier to Tierradentro, when the *caciques* defended their people against the Spanish aggressors and founded the *resguardo* system. For the Páez, the post-independence era is truly a second conquest, since in this period lands were stolen from them, and they forfeited political power with the creation of smaller, weaker *resguardos*.

Narrations about these two periods are very distinct in terms of style. Accounts of the early period are highly stylized, and emphasize the actions of individual culture heroes, closely following the colonial titles upon which they are based. In contrast, stories about the post-independence period incorporate more historical data into their plots, and concentrate more on human society than on supernatural culture heroes. While the earlier stories are recounted by many, differing from one another in a few details, the accounts of the 19th century can only be heard from a small number of narrators: they are not oral traditions *per se*, but recent interpretations of historical process.

Whether accounts focus on the colonial or the post-colonial periods or not, most Páez historical analysis takes as its central focus the *resguardo* system. The supernatural *caciques* serve as vehicles for highlighting the importance of the integrity of the *resguardo* in the face of the dominant society. Páez histories do not recount events as such, but the growth of indigenous institutions. Moreover, they deal little with the dominant hispanic society, preferring to concentrate on Páez actions, Páez innovations in the face of change.

Many times these stories apologize for indigenous loss of power. Other stories appear to grant more power to indigenous communities than has really been the case in the historical record. Sometimes accounts contradict each other in their descriptions of confrontations with the dominant society or with other invaders.[5] What is actually occurring in these narrations is that the Páez are recounting 'what should have happened', instead of what really occurred.

Integrated into a continuous narration, these accounts and bits of accounts have a clearly chronological nature. They delineate two broad periods – the period in which *caciques* ruled and the period in which they lost power – which roughly correspond to our colonial and republican eras. They exhibit a clear understanding of historical process and of change over time. They depict quite clearly the changing relationship between the Páez and the State. Nevertheless, the history is never told in its entirety, but in fragments which must be put in context by the listener who has at his or her disposal a store of historical knowledge derived from listening to and recounting other historical episodes. Although the chronological nature of these accounts is implied, the narrators use time in a distinctive manner. Time is compressed in the narratives, so that events taking place over a period of a century are recounted as though they took place simultaneously. This telescoping does not arise from a lack of historical consciousness among the Páez. What is more likely is that it is a means of placing emphasis on certain themes as opposed to others, and for stressing institutions instead of events. These institutions are described within the framework of what could often be fictional or mythological events, so that the narration takes on the flavour of a historical novel.

Breaking the chronology

Although in an integrated version these accounts cohere into a clear chronology, they are never told in this integrated fashion, but are recounted as short episodes or fragments. These bits of historical interpretation are associated with sites of historical and symbolic importance, dispersed across Tierradentro's landscape. For example, the place at which Juan Tama is believed to have been fished out of the waters, the mountain atop which the *cacica* Angelina Guyumús distributed indigenous lands at the time of the Spanish invasion and the highland lakes, where the *caciques* disappeared, are talked about in oral histories and acted upon through pilgrimage and ritual.

On the one hand, the sacred precincts which serve as referents for historical narration are mnemonic devices which aid the Páez in remembering their history. Most of the people of Tierradentro are illiterate or only semi-literate, and cannot record their history in writing. The sacred geography serves as a means for encoding historical referents. Moreover, these same sacred sites form the boundaries of individual *resguardos*, and also delineate the major historical *cacicazgos* of the colonial era. Thus, a knowledge of history as lodged in the landscape also serves as a means for remembering political boundaries: history is a direct means for defending territory (Rappaport 1982, 1985).

However, space serves as more than a simple mnemonic device for Páez historians. It is a tangible link with the past, something that can be seen, touched and climbed, something that merges past with present. Space is part of the process of interpreting history. It is not just a medium which records the past, but a means for making sense of it. This use of space as a framework for interpretation breaks down the chronology of the spoken narration, creating new relations among historical referents. This redefinition of chronology takes place along two lines: visual relationships among sacred precincts link their historical referents into a spatial, as opposed to a temporal, framework; and historical referents reordered as their spatial representations are linked through ritual activity in an annual calendar.

Visual relationships

Tierradentro is a mountainous region, and many of the precincts sacred to the Páez are located on mountain peaks. From one of these mountain-tops the observer can see many other mountains, some of which are also sacred sites. Villages or places of residence are also linked with sacred precincts in this manner. Because certain historically important mountains block the line of vision of a community, forming its horizon and often the limits of its domains, many of these peaks are the focus of rituals which define the community. Even though a village and a mountain, or a mountain and a mountain, might not be closely related in a chronological manner, the visual or geographical relationship between them lends an immediacy to the relationship between its historical referents. A good example of this is Chumbipe Mountain, located in southern Tierradentro. Here, the great *cacica* Angelina Guyumúa viewed her dominions and created the colonial *resguardo* of Togoima. Chumbipe is also believed to be a petrified Pijao chief who was transformed into a mountain after he was defeated by the Spanish invaders. The same mountain lies on the southern limits of Togoima, beyond which the *caciques* of the northern community of Calderas banished the Pijao invaders. One of Calderas' mythical chiefs disappeared into a lake behind Chumbipe. Standing atop the mountain it is possible to see Cuetando Bridge, where Páez Liberals were massacred during the 1950s civil war. Thus, a single peak encodes a variety of historical referents occurring at different times, all of which are related by having taken place at the same site or by having used it as a visual reference point. The relationship among these referents is not chronological, but spatial or territorial.

The calendar

Similarly, the ritual calendar regroups historical referents linked with sacred precincts into a new order. Most of the sacred sites of Tierradentro are in some way related to the December or the June solstice, or to atmospheric phenomena related to changes in the seasons. In some cases, on these dates rituals take place at these sites. In other instances these are the months in which the Páez engage in ceremonies which refer to the site and re-enact historical events that took place there. Finally, several of the narrations which mention particular topographic features also locate historical events as taking place at the winter or summer solstice. Thus, historical referents are arranged through the activity of ritual into a new order which corresponds to the annual calendar, an order which does not necessarily correspond to the chronology outlined above. A good example of this is the relationship between Alto de Tama, where Juan Tama is believed to have been born, and Vitoncó, where he lived. These two points associated in mythical narration are also astronomically related to each other: Alto de Tama is the point at which the Sun emerges on the June solstice when viewed from Vitoncó. Another nearby mountain, Chuta, is called the 'Mother of the Rains' because the appearance of clouds around its peak as viewed from Vitoncó marks the onset of winter. Chuta is a pilgrimage site at which the staffs of office carried by the *cabildo* are ritually refreshed (Rappaport 1985), linking the contemporary Páez political leaders with their mythological progenitor who lived in Vitoncó. Thus, these sacred precincts will be remembered in an order which corresponds more to calendrical or annual markers than to a chronology marked in years or eras.

The close relationship between space and time is also evident in other, non-ritual, activities. For example, Bernal Villa (1954) notes that the Páez describe extensions of land in terms of the number of harvests they will produce, since the Páez practise slash-and-burn agriculture.

Rebuilding the chronology

The Páez arrange historical referents into a variety of coherent patterns, defined both temporally and spatially. While the insertion of history into physical space serves to alter the chronological character of the narrative, linking referents from different periods, an examination of the movements of mythico-historical figures through space reveals that this very process of spatializing history also rebuilds the original chronology.

In her study of memory techniques in the Western world, Yates (1966) describes how the classical Greeks utilized buildings as mnemonic devices, so that architectural features became the repositories for facts, which could be recalled in a fixed order corresponding to the order of the features in the building. Harwood (1976) expands on this example in her analysis of the arrangement of Trobriand mythic episodes within and across sacred geography. She asserts that the temporal order of Trobriand mythic episodes is recapitulated in geography: the directionality of mythico-historical sites corresponds to the chronology of the myths. This relationship between sacred place and mythic episode is not static; the myth is merely a reference to a whole series of further episodes which might be recalled, reformulated or recombined.

In Tierradentro an interesting situation results when we apply the ideas of Yates and Harwood to the relationship between myth and geography. At the time of the Spanish invasion the Páez occupied the valley of La Plata, to the south-east of Tierradentro, and what is today the Páez heartland was then a rustic outpost for the more developed La Plata settlement (Velasco 1979). The Páez migrated up the cordillera during the first few centuries of colonial rule, and it is only in the late 17th century that we first see Páez settlements at the higher altitudes of Tierradentro itself. Seventeenth century *caciques* living on the western slopes of the cordillera are mentioned in the documentary record as hailing from Tierradentro (Archivo Nacional de Historia [ANH/Q] 1703). The great

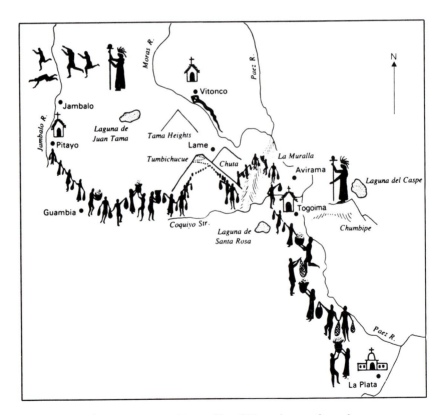

Figure 7.1 Schematic topographic profile of Tierradentro, from the Spanish invasion to the present.

Páez *cacique*, Don Juan Tama, claimed to have inherited his *cacicazgo* from Jacinto Muscay (ACC/P 1881), a Guambiano. It was only at the beginning of the 18th century that the Páez established stable communities in this area.

Páez oral tradition recapitulates this chronological and geographical trajectory, lending it immediacy by framing it with mythical concepts. The Páez believe that, after having destroyed the colonial city of La Plata, they transported the riches of this mining town to Tumbichucue, a mountain in the centre of Tierradentro. The treasure was passed from hand to hand along a huge line extending from La Plata to Tumbichucue, the petrified remnants of which can be seen in the ridge called La Muralla. Some time before the Spanish invasion the *cacique* Juan Tama was born in the heart of Tierradentro. Some of his unbaptized siblings were transformed into evil serpents that ate people. The villagers killed these serpents, cutting them into pieces, which fell into the river, their heads oriented upstream, pointing toward the western slopes.[6] One of the best-known of these supernatural beasts lived in the village of Lame. When he was cut into pieces, his head fell into the Moras River above Lame and his tail, in front of Suin (see Figure 7.1). Juan Tama himself settled in the village of Vitoncó, chosen after repeated attempts in which crosses were placed at various sites overnight so as to choose a place at which the cross was left standing in the morning. Tama saved his people from the Guambiano, neighbouring Indians who were sacrificing Páez children to a sacred lake in order to acquire gold.[7] The decisive battle between Guambiano and Páez was fought at a point near the modern village of Jambaló. At the end of his life Juan Tama travelled to Juan Tama Lake, located in the high grassland (*páramo*) between the two slopes of the cordillera, where he established the *resguardo*, passed on his inheritance of power to the shamans and finally disappeared into the lake. Tama's journeys are marked by sacred places. Thus, the life of this *cacique* is represented by a journey up the cordillera, recapitulating the historical ascent of the cordillera during the colonial era, a migration which marks the founding of many contemporary Páez villages and *resguardos*.

Here we have an interesting case in which the very arrangement of Tierradentro's sacred geography recapitulates historical migrations of the Páez nation. In both cases there is a clear movement from east to west, from lower to higher ground. The same sacred geography that reconstructs temporal experience in non-chronological form is also a vehicle for regrouping episodes in a chronological account which, moreover, follows the same temporal and geographical trajectory that we can reconstruct on the basis of colonial documents and chronicles.

Innovation in geography and history

Páez historical referents are encoded and interpreted through a localized sacred geography. Each community has its own topographical referents which structure its local historical accounts. Few Páez are able to interpret their history on a broader regional basis, using the regional system of sacred geography to construct a pan-Páez history, because they are familiar with only a small number of localized sacred sites and only their own local culture heroes. They confine themselves to the local level, where sacred places are immediately observable. This aspect of the nature of Páez historical thought might be construed as a handicap obstructing the development of a broader historical consciousness, and it has, indeed, forced both observers and the Indians themselves to understand Páez history as a series of histories of discrete territorial units.[8]

An attempt has been made in the past decade to transcend this regionalization of historical consciousness among the Páez. A solution was found in a series of maps which span the entire Páez area and which illustrate in pictorial form the various historical actions taking place over the landscape (Bonilla 1982).

An interesting result of the use of these maps is the development of a Páez coat of arms which depicts a hand holding a staff of office, superimposed over a circle containing a mountain range. The circle is said to represent the boundaries of *resguardos* (Alvaro Velasco pers. comm.). The mountain range undoubtedly represents the sacred peaks in which historical information is lodged. The hand holding the staff of office might possibly be Juan Tama's. This coat of arms is carried by Páez activists to political meetings, and it can be understood as a regional application of the traditional ritual of refreshing a *cabildo*'s staff of office, a ceremony which generally takes place at locally important sites. Movement through space with this innovative but traditional symbol lends a broader regional significance to the localized sacred geographies which encode the history of individual *resguardos* or groups of *resguardos*. A very simple innovation, this new symbol permits the Páez to continue to engage in their own mode of interpreting the past within a new and broader regional context.

By way of conclusion, it can be stated that Páez historical thought is spatially organized, its chronology understood and alluded to in geographic referents rather than being stated directly through the order of narration. Although this brand of historical analysis is quite different from a European one, it does not prevent Páez from using their own mode of historical interpretation as a very effective arm of resistance against a nation that orders its narration of temporal experience according to a more chronological (or Historical, with a capital H) mode. Páez historical thinking makes the past immediate, tangible and relevant for contemporary concerns which pertain, as does the history, to territorial matters.

Acknowledgements

Research for this paper was conducted from 1978 to 1980 under the sponsorship of the Fundación de Investigaciones Arqueológicas Nacionales, Banco de la República (Bogotá) and for four months in 1984 under a Grant-in-Aid from the Wenner-Gren Foundation for Anthropological Research and a faculty summer fellowship from the University of Maryland, Baltimore County. Field research was conducted largely in Tierradentro, Cauca. Archival research was conducted at the Archivo Central del Cauca, Archivo

Nacional de Colombia, Archivo Fundación Colombia Neustra, Biblioteca Nactional de Colombia and Biblioteca Luis Angel Arango. My thanks go to the Instituto Colombiano de Antropologia for giving me permission to conduct ethnographic research in Colombia. During the 1978 to 1980 ethnographic research, Gustavo Legarda served as my research assistant. Sofia Botero assisted me in archival and bibliographic research during the summer and autumn of 1984. This contribution is the result of long-standing discussions with many colleagues. Among them I especially thank Catherine Allen, Victor Daniel Bonilla, Maria Teresa Findji, Jonathan Hill and Deborah Poole. Finally, all my thanks to the Páez of Calderas, Jambaló, San José, Togoima and Vitoncó for their support, collaboration and hours of discussion.

Notes

1   At the time of contact the Páez occupied the eastern slopes of the cordillera, and it is only in the 17th and 18th centuries that an expansion to the western slopes took place. In fact, the conquest-era Páez were settled further down the cordillera, near La Plata, and even the inhabitants of Tierradentro were thought to be a rustic outpost of the more-established La Plata Páez (Velasco 1979; for an analysis of colonial history, see Rappaport 1982).

2   This brings to mind the ancient Greek mode of remembering, which was based on the mental location of ideas in distinctive points of architecture (see Yates 1966).

3   For a detailed recounting of the *cacique* stories, see Bernal Villa (1953, 1956) and Rappaport (1980–1, 1982, 1986).

4   The War of the Thousand Days was only one in a long series of civil wars which raged in the newly formed Colombian nation. This war, which was the last of the 19th century and thus the most recent in Páez memory, occupied the last few days of the 19th century and the first few of the 20th.

5   An interesting case of this sort of contradiction is the set of *resguardo* titles secured by the *cacique* of Pitayó and Vitoncó, Don Juan Tama y Calambás. In one account Tama claims to have inherited the *cacicazgo* from his Guambiano uncle (ACC/P 1881). Only a few years later, in another title, he claims to have been born of the waters of the Tama Stream, and to have won the *cacicazgo* by military means (ACC/P 1883).

6   Of interest here is the parallel between this Páez account of the liquidation of a mythical destroyer, and the Desana origin-myth which recounts the journey upstream of a primordial anaconda who creates Desana communities (Reichel-Dolmatoff 1972). These similarities in symbols utilized in the accounts do not indicate a lack of historical content in them, but point to the fact that mythic concepts can serve as useful conceptual frameworks for making sense of historical process.

7   This same narration is recapitulated in ritual in the western Páez community of La Ovejera, where bread children are eaten in remembrance of the sacrifices at the lake (Diego Berrio pers. commun.).

8   The largest divisions of the Páez nation, which are both historically-based and conceptually defined in the present, divide Tierradentro into a northern and a southern portion separated by a high mountain range, and distinguish Tierradentro as a whole from the western slopes of the cordillera, separated from Tierradentro by the *páramo*. These divisions were the basis for colonial *cacicazgos*, are separated from each other by hours of travel, and each provide for their residents a different horizon of sacred peaks.

References

Archivo Central del Cauca, Popayán (ACC/P) 1881 (1700). Titulo de las parcialidades de Pitayo, Quichaya, Caldono, Pueblo Neuvo y Jambalo. Protocolo Notarial, partida 843.

Archivo Central del Cauca, Popayán (ACC/P) 1883 (1708). Titulo del resguardo de Vitonco. Protocolo Notarial, partida 959.

Archivo Nacional de Historia, Quito (ANH/Q) 1703. Campo vs. Miera sobre la encomienda de Guanacas. Fondo Popayán, caja 20.

Bernal Villa, S. E. 1953. Aspectos de la cultura páez: mitologia y cuentos de la Parcialidad de Calderas, Tierradentro. *Revista Colombiana de Antropologia* 1 (1) 279–309.

Bernal Villa, S. E. 1954. Economia de los Páez. *Revista Colombiana de Antropologia* 3, 291–368.

Bernal Villa, S. E. 1956. *Religious life of the Páez Indians of Colombia.* MA thesis, Columbia University, New York.

Bonilla, V. D. 1982. Algunas experiencias del proyecto "Mapas Parlantes". In *Alfabetización y educación de adultos en la región andina* J. E. Garcia Huidobro (ed.). Pátzcuaro, Mexico: Unesco.

Cohen, D. W. 1980. Reconstructing a conflict in Bunafu: seeking evidence outside the narrative tradition. In *The African past speaks*, J. C. Miller (ed.), 201–20. Hamden, Connecticut: Archon.

González, M. 1979. *El resguardo en el nuevo reino de Granada,* 2nd edn. Bogotá: La Carreta.

Harwood, F. 1976. Myth, memory, and the oral tradition: Cicero in the Trobriands. *American Anthropologist* 78 (4), 783–96.

Price, R. 1983. *First-time: the historical vision of an Afro-American people.* Baltimore: Johns Hopkins University Press.

Rappaport, J. 1980–1. El mesianismo y las transformaciones de ideologias mesiánicas en Tierradentro. *Revista Colombiana de Antropologia* 23, 365–413.

Rappaport, J. 1982. *Territory and tradition; the ethnohistory of the Páez of Tierradentro, Colombia.* PhD Dissertation, University of Illinois at Urbana.

Rappaport, J. 1985. History, myth, and the dynamics of territorial maintenance in Tierradentro, Colombia. *American Ethnologist* 12 (1), 27–45.

Rappaport, J. Their idea of civilization and ours: Páez historical consciousness. Unpublished manuscript.

Reichel-Dolmatoff, G. 1972. *Amazonian cosmos.* Chicago: University of Chicago Press.

Velasco, J. de 1979 (1789). *Historia del reino de Quito en la América meridional,* (3 Vols). Quito: Casa de la Cultura Ecuatoriana.

Yates, F. 1966. *The art of memory.* Chicago: University of Chicago Press.

8   Past and present of Andean Indian society: the Otavalos

ANTONIO MALES

(translated by Joanne Rappaport)

> Cunan tiempupica, taitacunami
> cancunamanta rimanajun.
> Na cayaca quiquincunami
> cunami taitacunamanta rimana
> canguichic.
>
> In these days, the elders
> speak for you.
> Tomorrow, you must speak for them.
>
> Omen of the *taitas* (the old) to the *guambras* (the young).

Introduction

This chapter presents part of a communal body of experiences and ideas that has been developing over the past years in indigenous communities and organizations of Ecuador. It grows out of the struggle to achieve basic rights and guarantees for the legitimacy of indigenous autonomy and independence, which have been under attack by the dominant classes of Ecuador throughout history. In the face of this situation, the indigenous peoples and organizations of our country have struggled, day by day, to transform the cause for equal rights and a respect for our culture, language, organizations and historical traditions into a living reality.

Obviously, these objectives must be understood within the broader context of the work accomplished by Ecuadorian Indians in bolstering their historic presence in the nation's destiny, after having been ignored, oppressed and exploited for centuries. In this sense, indigenous organizations have oriented their political and historic activities in various areas: production, education, culture and art, technology, science, and social and political organization, all keys to laying foundations for the 'multicultural' and 'multiethnic' nation that they hope to build in concert with other oppressed social forces.

In this chapter I study my own people and record our testimony, lending continuity to the actions and the memory of past and present generations in an attempt to link past and present in Andean Indian society: in this case, the Otavaleños of yesterday and the Otavaleños of today.

Within this process, the efforts of indigenous organizations must be high-lighted: these groups use the past as a taking-off point, intermixing it with current historical reality in order to draw from it inspiration, knowledge and experience. All of this translates into a communal effort to forge an absolutely different and renewed tomorrow.

This indigenous quest has taken permanent root in the conscience of communities and their leaders. They are deepening their commitment in the face of the thoughts and actions of the powerful who have historically ignored and reviled us. In response, organized groups of Indians are re-affirming their indigenous origins, re-invigorating their expressions of identity and culture, and orienting their demands toward the creation of a unified and strong Indian movement. In accord with its vast potential resources, the movement is confronting and lessening the impact of the ideology and power of those who have persisted in ignoring the obvious presence of the Indian peoples of Ecuador, and promoting an alternative account of our history.

Background

The Otavalo territory is located in the northern Ecuadorian highlands. Otavalo was one of the most important indigenous communities, even in the prehispanic period, part of a complex social, economic and political web fuelled by a dynamic exchange among communities, each with its own traditions and customs. The contributions of each group bolstered the communal institutions that comprised the regional social system.

It is impossible to understand the dynamics of the evolution of the social and political institutions that characterized the region during the early colonial period, immediately before and after the Spanish invasion and conquest, unless we consider the interrelationships that existed among the diverse indigenous communities of the zone. Here, we want to underline two fundamental aspects:

(a) The existence of a territorial structure administered by the Indian communities of the region;
(b) the transformation of indigenous social and political systems wrought by the Spanish conquerors.

There is no doubt that the complementarity of human and material goods and resources that existed among communities, gave rise to relations and alliances guaranteeing, to a large degree, the peaceful coexistence of these territorially based groups, mediated by a flow of reciprocal exchange and by the establishment of 'horizontal' and 'transverse' connecting routes, as is apparent from Figure 8.1. In other words, indigenous communities of the northern Ecuadorian Andes were organized socially and politically around *ethnic lords*. In addition, the presence of *mindaláes** added to the complexities of the regional economic system.

*Translator's note: *mindaláes* were politically sponsored traders, specializing in sumptuary goods, an institution characteristic of the northern Andes.

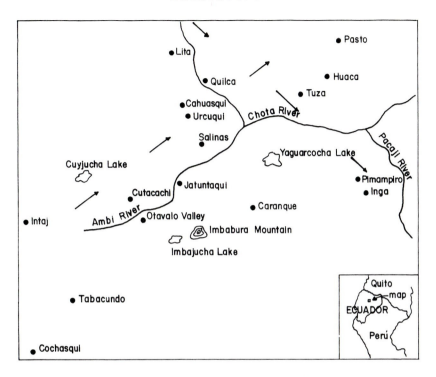

Figure 8.1 Northern Ecuadorian highlands in 1532
(sources: Caillavet 1985, Males 1982).

The transformation of the aboriginal regional system radically affected the nature and function of social institutions. Pre-colonial customs were replaced by a corpus of norms that 'legally' expressed the changes undergone by the Indians, and the obligations under which they were now placed. This began with the usurpation of communal lands and the exploitation of indigenous labour in production centres quickly established by the Crown and its agents. In the region in question, the institutionalization of *encomiendas* and *obrajes** was a new application by the colonial administration, of systems of domination implemented in Spain and administered by Iberian functionaries established in these territories.

In 1557, in order to dominate the Indians more effectively, the Spaniards established Otavalo as a *corregimiento*,† permitting better administration of Crown interests. Otavalo became an important colonial centre by the end of the 17th century, while new centres of regional power, such as Ibarra (founded in 1606) arose as part of a policy of establishing 'Spanish towns'. All this occurred in the wake of the appropriation of communal lands, and was brought

*Translator's note: the *encomienda* was a royal grant made to Spaniards in recognition of certain contributions made to the interests of the Crown. It gave its recipient the right to a percentage of the tribute of community members. The *obraje* was a colonial textile sweatshop.

†Translator's note: the *corregimiento* was a provincial unit of administration in the colonial era.

about by Indian labour, forced to erect a replica of the Spaniards' native architectural style.

Arising from these events, a number of enduring social institutions can be identified which persist in various forms to the present. Indians dismissed the republican period, beginning in Ecuador in 1830, as the 'last day of despotism and the first day of the same thing' because the Indians did not perceive any historic change at all. Their exploited and dominated condition was maintained, and there was no foreseeable possibility of escaping from the violent constraints imposed by generations and centuries of governors. Moreover, post-independence indigenous communities continued to maintain their own strategies and alliances that they had forged historically, so as at least to keep in step with the colonizer. The Indian turned to his own mode of administering and exploiting his territories and maintaining an intimate relationship with community life. He continued to uphold as living realities those social and political institutions characteristic of the pre-colonial Andean world (such as reciprocity and redistribution, mutual assistance, the lending of labour, the *rama*, the *tumin*, the *minga*,* etc.). These traditional institutions have acted as a barrier to state policy, allowing Indians to escape the constraints erected by those in power. Their legal strategy has been to grant citizenship to the Indians of Andean communities and *ayllus*†.

The immediate past

Now that we have touched upon that distant past, we must ask ourselves certain questions. Wherein lie the causes of the Otavalos' success in maintaining their deepest traditions across the generations, in spite of conquest, colonization and the devastation that arose through the textile industry? Their oppression is comparable only with the situation of anguish and super-exploitation of the Potosi mines (silver) and the Cauca Valley (gold), among all those regions dominated by the colonizers. From whence was such rebelliousness born, that stubbornness that, even in prehispanic times, drove them to form natural alliances that resisted Inca expansion and domination, and later that of the Spaniard? What is the cultural inheritance enjoyed by Otavaleños of succeeding generations, and how have these traditions been transformed in order that they continue to be effective?

The answers to these questions are not readily apparent, even to those who ask them. The answers undoubtedly lie partly in the nature of thought and the notions of life and death of these people, the worldview of Andean Indians, still only partially understood. Their components are signs, symbols, gestures, movements, representations, colours, mixtures, dialogues, prayers, laments, tears, laughter and irony, all of which are expressed openly, without restraint,

*Translator's note: *rama*: a communal fund to which everyone contributes; *minga*: a collective work party.
†Translator's note: the *ayllu* is an Andean kin group.

as though to absorb forever the purity of the *páramo* and the *puna*,* the freshness of the valley air, without schedules and without time.

This immediate past is replete with legendary milestones forged in the mountains, on the slopes and on the plains: in what hidden spaces are these gestures found? The Indians of Lita and Quilca rose up and protested against taxation back in the 16th century; just as in the 19th century the indigenous communities of the north rose against the political power that forced the peasants to work in 'communal troops' in the construction of public works. They have protested the abuses of local civil authorities and of the Church, with its taxes, the tithes and first fruits extracted from the harvest, and from the work – including weaving – that complemented agriculture. All of these were included in the high taxes required in exchange for religious services.

Then came the decisive protest of the 'Indian' Alfaro,† as he was called by Conservatives and their entourage: the general who transformed some of the institutions of the republican state that had maintained the Indians subject to the fluctuations of government interests. The Indians from northern and central Ecuador did not hesitate to support the Liberal general's programme, culminating in his taking of power in the revolution of 1895. As a consequence indigenous participation in the battles between Liberals and Conservatives lives in the memory of the generations whose immediate ancestors participated at the side of Eloy Alfaro and his Council of Generals.

Then came demands and community pressure to defend lands acquired from the Church by Liberal governments, in accord with 1908 legislation that ordered the expropriation of haciendas and church lands. Years later, when the coastal agricultural export economy declined, the owners of coffee and cacao plantations and their financial backers planned to transfer title to the workers and the people of Guayaquil, giving rise to the bloody confrontations of 15 November 1922. At that time they attempted to silence the people of Guayaquil, largely migrants from the central highlands who had migrated there at the beginning of the 19th Century to escape oppression by landowners. Among the fighters of 1922 there were Indians and mulattos who hoped to settle on coastal lands – another form of struggle and resistance against oppression and domination.

In 1937, when the state apparatus was modernized and certain state structures such as the Social Security Bank and the Labour Division were established, struggles for the demands of rural workers, especially those associated with haciendas, began to spread throughout the northern region. Especially targeted were the haciendas in Church hands, where memory and tradition had been maintained by the Indians of the *páramo* and the valleys.

---

*Translator's note: the *páramo* is the high swampy grassland of the northern Andes. The *puna* is the even-higher arid plain of the central and southern Andes.
†Translator's note: Eloy Alfaro was a 19th century Liberal leader in Ecuador.

Another view of history

In the course of this retelling of the events and acts lived by the Indians, we cannot forget the quite different perspective of the dominant class and its ideologues with regard to our own past. In response to economic and political interests, the educated men never saw in the Indian any real and concrete potential for transforming the country. Of course, they were never concerned that Ecuador should build an alternative to backwardness and ignorance. They never saw the value of the roots and the potential of our people. Disgracefully, they impeded the self-expression of our people, they did not allow them to transmit their voices and their thoughts. They preferred to claim the role of those who 'understood' the condition of those very men and those worlds that they scorned and underrated. They wrote the history of this country, and claimed to have discovered the vestiges and the ancestors of the first men and the first cultures of these northern Andean lands. However, they never gave a place to the Indians of this country. Although, on the one hand, they said they had discovered the roots of the 'Ecuadorian nationality', on the other hand they did not do justice to the efforts and the valour of the Indians, who at best could have contributed to the affirmation in Ecuador of an historical consciousness that would have filtered the past through the lens of our authentic identity. Nevertheless, those who always claimed to have 'understood' have not 'conceded' to us our identity, flagrantly violating our legitimate right to be as we wish to be – that is, as distinct peoples, autonomous in the face of a national project lacking any real base, a project that does not allow us to participate as substantial components in the future of the country, even though, quite simply, we are the majority of Ecuadorian society.

The present

In the trajectory of the indigenous communities of northern Ecuador, historically assaulted by those who hold political and economic power, especially the landlords who held 53 haciendas in the province of Imbabura until 1960, the Indians reinitiated their process of resistance and defence of communal lands that historically belonged to their ancestors. To this struggle they gave their strength for their entire lives. Moreover, they organized themselves to block the theft of their basic resources, such as water, pasturelands and access to natural resources guaranteeing family subsistence.

The indiscriminate abuse inherent in the inconsiderate exploitation of those natural resources that are vital for our community life is exemplified by an attempt on the part of Otavalo mestizos linked to local and regional politicians to expropriate from the Indians large stretches of land along the shores of Lake Imbajucha or San Pedro, with the goal of erecting an infrastructure for tourism, all for their own benefit. This was executed without regard to the objections raised by indigenous communities, complaints that went unanswered by the local authorities. This situation provoked an uprising of the communities along the lake shores and, immediately, neighbouring communities joined the struggle. So, during many days and nights of 1959, the police and the army assailed the thousands of Indians who had come in support of the communities directly affected. The blood of the dead and the wounded flowed in the hills and cliffs along the shores, under the watchful eyes of Taita Imbabura*, a mountain of profound mythical and human significance for the Otavaleños of the past and of today.

Here is one of the many episodes encoded in oral tradition, which clearly illustrates the clash of values that took place in the region:

The Indians:
Taita Priest, please say mass to Taita Imbabura. There is no water, and the corn is drying out. Everything is going badly. We want a mass, and want you to say it!

The Priest:
My children, how can you possibly believe I could say mass to a mountain? No! Mass is only said to Taita God. I cannot give you this mass!

The Indians:
But Taita Priest, we want to say mass to Taita Imbabura. He seems to be angry, and he doesn't give us any water for our corn, and everything is dry!

The Priest:
I've told you *no*! I simply cannot say mass to a mountain!

The Indians:
We will pay whatever you ask, Father. But, please say the mass. Just say mass to Taita God and at the same time, say mass to Taita Imbabura.

And the priest accepted the proposal.

Thus, at the foot of Taita Imbabura and along Lake Imbajucha, the Indians of Pucará Bajo rose up, fighting battles and engaging in struggles that provide a lesson to present generations, who must deepen the unity and solidarity that exists among the communities of the zone and the region where the Otavalos live. There, the most fertile traditions of the past three decades have been forged, ritually marking a crucial period in the modern history of Otavalo: the original and immemorial Otavalo, not the place tied to the urban life-style, where social and ethnic contradictions are expressed in all their varied and elemental forms. For this reason, the difficult moments of Pucará Bajo in 1959 are

---

*Translator's note: *Taita*: old. For location see Figure 8.1.

harboured in the deepest memory and in the consciousness of the *taitas* and the *guambras** of the region.

More recently the struggle for changes in agrarian structure mobilized indigenous organizations who, on their own initiative, have ably confronted the State and its offers of an agrarian reform initiated in 1964. Then began a period of 'ups-and-downs', of striving to resolve the problem of land tenancy. This was resolved successfully, in that a partial resolution favourable to indigenous needs and interests was reached. Nevertheless, the primary beneficiaries of the reform were the landlords, who 'walked off' with extensive oil-derived economic resources provided by the Ecuadorian state. Without doubt, the second agrarian reform law of 1973 favoured, again, those sectors linked with political power.

These events also gave way to the constitution of Indian organizations to lead the growing political action. Their objectives were to confront and resolve in a unified manner the problems affecting the countryside. The Peasant Confederation of Imbabura was created in 1974. In the course of the struggle it has transformed its name and its objectives so that, by its third congress in 1984, it decided to rename itself Imbaburamanta Runacunapac Jatun Tantanacui-Inrujta (Indian-Peasant Federation of Imbabura, or FICI). Among its objectives were an orientation toward permanent struggle against colonialism, neo-colonialism and racism; the struggle for national liberation as indigenous peoples in unity with all the exploited; the struggle for equality in social and political rights; the defence of land and culture. Its success in local struggles led to the 1977 founding of the Federación de Comunas de Cotacachi (Federation of Cotacachi Communities), its goal being to unify the people of one of the most exploited and poverty-stricken areas in Imbabura. Its actions have transformed living conditions in rural communities, and it has also participated in political decisions on a local level. This has been a difficult task, given the complex social relations that exist between the villagers of Cotacachi and neighbouring Indian communities.

In the process land has been distributed to Indian communities, a redistribution associated with indigenous notions of territory and with indigenous culture. This has permitted the creation of an economic base which, although still insufficient, provides minimal conditions for family survival and the maintenance of those basic structures that ensure the effectiveness of communal institutions.

Equally important is reference to the situation of land tenure in other parts of Ecuador. The fundamental characteristics of state agrarian policy have not, in general, differed qualitatively in the various regions, although on the quantitative level there have been significant variations. There are regions where large land-holdings still exist, precisely where indigenous populations are larger. These include the provinces of Imbabura, Cotopaxi, Chimborazo, Tungurahua and Cañar. Here, former hacienda employees of indigenous origin and 'unattached' Indians, have begun to participate in a process of political

*Translator's note: *guambras*: the young.

organization aimed at increasing their capacity to exert pressure on the State and on those social sectors with interests in the countryside. All of this has brought with it risks, of course.

The reality of Ecuadorian Amazonian Indians is diverse and complex. Their organization and use of space is substantially different from those of the highlands. Their economy is based in the collection of resources in open territory, where man's action is broad and natural technologies perfected by the Indians are still used, where cultural practices remain strong. Here, Indians have been subjected to pressures to cede their lands to colonists and people from the highlands, who were avid to exploit lands as though they belonged to no-one. The situation is aggravated by the presence of multinational oil companies and their Ecuadorian backers, as well as by plunder on the part of native investors supported by the government, who have initiated agro-industry in the form of African palm production and the devastating lumber industry, all under the benevolent eye of the Ecuadorian authorities.

Amazonian Indian communities, heirs to a deep tradition of resistance and struggle against the exploiters, have recommenced the arduous task of defending their lands and their culture in order to guarantee life for future generations. They have also turned to the creation of organizations as a legitimate right, in order to defend themselves against, and liberate themselves from, the oppressive system. Thus, in 1964 arose the Shuar Federation, in 1973 the Federation of Indian Organizations of the Napo, and in 1980 the Organization of Indigenous Communities of the Pastaza. The three organizations also founded the Confederation of Indigenous Nationalities of the Ecuadorian Amazon (CONFENIAE) in 1980, born out of a necessity for total unity among indigenous organizations and nationalities of the region. This move enabled them better to defend their basic rights and to seek better paths to justice and liberty for their people. Moreover, in the Andean region, the Movimiento Ecuador Runacunapac Riccharimui or ECUARUNARI (Indian Awakening) was founded, initiating its activities in those areas of highest indigenous population density.

Ecuador's Indians have initiated an organizational process leading toward the constitution of a single national movement. Important steps have already been taken toward this goal, including the formation of the Council for the Coordination of Ecuadorian Indigenous Nationalities (CONACNIE) in 1980.

The indigenous peoples and groups of Ecuador have, since the second half of the 20th century, opted for a diversity of organizational modes, each subject to the characteristics of the region in which the group lives, and each taking into account the internal and external factors that determine the success and the social and cultural perspectives that they must assume. To this degree, indigenous organizations comprise a broad range of characteristics, although their final objective is the consolidation and maintenance of the fundamental institutions of Indian society and the strengthening of indigenous culture, which naturally constitute the foundations of the power that they seek to forge and of the society they seek to construct. Our past lives in the achievement of this historic objective, as much in those apparently silent and immovable expressions that are the fruit of the multiple generations before us, as in the messages and signs that are still not well-decoded, and which silently wait for us to take them up again to continue on the indelible path marked by our societies and peoples. This path leads us to learn from their wisdom, and to contribute to surmounting the errors of so many years of oppression and domination, from 1492 to the present. During these centuries, today's Otavalos and many sister peoples of the Andes have worked to forge the present as a guarantee of what, as a people, we want for the future.

References

Caillavet, C. 1985. La adaptación de la dominación incásica a las sociedades autóctonas de la frontera septentrional del imperio (Territorio Otavalo Ecuador). *Revista Andina* 3.

Males, A. 1982. *Crónicas de un pasado reciente: notas y reflexiones*, Otavalo.

9   *Oral tradition and the African past*

PATRICK MBUNWE-SAMBA

It is no longer news to state that the customs, beliefs, values and opinions of the African society have been handed down from their ancestors to posterity by word of mouth or by practice since the earliest times, until the advent of European colonization and its stress on literacy and the written word barely 100 years ago, changed the trend. Before this so-called 'civilizing' contact the African had lived his life and had maintained his tradition in his own way. He had made things and had acquired property; he had believed, loved, hated, fought, wandered and wondered, and had learnt many things by his own empirical existence. His dreams, fears and his hopes had existed since the most primitive days when his life began.

All these, and more, are an eloquent testimony of the way of life of a people – they represent the spirit, attitude, wisdom and life-style which the African had lived, had believed and had passed on from generation to generation for many centuries. They are the product of his experience rooted at a particular time in the life of the society. This built-up wealth of African oral tradition has lived, is living and will live in the folklore of the people. It is enshrined in the memories and hearts of the people, particularly in the minds of the talented tenth – the bards, *griots* (skilled performers of oral narrative), praise singers, raconteurs and story tellers, as they are called variously in different areas in Africa. These tradition-bearers have kept alive the totality of our life-style and philosophy, the entire wisdom of the tribe, the cherished values of our society, the unique system of our beliefs, the pristine virtues of our humanity and the rich cultural heritage found in the folk tales, myths, legends, proverbs, superstitions, songs and recitations of our ancestors, which have come down from the remote past of our history.

A vast amount of the African oral tradition has still not been documented, in spite of the influence of the literary tradition on a so-called simple rustic people and their 'primitive' societies. These untutored folk still compose orally from their common themes and experiences, besides the information that can be obtained from arts, crafts and customs of the various tribal groups with which the folk culture abounds.

However, for quite some time, many of our African values and practices were not understood by Westerners – people whose civilizations were different from our own. The tendency was to laugh at those things which looked queer from the standpoint of those who made themselves judges. These were labelled primitive and uncivilized, because they did not conform to 'civilized' standards. For the values of a particular culture to be authentic it can only be judged in terms of itself or compared with values of similar traditions. Unfortunately this was not the case. Scholars on African oral traditions who considered the folk-lore as rustic and primitive, without depth or sophistication, missed the point completely. Although there are some puerile and common-sense beliefs and superstitions in the uncivilized communities, it must be noted that these have existed side-by-side with some of the most profound philosophies as well as some of the deepest truth of humanity.

As a result of this attitude, the oral tradition in Africa was at first studied rather as a curiosity than for its authenticity. Some of the customs and practices were viewed with surprised amazement and with cynicism by many scholars of the civilized world – which is the case even today!

The practice of polygamy, communal living or African socialism, the love and care of the elderly, the extended family system, the love and respect for neighbours and strangers, and the sanctity of human life are some of those prac-tices that the peoples of other civilizations find hard to understand. Just as many Africans will find it difficult to understand how a human being could prefer his aged parents to live in old people's homes and be cared for by charity when the children are still living. Nor can the African understand the attraction of marriage for companionship or the excessive obsession with accumulation of material wealth. Many Africans are now even beginning to wonder why Jesus Christ, the son of God, was not a black man since most of what he came to preach tallied with what the African has believed in and has practised for many generations in the past! What is obvious from the argument above is simply that to isolate and judge aspects of a people's culture out of context is to expose our own ignorance to ridicule by others.

Thus, one of the best ways of knowing the African past is to learn its oral tradition. Through an intimate and an on-the-spot investigation into the folk culture of the people, we can come to understand their belief system, their values and history which are embodied in the whole range of the African folklore and mythology, as well as in the artefacts and customs inherited from the remotest past of that civilization.

The stress on an intimate on-the-spot investigation is important because, in an African oral performance, both the text and social context of the folklore as well as the time and circumstance of performance are equally important, as Malinowski emphasized:

> The text, of course is extremely important, but without
> the context it remains lifeless . . .
> The stories live in native life and not on paper,
> and when a scholar jots them down without being
> able to evoke the atmosphere in which they
> flourish he has given us but a mutilated bit of reality
>
> (Malinowski 1954, p. 90).

There is very much that can be drawn from the African traditional heritage. The stories of fairies, witches, dryads, spirits, magic, gods, ghosts, devils, animals and the underworld, which hold many societies spellbound even today, came from the expressions of rustic folk many generations ago. The systematic investigation and documentation of the culture and tradition of these people by drawing from their folklore, their arts, crafts, beliefs, customs and practices is an invaluable and priceless venture, not only for the men of letters, but also for archaeologists. By preserving the written versions of our oral tradition we are trying to immortalize the folk culture of the nation of Africa, because, even in the remotest of village homesteads today, primary orality is no longer tenable, although the majority of people in Africa subsist largely within an oral rather than a literary culture.

How, then, can one know about the past from the present? What surviving elements of the past oral tradition can be traced in the various genres of our folklore and customs? Does anything in African oral tradition show that Africans share the long roots of the life of their ancestors? Is it possible to interpret some of those elements and past material remains as the things that happened in the far, far past of their history that have effects on us today? Is their past important to our future? The discussion that follows is designed to provide answers to these questions.

The practice of superstition and rituals in African society

Apparently subconscious beliefs are so strong among Africans that it is no use thinking that they will all be eradicated one day. Whether they are based on ignorance, lack of information or gullibility, there is no doubt that many things are hidden from man by some almighty power.

Nobody understands, for example, why man is born, grows old and dies. Nobody has yet found the medicines for stopping death. Why is there water everywhere? Of what substance is the Sun made? Who made the world? When did it begin to exist? At the present state of technological advancement, the superpowers have yet to explore all of outer space. Thus, the human being's concern for the imponderable and the tantalizing forces of nature hidden behind the visible universe, the myriads of unexplored and unexplained facts, the hazards and uncertainty of life – these baffling and unknown infinity of creation (Lantum 1969) augur varying degrees of fear and bewilderment in every heart, whether in primitive or in advanced societies.

These are the basis of superstition, although simple folk will believe even in ridiculous things because sense, mind and feelings are untutored. Because of the concern for survival, man speculates on all hidden forces which he is unable to prove objectively.

There are literally uncountable numbers of strong beliefs and superstitions all over Africa, embedded in almost all aspects of life, which have survived from our forebears – and some are still being produced in our time. A large number of the examples quoted here are of communities with which I am familiar, but the truth is that these beliefs are similar in many societies all over Africa.

In many farming communities in Iboland in Nigeria, and also in the grassland region of Cameroon, there are some days in the eight-day week-cycle when farmers dare not go to their farms to work. Those special days are reserved for the reverence of the village gods and ancestral spirits of the land. Any farmer who breaks this custom may meet with the spirits in the farm, and may get his just reward in sickness or even death, or something unbecoming may happen to him. It is worst if some people of the community see him, for, as the news spreads like a dry-season bush fire, everyone anxiously waits to see what will befall the transgressor. Sometimes the sheer physical isolation alone affects the individual. It has been difficult to discover any examples of a transgressor because the belief is so total that no-one seems ready to tempt the ancestral spirits so far.

If today you visit any farm in the Bamenda area in Cameroon, you will see some traditional medicines like the draceana plant, old raffia bags, palm fronds and roots suspended on sticks and displayed on the farms to ward off thieves. This is common practice to taboo the farm and the ripe crops against children, wayfarers and thieves. It is also an old practice to offer seeds to the village spirits before planting. The first crops are also offered to honour and thank the ancestral spirits for the abundance of the harvest, and usually the first harvest of a new crop of the season is tested by the head of the household before others, whether it is the new yam in Iboland or a new maize crop in the Bamenda area. Although in some areas in the Bamenda grassland the Catholic church has tried to convince Christians to be satisfied with the blessing of holy water on their seeds, many Christians prefer both – the blessing of holy water and the traditional blessing of their ancestors.

Many of these beliefs are highlighted, solemnized and made sacred by ritual ceremonies. Ritual incantations are usually highly ceremonial verbal adjurations addressed on special occasions, sometimes accompanied by a dance. Rites can be conducted to appease the spirits of the ancestors, who should intercede with the spirits for the general well-being of the living, for the fertility of women, for the fertility of land and abundant harvest and rain, to ward off epidemics and to ask for good luck. There are rituals conducted during circumcision, burial, twin rites and those at the death of traditional rulers. During the ceremonies, which are usually short, all sorts of things are invoked. It is usually conducted by the eldest member of the group, it sometimes involves dance, and what is said depends largely on the occasion and circumstances.

A common ritual today, among a large number of native élites in Cameroon particularly, concerns the celebration of some achievement – promotions or births, or the fortification and cleansing of individuals or the members of a family to render them invulnerable to all sources of evil. It also helps in the promotion of the family well-being and welfare. A typical ritual ceremony by a Wimbum father when the son is leaving home, runs thus (when translated from the Wimbum vernacular):

Haaa the spirits of *Ta Tata* and *Ta Nfor*, (the ancestors)
We are gathered here in your name,
To leave this grand son in your hands
Protect him as you have done in the past
Be his guide wherever he will be.
Although you were gone for many, many years from us,
Do not forget your children.
Protect them from all adversities
Accept this (pours wine) from the hands of your sons.
As a token of our union with the underworld
Prepare a place for us as you go,
So that we meet you in glory when our time is out.

In the past, for a ritual ceremony to be accepted by the ancestors, the elders used a traditional cup (horn) to pour the libation, but today the urban élites are using liquor for the same purpose – thereby adulterating the culture.

A fetish that needs mention is a specially designed bamboo which is displayed particularly at the entrance to a palm bush to stop people from stealing palm wine. This fetish is also supposed to protect people from witchcraft practices, and even from death, when it is planted at the door of the victim against whom witchcraft is intended. Some very highly placed people in our society still plant these sticks for protection.

There are many widespread beliefs in Cameroon society that women and children should not eat the gizzard of a chicken, lest they become thieves. Also in Cameroon, the eating of eggs by women and children is only a recent practice; the Bakwerians of Buea believe that the house should not be swept at night or else you invite evil spirits, and also that if their women eat palm birds their offspring will cry too much. In Babanki, Ndop, Bamenda women are not allowed to walk over egusi peelings and in Bakossi, Kumba, profuse bleeding in labour is associated with eating a deer (Lantum 1969). It is strongly believed among the Wimbum people of Donga Mantung, Cameroon, that if an owl (the archetypal harbinger of misfortune) cries at night, then some important person will die. There is superstition about thick forests, deep pools and huge rocks, which are the abode of the gods, and very often Africans offer periodic sacrifices to the ancestral spirits in them.

Many people in Africa wear protective charms on wrists, ankles and necks to ward off danger from witches and evil spirits. Twins are not supposed to see a corpse, lest they die and follow the deceased. Moslems do not eat pork at all, nor any meat killed by a non-Moslem. In Nigeria the Ibos have institutionalized trial marriage in order to avoid divorce which can come as a result of sterility of the woman.

There are also many mystical things which can be thought of as superstition, but which actually happen even though we cannot rationally explain how they actually do. To some of them I was an eyewitness.

A 13-year-old girl from Baba I in Ndop, Bamenda, Cameroon, went out on 4 December 1983 to watch the Sun's eclipse and felt an irritation on her right lap. When she lifted her dress to see what caused the irritation, she noticed something in the shape of a New Moon on which words began to appear. The first word was GOD and then *God helps you*. She got frightened, reported to her father, mother, then a priest and the district officer, who were all mystified and did not know what to do. Still a series of writings continually appeared and disappeared. When we heard of it, we mounted an investigation into the mystery. After two months the writing stopped and, thereafter, the girl started to cure people and make barren women fertile.

A second incident happened in Yaounde in 1979. A young Bayangi man from Mamfe, Cameroon, was tormented by spirits. He could not sleep, and whenever food was cooked for him in his house and he began to eat, it turned automatically into sawdust. On his bed and on his floor there was a drawing of a coffin. He became alarmed. For many days priests and medicine men from far and near were brought in, but to no avail. Then the people began to isolate people and things in his house and when his junior sister was taken away the strange happenings stopped. It was said that his mother, through the sister, was responsible for those happenings for some strange reason. Other examples of actual events exist, like the control of rain, the sending of thunder and transforming people into animals. Some of these cannot be explained rationally, but do happen. What name should we give these strange miracles of our day? Are these superstitions?

Myths and legends

Myths are made by man. They come out of the far, far past of humanity, and are an attempt by man to answer the many questions that have bothered him since creation. The African has developed a whole series of myths about gods, culture, nature and heroes, that try to unveil some of the mysteries of life. Here are two examples of myths from some societies in Cameroon. They are similar to many others found in other societies all over Africa.

The wicked step-mother – how evil came to the world

This popular story is told all over Cameroon. It is about a wicked step-mother who treated an orphan child very badly and sent him out to search for a vessel he lost. The child returned after a long time with a golden egg which, when he broke it, transformed the whole place into a kingdom over which he presided. Seeing that, the jealous woman sent her own son to bring her the same glory. The son was disobedient, and the gods of the underworld gave him his own egg. When he arrived home the whole society was invited to see him break the egg. He did, and as I recount it:

Pooom! Down went the egg and up came the doom!
Instead of the long awaited city of worth,
The egg gave rise to wild beasts of all sorts,

And stinking insects and dangerous reptiles
All made chase, following the people
Corpses lay there and all about
That of course was a worthy price to pay
of jealousy and disobedience
Which, like the fruit of Eden
Brought the origin of all the animals
To this world of ours
In this way shame and ruin came to the world

The origin of death

At first death did not exist. People grew old and rejuvenated. But the dog and the chameleon had a fierce argument. The dog argued that people should live for ever, so that there would be no sorrow. The chameleon felt that people should die. They went to convince God. The argument was evenly weighted, and God decided to organize a competition for them to run to the top of a hill. 'Whoever arrives there first', He said, 'should drum his message and his pleas will be accepted.' When the race began the chameleon went on steadily. The dog ran at full speed, but then fell into eating and drinking on the way, on the assumption that he would overtake the chameleon. Then he slept, only to be awakened by the sound of chameleon's plea on the drum – 'there should be death', 'there should be death' – and God accepted this plea. And so death came to the world.

Folk tales, fairy tales and folk songs

There is hardly any culture in the world that has no kind of story-telling. In non-literate societies in the past, and even today, folk tales, fairy tales and folk song played an important role as instruments of self-control and by the morals they teach, thereby helping to bring order to the society. The folk tale, like other genres of literature, was one of the principal features in the education of the child. Folk tales, folk songs and fairy tales were and are the largest and most common genres of our oral past, and they still play an important part in the regularization of the lives of many people in the developing world. When children listened to fascinating stories around a bonfire after the evening meal, they enjoyed them and at the same time they were learning. Thereafter, they would be initiated in a dramatization of scenes in fake arenas of war, where they would play at fighting in preparation for real battle over anticipated adversaries, or would imitate the movement and pacing in a game-hunting scene or a practice to defend a title or undergo an initiation into a tribal rite. Through these simulation exercises, the boy is developing his manhood tactics while the girl practises motherhood – all this knowledge is passed on by the tradition-bearers of the tribe. These stories also give the young a wider cultural dimension in which they are schooled quite early in their lives, when habits are easy to form and impressions are indelible in the mind.

These examples give us an insight into what we can now learn of the life that was lived many years ago by our forebears.

A folk tale in which a young, beautiful princess marries a stranger who later becomes a skull, or where a pretty, dandy girl later marries a monstrous dragon, are told to warn young women to beware of love at first sight and of the necessity of making a reasonable decision in each circumstance. In another tale a notorious thief is caught. The chief gives everyone a stick of equal length and threatens that whoever stole from the village will find his stick has grown by two inches. The thief, believing this, cuts two inches from his stick and is thereby discovered when the sticks are brought together. Here we see a classic case of the wisdom of traditional justice.

Some tales are meant to warn against disobedience and disrespect for elders. Because a baby-sitter disobeys and takes her charge to an enchanted rock near a pool, the baby is glued to the rock and all attempts to rescue it fail. A wild hyaena later eats the baby and three other relatives who come in search of the baby. Later, the hyaena is killed.

There are trickster tales in which the tortoise, bat, hare and spider are prominent personalities. In one of the tales in this series, the tortoise defrauds the pig of his money, and in another he tricks two giants, the hippo and the elephant, into a tug-of-war in which he does not take part. In many stories of this narrative cycle, the trickster character succeeds against all his adversaries, and his schemes hardly ever backfire. These stories tell the child much about the use of his common sense, and that the 'pen is mightier than the sword'.

Many tales are told to inculcate the habits of kindness and sympathy to other people. The idea of sharing what you have with others, particularly with strangers, is deeply rooted in the culture. It will be difficult for a person in a traditional African society to laugh at someone afflicted with a disease, because in some stories some of these people sometimes turn out to be a god disguised as a beggar to tempt people. Thus, whatever we have, we share with others, lest one may face the wrath of a vindictive spirit or an angry ancestor. Moral dilemma tales are usually intriguing to young children. One example, where a father, mother and an only child have to decide which of them should die in order to save the others when they come by a river which only two people can cross, ends in a dilemma because a resolution is hard to come by. Many of the tales that satisfy young people are those in which the weak, the orphan, the poor and the despised are shown always to triumph. In one example, a poor, badly treated orphan becomes kind, and in another an ugly and deformed character marries the princess amidst very stiff competition from his betters. One believes that these tales have many good lessons for everyone, no matter what the society or the civilization.

Like the folk tale, the African traditional folk song has lived primarily in the memories of the Africans, and has been passed on from one singer to another by word of mouth. Of all the genre-types, the folk song has survived best because the tune, the rhythm, the refrain and the poetic nature lend themselves to easy recall from memory, and it is also the most migratory of the genres because the tunes are easily picked up and transported to far-distant lands within a very short time.

There are many types of traditional folk songs in Africa, and many of them are very solemn, enchanting and profound. Nursery rhymes and lullabies play a very useful role in the care of screaming babies whose mothers might be returning late from the farms. At the village level in the traditional African societies, most work – like the hoeing or clearing of a farm, the harvesting of crops and the daubing or thatching of a new house – was done as a communal service by the people. During this time songs are sung for entertainment and also to accompany the rhythmic movements so as to lighten the burden. In the Cameroon Development Corporation (CDC) – an agro-industrial complex which employs thousands of work-hands – many new songs are made up to describe current events, and especially gossip and scandals in the camp. The famous 'Nkum Nkum massa' (see Appendix) is extremely elegant and versatile, and is sung by CDC banana plantation workers. (Notice the way the illicit love affair of a CDC worker is being handled.) Many such examples abound. Usually the singers, like the *griots* or praise-singers in a folk tale, are very smart, and once in town they try to identify themselves with the potential victim of satire and to acquaint themselves with the latest gossip and scandals involving such persons. These are used to embellish the songs. It is in these song performances that serious happenings – like the beating of a juju, the iniquity of the chief, scandal concerning a priest – things about which everybody knows but dare not talk of openly, are used by the singer to ridicule prominent persons. Love songs, religious songs, dance and game songs also perform useful functions in our traditional societies. Dance is present throughout Africa – it is central to ritual and ceremony.

Proverbs and riddles

Because of their pungency and terseness, proverbs and riddles have been described as wisdom literature. Proverbs are the distilled wisdom of past generations and the authentic voice of history. In most African societies, where moral behaviour of the group is governed by social norms, proverbs are very effective checks on people's behaviour, as well as censoring defaulters or praising those who conform to the ethics of the group or tribe. Although many African proverbs are similar to or have been adapted from Western civilization through education, there are many more that are local, because their referents are the environment and local activities.

The Cameroon proverb which states that 'You cannot judge a Hausaman/ Moslem from his size' is drawn from the fact that most Hausa people are tiny, and the meaning is that size is not might. This proverb is similar in meaning to the Yoruba proverb 'No matter how small a needle is, a chicken cannot swallow it'. Both proverbs are a warning and a lesson to more-powerful people who can be embarrassed by apparently weaker individuals.

Other common proverbs such as:

A goat eats only where it is tied.
No one expresses his poverty to a stranger.
Nobody is the father of wealth.
One hand cannot tie a bundle.
The dog's rump is cleaned by God.

are among many that are created daily. They are witty and terse, and are made by the older members of the society in conversations to prop oratory, and in court, to retort to a sharp rebuke and rebuff and as a lesson to the young. Proverbial language and idioms are so profound that sometimes it is hard to follow the conversation of elders unless one's mind and tongue have been tutored to grasp that traditional rhetorical repertoire.

Riddles, on the other hand, are an entertainment device and a 'warming up' exercise before the family story-telling session after an evening meal. Some riddles have become hackneyed, so their answers are shouted out by those listening long before the riddler has finished the statement. Others are intriguing, perhaps remote and far-fetched, because they can be created about any subject/object of which the riddler has experience. Because some riddles are so localized, they are difficult for people from outside a particular culture and society, although common sense is very useful in answers to many riddles. Others are more generally known. Here are three.

Who am I?
    (a) *Riddler*: I am an army that uses only one gun
         Answer: A broom
    (b) *Riddler*: You can feel me but you can't touch me
         Answer: Air or wind
    (c) *Riddler*: I walk on all fours in the morning, on two legs at noon and on three legs in the evening
         Answer: A baby, a grown-up man and an old man

Many riddles depend for their success on a hidden ambiguity and a trick which the people listening must be trying to unravel.

Although many proverbs and riddles are also created today, they too are part of our past, and we can get into the minds of our ancestors by studying the make-up of their proverbs and riddles, as well as knowing how they spent their leisure.

Some material remains of the past

Very similar to myths are legends. Many legends in Africa relate to tribal origins and migrations, and they have usually proved to be very accurate and reliable. Some deal with people, places and events, and are usually known to the entire society. The people believe in them absolutely, and no scientific explanation can convince them to the contrary. One main characteristic of a legend is that it is fraught with many supernatural elements that are extremely systematic. Many legends are also situated in particular societies.

There is a legend among the Tang people of Donga Mantung Division in Cameroon that a small dark-striped rat (mukie) saved the clan from extinction. The story goes that, while escaping at dead of night from an imminent attack from a neighbouring tribe, the Tang people came to a big stream at Mbajeng, in Ndu. All of the people who entered the stream to wade across were drowning, unknown to the rest until they heard the sound of a gong which one of them was carrying rattling on the stones far downstream. Then their chief realized what was happening and ordered that no one else should enter the stream. At dawn, it was clear that many were drowned and, as the rest sat by the bank, a small dark-striped rat (mukie) ran across the stream on a twig to the other side and back again. This gave them the idea that if they cut a tree that was by the bank so that it fell on the other side they could cross on it, as the mukie was do-ing. This, they did and the rest crossed over. At the other end they took count, family by family, of the missing people by counting stones – a large pile of which is still found at Mbajeng in Ndu today. That is why the Tang clan does not eat the mukie, which is believed to have been their saviour.

There is a similar legend among Moslems, who were also saved by a pig which provided a clue to water during a devastating drought, and for that reason Moslems do not eat pork.

Another legend which is very popular in Bamenda concerns the Kom people. We are told that when the Kom people came from Tikari and settled in Ndop plain, their neighbours, the Babissi people, were very belligerent and menaced them frequently. It is said that one day the Fon of Babissi tricked the Fon of Kom and burned all Kom able-bodied males. In a dramatic twist of events the Fon of Kom committed suicide, which later was to be the cause of the destruc-tion of the Babissi people. Thus, the Kom people had to leave for their prom-ised land. Led by a snake-god, they travelled all the way to Laikom, where the snake disappeared and there, on Laikom Hill, the Kom people built the Kom palace which is the sacred headquarters of the Kom Fondom, free from the incessant battles and the menace of belligerent tribes. Many thousands of such fascinating legends abound among the many tribal societies in Africa, which need much more documentation than exists now.

The basic question now is why we still study myths and legends today. Has the introduction of literacy and religion demystified our beliefs in myths and legends? Why are myths still being created? For example, the stories about the late Abendong in Mankon, Bamenda, a mystic politician, or about the Zulu leader, Chaka. Can archaeologists use these beliefs to discover more about the people, or can the universality of some themes and recurrent motifs in many civilizations tell us more about mankind?

However divergent our answers may be, perhaps because of our various backgrounds and our different civilizations, one thing is clear: even today, we have not yet found all the answers to many intriguing problems in life. Literacy and religion can only explain things up to a point. It will take a very long time indeed even for modern technology to discover who the Big Brain is behind all the forces we are trying to uncover, and how they came to be. Many of our scientific theories and explanations are still speculative, and because of that myths and legends will continue to be created even in the 24th century.

In most traditional African societies there can still be seen today some surviving elements of what one can describe as materials or concepts providing direct evidence of the past.

The first institutions that come to mind are the many museums, with their wonderful arts and crafts. African museums are the vanguard in the battle to protect our cultural heritage. In many chiefdoms in Cameroon, for example, there are museums that pre-date colonization. There are carvings, brass works, pottery and masks, among other things, that have lasted for more than 200 years. In East Africa many fascinating works of art and relics are preserved in the museums in Tanzania and Kenya. In Nigeria the Yoruba arts and crafts have won world acclaim, and the Ibiobio and Ibo masks have stood the test of time. African museums may not have any antiques or works of artistic value to fit foreign definition, but African arts and crafts are of intrinsic value which is specifically African.

Another typical feature of African life that is still visible in some societies today is the institution of titles. In Cameroon there is presently an upsurge in the acquisition of traditional titles by the urban élite, and some of these titles go with their full regalia and ceremonial observances. The title *Nformi* in the Wimbum tribe was an honour to a strong leader of the war club called the *Mfuh*. He was a strong, intelligent master-planner, and the title was given for nis part in the defeat of a warring tribe from which he brought captives as well as booty. Today, there are no inter-tribal wars, but these titles are still being given, but now for some achievement for the society. Other titles in this war club are *Ngwang, Ngwayi* and *Gwei*, the last of these being spies.

In many African societies there is respect for the tombstones of certain family lineage heads, where libation is still being poured so long as there are family members. There are still weapons, utensils, grinding stones, traditional ceremonial houses in many chiefdoms in Cameroon.

In some villages in Cameroon there are remnants of compounds and dilapidated houses. On asking what happened to the people in these compounds, one is informed that the people were exiled for practising witchcraft. In the past the chiefs had the power to exile people who were suspected of witchcraft. Only recently, a chief was taken to a modern court by one such suspect. The chief was seriously warned, and this is the first test case for a traditional authority in this area. It generated a lot of talk and discussion, because this was the first time the traditional institution was facing reality in a modern setting.

We have already discussed several fetishes and taboo practices which are still seen in some African societies. These, and many more, are parts of our past which are still present in our society. Our present is a re-embodiment of the past for, although some values have changed and are still changing, the past is with us today. We can re-interpret it today in order to understand the present and find solutions for the future.

Conclusion

Many scholars of Africa have lamented the fate of our folk-life, for they said that our oral tradition is in sharp decline because of the barrage of Western civilization and Western-type education and its stress on literacy and the written word. In Mali, for example, where the tradition of training bards is still continuing, it has been noticed that the situation of the *griots* is in decline because even they are now sending their children to school. *Griots* today are not like they once were, and there is no doubt that the art of story-telling and the initiation into tribal apprenticeship is not being pursued with the same rigour. It is clear, then, that there are few authentic practitioners of the art of story-telling, and the way the onslaught of modern communication – transistor radio, television and other media – is affecting life even at the village level is an indication that bards, *griots* and story-tellers, who rely on patronage and gifts for their living, can now exist only in very difficult circumstances.

In spite of the pessimism, which is justified, we do know that our oral tradition will never be the same again. However, it could be for the better, because by collecting, retelling and archiving our folk culture, we are immortalizing it. Also, there is no greater treasure for the modern man than to know his past well as a basis for assessing and understanding the future: 'When we study our oral tradition, we are in a sense studying ourselves. And knowing ourselves is still a challenge to the modern man' (Talla 1984).

If African scholars and researchers are pessimistic, they would probably say (to borrow Richmond's idea) that: 'Today our oral tradition is a fossil, a magnificent specimen to be studied and exhibited but, like all fossils, a mere shell of its former self' (Richmond n.d., p. 111). Who are more qualified to study shells and fossils, than archaeologists?

Appendix

Soloist	*Chorus*
Nkum nkum massa	Ha!
Nkum nkum tam i no day	Ho-nkum nkum
We go for bar o	Ha!
Manmi polina go weti we	Ho-nkum nkum
As Polina i inta	Ha!
I miti massa Johnson	Ho nkum nkum
Ho a ho	Ha ha no nkum nkum
Ho a ho	Ha ha ho nkum nkum
Massa Johnson i tanap	Ha
I tanap I go for upside	Ho nkum nkum
Polina I tanap	Ha
I tanap follow massa	Ho nkum nkum
Dem go for upside	Ha

Dem waka go for backside	Ho nkum nkum
Dem fall for ground-o	Ha
One tam chop i don done	Ho nkum nkum
Dem chop one tam	Ha
Small taim dem chop two taim	Ho nkum nkum
As dem day for ground-o	Ha
Man Trouble come catch dem	Ha ha ho nkum nkum
Ho ha ho	Ha ha ho ha ho
Ho ha ho	Ho nkum nkum

Source: Talla (1984, p. 30).

References

Lantum, D. N. 1969. Superstition. *Abbia: Cameroon Cultural Review* **22**, Yaounde.

Malinowski, B. 1954. Myth in primitive psychology. In *Magic, science and religion*, B. Malinowski. 93–148. New York: Doubleday.

Richmond, W.E. n.d. American folklore. *Voice of America forum lectures*. Washington, DC.

Talla, K.I. 1984. *An introduction to Cameroon oral literature*. Yaounde: SOPECAM.

10   *Classical Greek attitudes to the past*

BRIAN SPARKES

The 'Classical' of the title distinguishes the subject from the preceding pre-historic periods, and from the later Christian, Medieval and Modern periods. What follows is mainly concerned with the historical period from Homer down to the 4th century BC, when Philip of Macedon and his son Alexander took over the Greek city–states.

Evidence for Classical Greek attitudes to the past is irregular in quality and quantity. Time and chance have destroyed or preserved different bodies of evidence, and there is no specific work on the subject in antiquity, and references are only allusive. The casual remarks we encounter may have real significance or only the semblance of it. The works we have are biased in different ways: politics, local pride, philosophical theorizing, etc.

The chronological list in Table 10.1 is brief and approximate; it is for those who are unfamiliar with the period to get their bearings.

Mycenaean society of the Late Bronze Age in Greece was centred on a few rich and powerful palaces, such as Mycenae itself, Pylos and Thebes. Life under the domination of the palaces was highly organized, and a form of writing (the Linear B syllabic script) was used by scribes for the palace administration. Outside contacts with other societies were widespread. By the year 1100 BC the collapse of the Mycenaean way of life was complete, and this was followed by some generations of low-level inward-looking existence (the Greek Dark Ages). Literacy came to an end with the destruction of the palaces, and emigration from long-established settlements on the Greek mainland to new foundations on the coast of Asia Minor altered the demographic pattern. The 8th century BC saw an accelerated improvement which led to the development of a new social and political organization: the small independent city–states of the Classical Greek world. Horizons also widened, with contacts with outside powers re-established, and literacy returned.

In many cultures such a combination of circumstances – a decline of a once-powerful nobility, a drop from high to low living conditions and a change of settlement – produces a nostalgic attitude for the days when life was materially richer, when men were more courageous, and when there was a taste for warfare and adventure. This is true also of the Greek attitude – the Heroic Past was something from which they were never free; life had always been better in earlier days. During the Greek Dark Ages, stories of earlier exploits and adventures were accommodated to this attitude and crystallized. Most stories that had

Table 10.1   Chronology (approximate) from Mycenaean culture in Greece to loss of
Greek independence.

1500 BC	Late Bronze Age Mycenaean culture in Greece
1250	Trojan War Linear B script
1100	end of the Bronze Age fall of the Mycenaean kingdoms
	Greek Dark Ages
800	the alphabet and the beginnings of Greek literacy
700	Homer Hesiod epic poets
600	lyric poets Xenophanes
500	Persian Wars (490–479) Pindar Athenian tragedians Herodotus Peloponnesian Wars (431–421, 415–404) Thucydides
400	Plato Athenian orators Philip of Macedon (*d.* 336) Chaeronea (338) loss of Greek independence

existed before were now developed and became fixed in the princely society of
that Mycenaean Age generations before. The location of the main characters
was centred on the palaces which lay in ruins on the hilltops. This past was
recalled by bards who sang of heroic exploits in epic verse – memories had
travelled with the emigrants, and were one of the chief links they had with that
more glorious past. If any stories had existed in the Late Bronze Age and had
been recounted in the courts, we do not know what sort of past they recalled,
but it was unlikely to have been the same as that sung in the Dark Ages; too
much of importance and change had happened in the meantime.

An important factor which affected the Greeks' attitude to their past was the
late arrival of literacy. In the Mycenaean period there had been the complex
system of syllabic writing we know as Linear B, serving the administrative
needs of the palaces. It was a system operated by palace scribes, and is unlikely
to have been widespread outside the palaces themselves. Illiterate generations

followed the collapse of the palace system, and it is not until *c.* 800 BC (i.e. three centuries later) that the more flexible alphabetic script was adopted by the Greeks from the script of the Phoenicians, within whose orbit they had begun to trade. It was a much simpler script, widely available and useful for a range of purposes – administrative, to be sure, but more importantly commercial and private, it was not an official organ of power. It was eventually used for committing to writing the oral songs of the bards. Anything that had happened and was remembered, before alphabetic writing, was transmitted by individual report through word of mouth or by the 'corporate' memory of the bards. The writing down of the songs meant that the remembered past was crystallized at that stage in its development. Although this was not a total ossification, a fixed, written version was now in existence, and the fluid and creative version of the past was circumscribed. Bards now largely became reciters of a 'received text'.

Even after the adoption of writing, story-telling was the main medium for recollection of the past, as many people would still have been illiterate. The stories learnt at mother's or grandmother's knee were no doubt a mixture of family histories and the legends that were the common property of the community. With the fixing of the epic tales in writing, freedom to alter the major lines of the tales may have been reduced, but piecemeal alteration must have been taking place all the time. The informal telling may have been prone to alter more freely, as it was unfettered by the stricter demands of poetic form. Our main evidence for the Greeks' attitude to the past derives from their different genres of literature – epic, tragic, historical, etc. For most Greeks these literary genres, although composed and preserved in written form, would have been communicated orally – in recitals, choral singing, performances in the theatre, and so on. Audiences would have absorbed the work as it unrolled, few would have studied a written version.

Epic songs, particularly the songs that went under the name of Homer, were a vitally important factor in the Greeks' view of the past. We know that the epics of the *Iliad* and the *Odyssey* were fixed by the 6th century BC, perhaps on the basis of written texts, and were recited at public performances every four years. Crowds of thousands went to listen (Plato, writing in the 4th century BC, mentions the figure of 'more than 20 000' in an audience; *Ion* 535d), and they no doubt thrilled to hear the traditional tales and absorbed the values which they inculcated. They also doubtless accepted the stories as true tales of their own past, as they heard the singers assure them of their own veracity or of that of their heroic predecessors within the epic itself, as Odysseus flatters the singer Demodocus (*Od.* 8, 487–91, transl. Shewring):

> 'Demodocus, I admire you beyond any man; either it was the Muse who taught you, daughter of Zeus himself, or else it was Apollo. With what utter rightness you sing of the fortunes of the Achaeans – all they achieved and suffered and toiled over – as though you yourself were there or had talked with one who was!'

The very repetition of the stories in fixed form helped to underline the notion that this was what had, indeed, happened. The stories recounted were set in a timeless age, with no connection with the present. The poet distinguished the heroic period by simple devices which enhanced and enlarged the earlier ages and set them apart (for example, *Il.* 12, 445–50, transl. Lattimore):

> Meanwhile Hector snatched up a stone that stood before the gates
> and carried it along; it was blunt-massed at the base, but the upper
> end was sharp; two men, the best in all a community, could
> not easily hoist it up from the ground to a wagon,
> of men such as men are now, but he alone lifted and shook it
> as the son of devious-devising Kronos made it light for him.

The Homeric poems are sophisticated literary products, and thus their effect on an audience is likely to have been strong and impressive. Also, the stories, characters and values were accepted as models for conduct, morality, religion, education, etc. The poems were emotionally satisfying, and although some intellectuals such as Xenophanes of Colophon in the 6th century BC might reject the morality as unsatisfactory, the incidents themselves were unimpeachable. Our modern passion for distinguishing poetic imagination and literary artifice from a 'hard core' of history would have had no meaning – it was within the legends they heard sung that their past was firmly entrenched.

Composers of epics other than the *Iliad* and the *Odyssey* are more fragmentarily preserved, but seem no real loss. Some integrated the Homeric epics into a continuous set of stories by adding series of incidents that took place before, between and after the episodes contained in the *Iliad* and the *Odyssey*. However, even this larger epic raft still floats free of 'history'. Other poets compiled genealogies and family trees in verse, or sang of the foundation of cities; these could later be used by families and states as validating documents. The poet Hesiod (*c.* 700 BC) adapted a widespread Near Eastern tale of the metal ages and races of man, but does not bring them into any meaningful connection with historical periods – they are discontinuous groupings that need a race of heroes to link them in any way with the Greek concept of the past. The imported model could not oust the traditional view, and the man-in-the-street would have clung to his heroic paradigms, with no need to fix them in time (relative or absolute), and no means of doing so had the need arisen.

If one were writing of the development of Greek literature, much would need to be said of the rise of the voice of the individual in lyric and elegiac verse: Sappho, Archilochus and such, with their emphasis on personal themes and contemporary concerns. In the 7th and 6th centuries BC such poets chose to ignore the past, or to use it in an allusive way by choosing heroic characters as exemplars for their friends or enemies. Choral, as opposed to solo, lyric was performed publicly, and Pindar, the major poet of such lyric in the 5th century BC, uses major figures from the past as suitable and impressive prototypes next to whom he places his victorious athletes whose achievements he is praising. Here the past, as so often happens, is tailored to meet the needs of the occasion; for Pindar the past must conform to the values of the aristocratic society for whom he is composing. On occasion the poet claims to know that Homer's art has beguiled his audience into accepting an untrue tale (for example, *Nemeans* 7, 21–7, transl. Bowra):

> But I hold that the name of Odysseus
> Is more than his sufferings
> Because of Homer's sweet singing;
> For on his untruths and winged cunning
> A majesty lies.
> Art beguiles and cheats with its tales,
> And often the heart of the human herd is blind.
> If it could have seen the truth,
> Aias would not, in wrath about armour,
> Have driven a smooth sword through his breast.

Pindar favours the stalwart Ajax against the more resourceful Odysseus, and puts down the victory of the latter over the former to the skill of Homer – in fact he sees the heroic characters in literary terms. 'The human herd' continued to believe in the inherited stories.

For the Athenians of the 5th century BC tragedy was a more pervasive and important influence. Again, these were for public performance and were presented to audiences of tens of thousands. They were therefore 'popular' entertainment. The past which circulated through the medium of the heroic epics was the mine in which the tragic poets worked – slices, as Aeschylus said of his own work, from Homer's great banquets. It was only on rare occasions that a poet went outside the corpus of epic stories and chose what we would call an 'historical' subject – the only extant example being Aeschylus' *Persians*. Although the audience would have known that they were being shown a tragedy that concerned itself with events that happened less than a decade previously, it is doubtful whether they would have made a distinction between the *Persians* and such tragedies as *Agamemnon* or *Oedipus* – all concerned the past, indeed the traditional stories might be thought more trustworthy because more firmly embedded in the fabric of their collective memory.

However, like Pindar, the tragic poets were innovators, and as more research is done, it becomes clear that they were radical in their innovations. They were not content to accept the epic versions, indeed they were forced by the different conditions of the dramatic contests, in which time for each play was short, to alter, condense and trim. The looser epic structure was tightened for the new circumstances, and opportunity was also taken to update the morality of the tales, and occasionally to manipulate the plot to introduce a political slant favourable to Athens: Athens as a safe sanctuary for exiles or Athens as a steadfast ally. Such alterations and innovations were not slow to take shape; each year dramatists had to produce plots that held the interest of keen theatre-goers, and this meant rearranging and revamping the stories so that not only did the 5th century BC Athenian dramatic versions differ considerably from the traditional epic tales, but within a few generations these new versions had undergone greater or lesser transformations at the hands of the different dramatists. The Athenians were noted for their love of novelty, and the theatre must have been one of the places where that love was best served. Certainly the continual reworking of the themes over three or more generations suggests that it was popular with audiences and met with their approval, but it also raises the problem of quite what was the attitude of the audience to the 'truth' of these tales which recounted their past. Was it possible for audiences to divorce the theatrical versions, full of startling novelties and progressive morality, from the 'real' stories that they knew in their hearts told their past as it had happened? This must have been the answer for many of the audience; for a few the authenticity of the tales themselves was doubtless suspect.

The development of an historical approach to the past may go back to the 6th century BC, but again the myths, though mocked, were not jettisoned altogether. Hecataeus of Miletus (c. 500 BC) began his work *Genealogies* (of the great mythical families) with the statement (fr. 1):

> I write what I consider to be the truth; for the tales of the Greeks are many and ridiculous, as it seems to me.

His aim, as the title of the work suggests, was not to reject the stories altogether, but to bring order into the chaos of the myths, discarding variants, harmonizing and rationalizing where necessary. Such a simplistic approach could only dismantle and reconstruct the past according to one man's limited vision, and is sterile. Herodotus and Thucydides, both of the 5th century BC, are major figures in Greek historiography, but their very reasons for writing set them apart from any investigation of general attitudes to the past. Herodotus' reason for writing was (1.1, transl. de Sélincourt):

> to preserve the memory of the past by putting on record the astonishing achievements both of our own and of other peoples; and more particularly, to show how they came into conflict.

Thucydides tells us that he wrote his history (1.1, transl. Warner):

> in the belief that it was going to be a great war and more worth writing about than any of those which had taken place in the past.

Herodotus uses the word *historiē* to define his work: 'enquiry', a search for facts, chiefly by autopsy, then by questioning others, and finally by consulting written sources. No matter what the order of research might be, here we have a more systematic approach, seeking for explanations, analysing causes. This was no longer an accepting world. Herodotus realizes that generations beyond a certain number of years in the past are to be differently assessed from more recent times (3.122):

> For Polycrates was the first Greek we know of to plan the dominion of the sea, unless we count Minos of Cnossus and any other who may possibly

have ruled the sea at a still earlier date. In ordinary human history at any rate, Polycrates was the first; and he had high hopes of making himself master of Ionia and the islands.

This is a different view from that of Homer and 'of men such as men are now'. Herodotus was also faced with the vastness of the Egyptian past (2.141–2):

> They declare that three hundred and forty-one generations separate the first king of Egypt from the last I have mentioned – the priest of Hephaestus – and that there was a king and a high priest corresponding to each generation. . . . When Hecataeus traced his genealogy and connected himself with a god sixteen generations back, the priests refused to believe him, and denied that any man had ever had a divine ancestor.

Here the validity of the Greek view of his own past is called into doubt. Thucydides chose a contemporary subject for his researches, and for the most part disregarded the past or extrapolated it from observation and common sense, though willing to use Homer as an historical source when necessary. For both historians the present was a product of past change, but neither was willing to put much trust in, nor spend much time over, the Heroic Ages.

Other prose writings present different approaches. In philosophy Plato constructs views of the past that are too personal and theoretical to represent anything other than an individual creation. On the other hand, the Athenian orators of the 4th century BC, in their need to rouse their jurors and persuade to their point of view, are prime examples of the manipulation of popular stories of the past; they are important sources of evidence, as they enable us to see to what extent public speakers could use the past in their assault on the minds of their audiences. An example of this is considered in some detail later in this chapter.

As with the historians, documentary evidence, though vital for the reconstruction of Greek history, is less useful for understanding views of the past. The records of a city – treatises, laws and official lists – did not tell the citizens of their past in the way that they learned of it from the improving stories in song and play.

Written evidence must inevitably be our main source, but there are other ways of approaching the subject. We have seen that literacy arrived late, and that the past was presented in public performances of epic songs and drama. For the unlettered public, pictorial presentation must have been important. In Euripides' *Ion* the female chorus, on a pilgrimage to Delphi, exclaim at what they see there (vv. 184ff., transl. Vellacott):

> So holy Athens is not the only place
> Where the gods have pillared courtyards
> And are honoured as guardians of the streets.
> – Apollo's temple too has the twin pediments,
> Like brows on a smiling face.

- Look – look at this! The Lernian snake
Being killed by Heracles with his golden falchion –
Do look, dear!
                    – Yes, I see.
But who is this other next to him
Waving a flaming torch? Is it the man
Whose adventures we are told at weaving-time,
The brave fighter Iolaus
Who went with Heracles to his labours,
And stayed with him to the bitter end?
– Oh! and look here
At Bellerophon astride his winged horse . . .

The scene that Euripides paints of the reaction of Athenian women who have never before been out of their native city, and whose delight at recognizing their favourite scenes and characters is naive and immediate, rings true. Temple sculpture carrying such themes as the Trojan War, Lapiths versus Centaurs, and Greeks versus Amazons would have been recognized and appreciated as episodes from the past. In a similar way, paintings, whether in public buildings or on a smaller scale on painted pottery, presented a range of stories that comprised a vast panorama of their ancestors' exploits. As in the literary genres, changes occurred over the generations; some stories became popular, others lost their popularity. Local pride reshaped the past to enlarge the part played by the community and to enhance its prestige, the best-known example being that of the Theseus legend which around 500 BC was used by the Athenians to bolster their new development on democratic lines.

Apart from the artistic shaping and reshaping of stories in carved or painted form, there were other visual reminders of the past that demanded a reaction from the people of later generations. That reaction was usually one of wonder and awe – the Greeks referred the building of the walls round Mycenae and Tiryns (Late Bronze Age) to the Cyclopes, from the strength supposed to be needed to erect them, the sort of strength with which the Cyclopes were presumed to be endowed. By accident or design, Greeks of the classical periods excavated relics of earlier generations, and either treated them with respect and veneration (e.g. the Mycenaean tombs containing post-Mycenaean votives) or manipulated them for political purposes (e.g. the search for and discovery of the bones of Theseus on the island of Skyros – a coffin of a man of gigantic size, as Plutarch not surprisingly tells us – *Theseus* ch. 36 – and their reburial in the heart of Athens).

The sanctity of the past in a more complex setting is to be found in the rituals enacted at religious gatherings. The original meaning of the rite was in many cases lost, but the need to repeat the traditional actions was paramount. It has been suggested that the major role that women took in the worship of Demeter, the Goddess of agriculture, goes back to the customs of Neolithic society, when agricultural matters were women's concern. Naturally, the Classical Greeks would not have known this; they accepted the inheritance from the past, and handed it on as precisely as they could.

Apart from the public celebration of heroic deeds in song and action, transmission of isolated events and names continued in a random manner. However, remembrance of the past was often for a purpose, and was in the interest of those who kept the recollection bright. For individuals the past was doubtless personal; it was their own or that of their immediate family. A man's memory goes back to what his grandparents told him of their childhood. Unless recorded, genealogies are distorted beyond that same range, and there is the well-known example of Homeric heroes who recite the names of their ancestors for a few generations and then claim connection with a god or goddess. We have noted Herodotus' contact with Egyptian records which could trace descent through more than 300 generations. The higher up the social scale, the greater the need is for a collective memory within the family. The antiquity and standing of a family was vital at all times, but particularly when there was social unrest and political instability. Legitimacy, inheritance, marriage alliances, and claims to land and power – all may need to be justified by reference to family records, and this means the memory of the elders. The periods of emigration and the foundation of new settlements in the early centuries of the first millennium must have led to countless squabbles, as families staked real or pretended claims to privilege and status in the emergent communities.

Cities and states also needed a collective memory – the ability to refer back to the past as an appeal to a witness. The past had practical utility in justifying claims to territories being overrun, etc. Hence the importance of Homer and of the fixed text of the poems, for within those poems lay validation. The Athenian recension in the 6th century BC was an opportunity to tamper with the text in a way favourable to Athenian military pride. The best-known example of invention and intervention on the part of Athens is at *Iliad* 2, 557–8:

Out of Salamis Aias brought twelve ships and placed them
next to where the Athenian battalions were drawn up.

Even in antiquity the Athenians were accused of inserting the second line at this place to support their claim to the nearby island of Salamis in opposition to their neighbour Megara. Reference back to past glories as confirmation of present deserts took place also on the field of battle. Herodotus (9, 26–7) recounts the rivalry between the men of Tegea in Arcadia and the men of Athens for the position on the left wing of the battle-line at Plataea. The rival claims centre around past exploits (the sons of Heracles, the Amazons, the Seven against Thebes, the Trojan War), only Marathon belongs to their own time. The instances that the Athenians give of courage and unselfishness became the stock themes in panegyrics, and formed the basis for chauvinistic outbursts in the orators of the 4th century BC.

An example of the way in which orators in Athens played upon the susceptibilities of their audiences by references to past glories is Lycurgus' speech in prosecution of Leocrates. In 338 BC, when Philip of Macedon had defeated the Greek allies at Chaeronea in Boeotia and looked set to march on Athens, an Athenian blacksmith named Leocrates defected with his wife and children to the island of Rhodes. After a period spent there and in Megara, Leocrates crossed over the border into Athenian territory and in 330 BC was impeached for treason by Lycurgus. He was acquitted by a narrow margin.

Lycurgus was a well-born citizen of Athens who had distinguished himself in public service, particularly in the years after Chaeronea, when he had organized the revenues of the city and done much to improve the financial administration. His speech against Leocrates survives, and into it the speaker poured his passionate love of Athens for which he had done so much, and his equally fervent hatred of anyone who betrayed her. The effect of all this on the tone of the speech is clear, both in content and in approach. In his denunciation of Leocrates, Lycurgus parades before the jurors the past glories of Athens and the sterling figures who had acted in her interest, whereas the renegades, tyrants and malcontents get short shrift, including Leocrates himself. We have seen that references to Athens' past had by Lycurgus' time become the commonplaces of panegyric. Because of or in spite of this, the speech can be shown to contain inaccuracies and exaggerations. The speaker is carried away on a tide of conventional rhetoric and chauvinistic propaganda. However, Lycurgus has a case to make and an effect to create in the minds of the jurors; slipshod detail counts for little, provided that the points reach their target. With attitudes to the past, we are not concerned so much with the accuracy of statements made as with the use to which a speaker puts remembered events and characters in which his audience can be assumed to take pride or register contempt. The jurors in Greek lawsuits numbered some hundreds, it was the broad effect on them that counted.

Almost half of the speech is devoted to an appeal to the past. After detailing what he sees to be Leocrates' crime, Lycurgus launches into a list of examples of patriotism – the past furnishes a storehouse of models for right conduct, an appeal to tradition sets present attitudes in perspective. At more than one point in his speech Lycurgus claims that Athens was the oldest city–state in Greece – indigenous, never ousted from her territory (paras 41, 83, 100). This had been a traditional claim for generations; thus, whatever the truth or error in such a view, its diffusion amongst the Athenians gave it a credibility that was useful to the speaker and comforting to the jurors. To desert the longest-lasting city is the worst crime of its kind. What is interesting to note here is that, to give substance to his statement, Lycurgus does not go back to any early source, he does not quote a historian such as Thucydides, he recites (and at inordinate length) a passage from Euripides' *Erechtheus*, written and staged less than 100 years previously. The speech is that of a queen of Athens who prefers to sacrifice her daughter rather than lose her autochthonous city – stirring stuff. The past, to be effective, is best clothed in rhetoric and melodrama.

As an instance of bravery in the face of the enemy attack and certain invasion, King Codrus is cited (paras 84–7). Codrus was the last of the Mycenaean kings of Athens, as understood by later Athenian traditions. There is no primary evidence for him, or indeed for his predecessors – all evidence comes from later sources, many of them in imaginative literature. Lycurgus has taken his audience back to a time before hard facts could be known, before writing, before record-keeping. He knows the value of the 'once-upon-a-time' age when the roots of the past grew strong but were hidden from view. The likelihood that Lycurgus, or indeed any Athenian of his day, knew any real facts about Codrus is remote; indeed, Lycurgus is our earliest evidence for the version he is recounting, and may himself have invented the episode he recounts – noble sacrifice to save the city. Codrus dresses up in rags and goes out to provoke a quarrel with the enemy, who must kill him and so vindicate the oracle that had warned the enemy to avoid killing the king if they wished to capture Athens. Whether traditional, invented for the occasion or adapted from a folk tale, the story is the very stuff with which to kindle the patriotism of the jurors.

Another, even earlier, figure from the Athenian royal past is used as an example of the need for sacrifice: Erechtheus must sacrifice not himself but his daughter to avoid defeat at the enemy's hands, and he and his queen acquiesce. It is for this reason that the passage from Euripides is quoted, full of high-minded sentiments – the common good, the ancient laws and love of country more than love of child. Again there seem to be touches of folk tale, but it is none the less (indeed, perhaps all the more) acceptable to the audience for that reason. That Lycurgus expects the jurors to accept the stories of Codrus and Erechtheus as genuine 'history' is shown by his reference to the intervening example of molten lava studiously avoiding the pious as 'a somewhat legendary tale but suitable for the younger among you to hear'.

It is perhaps inevitable that Lycurgus should make reference to Homer (paras 102–3). We have seen how the values represented in the *Iliad* and the *Odyssey* were part of the everyday life of the Athenians, and the power of the poetry to demonstrate the usefulness of the past was paramount: it was with patriotic verses ringing in their ears that the Athenians marched out to fight the Persians at Marathon (para. 104). Now that five generations had passed, Marathon and Thermopylae had become well-established as quasi-legendary battles, fit to be used along with those older paradigms such as Troy and Thebes. It is interesting to note that Lycurgus' traitors and deserters are taken from more recent times, not from the heroic past. The Persian Wars provided their crop, as did the Peloponnesian Wars, and for these Lycurgus has decrees read out to back his statements and accusations. The more remote past supplies the models to emulate, the more recent past those to avoid.

As with other cultures, the past for the Greeks was not what actually happened, it was what was remembered and what could most practically be brought to bear on the present, it sanctioned the way in which later generations lived and thought. Historians in ancient Greece aimed at being critical and objective; the common man needed the past, and used it in an uncritical and subjective way.

References

Bowra, C.M. 1969. *The odes of Pindar*. London: Penguin.

de Sélincourt, A. 1972. *Herodotus the histories*, revised edn. London: Penguin.

Lattimore, R. 1951. *The Iliad of Homer*. Chicago: Chicago University Press.

Shewring, W. 1980. *Homer: the Odyssey*. Oxford: Oxford University Press.

Vellacott, P. 1954. *Euripides: the Bacchae and other plays*. London: Penguin.

Warner, R. 1972. *Thucydides: history of the Peloponnesian War*, revised edn. London: Penguin.

11 Ancient Egyptian concepts and uses of the past: 3rd to 2nd millennium BC evidence

JOHN BAINES

Introduction

In the words of a medieval Arabic poem, the Great Pyramid, the archetypal ancient Egyptian monument, is 'feared by time, yet everything else in our present world fears time' '*Umāra al-Yamanī*; Schäfer 1986, p. 24). The protagonists of such a culture defy the future to erode their achievements, and they may appear set against change. Yet their successors are aware of change, and they have the monuments of the past almost ineradicably before them; they too seek to construct enduring monuments; in looking to the future they emulate the past and extend its traditions. Such obvious paradoxes could hardly be suppressed by the actors. They form a context for involvement with past, present and future in a complex society – large monuments are characteristic of complex societies and archaeologically relevant, but tension between the transient and the enduring is common anywhere. A literate, complex society can supply a continuing, precisely formulated ideological context for such reactions to the past. Very restricted literacy, as there was in ancient Egypt, brings limitations: the chief evidence, which consists of texts and works of art, relates to the ruling élite. I do not study the cult of the dead and of ancestors, which might give evidence for uses of the past in slightly more of the society. The topic can only be sketched here; the 1st millennium BC, the richest period for uses of the past, requires separate study. (For a different treatment see Redford 1986.)

Most Egyptian texts are bland and ideologically homogeneous. However, the use of the past is diverse, between official ideology or mythology and works of literature, between different literary texts, and between literature and private inscriptions. The past legitimates the present order, but an order that needs legitimating is not perfect. Imperfection can be set against the perfection of the past, which may be a model or something more subversive; criticism of the present is in terms of the past. I study where and why Egyptians exploited different pasts. Like any other society, they constructed their present and projected their future out of their past, but the character of Egyptian evidence, its time depth, and the type of society which created it, are all exceptional. First, the past must be related to Egyptian time concepts. The dates in this chapter follow Krauss (1985).

Time and eternity; future-oriented royal 'history'

Egyptian creation set up and demarcated an ordered cosmos surrounded by, and shot through with, the disordered and the 'non-existent' (Sauneron & Yoyotte 1959, Hornung 1982, pp. 172–85). Time is part of the ordered world and a Western 'eternity' is not; the counterpart of eternity is in two much-discussed Egyptian terms, *nḥḥ* and *ḏt*, which appear when distinguished to refer to cyclical and linear time, respectively (Assmann 1975, pp. 41–8, 1983b, Hornung *et al.* 1982, pp. 102–5). Although *nḥḥ* and *ḏt* are neither infinite nor non-time, they denote indefinitely extended, positive time. In the *Book of the dead*, the creator says that the 'lifetime in life' of Osiris, the god who is archetypally subject to linear time, will be 'for millions of millions, a lifetime of millions (or years or people?)' ('million' is related to *nḥḥ*); then the creator 'will destroy all (he) created, and this earth will come to the primeval water and the flood, as in its first state' (MS *c.* 1250 BC; Allen 1974, p. 184). The created world will endure indefinitely until its final destruction when, to quote another such text, there will be a social reversal, and 'mounds will be cities and vice versa. Dynasty (?, or "estate") will expunge dynasty' (Otto 1977, Lichtheim 1973, p. 132 [inaccurate]). Society and the gods inhabit the same bounded cosmos, within which one may aspire to a vast extension.

These global time concepts coexisted with complex calendars (Krauss 1985). There were two lunar calendars used for religious purposes, and a schematic solar 'civil' calendar of 365 days, introduced in the early 3rd millennium BC, by which documents were dated. Despite the existence of lunar and 'Sothic' cycles (*c.* 1456 years; interaction of the civil calendar and the star Sirius), no epoch longer than a year was recognized; from the 4th dynasty longer periods were dated by biennial cattle censuses, and from the Middle Kingdom by regnal years (cf. Assmann 1983b, p. 193, for 'periods' see below). There was thus a sharp division between the limited yearly cycles of the present, which were important in religion and cosmology, and the distant past; remote dates had to be computed from annals or king lists.

Official ideology presents human action as royal; humanity is almost excluded and its position in the scheme of things poorly understood. In parallel with the creator god, the king establishes and maintains the created 'order'. We have a quintessential definition of what he does. The creator placed him on Earth 'for ever and ever (*nḥḥ ḏt*), judging mankind and propitiating the gods, and setting order (*m3't*) in place of disorder (*jzft*). He gives offerings to the gods and mortuary offerings to the spirits' (Middle Kingdom, *c.* 1975 to 1700 BC?; Assmann 1970, 22). The king's role reactivates the creator's and is 'everlasting', while standing between this world and others – the gods and the spirits – and between the present and the past, yet concern for the past is directed away from this world. The definition of his role is oriented primarily to the future (the succession of kings is not mentioned).

This orientation to the future is characteristic of the king's role in 'history' (for which Egyptian has no word) as recorded in his inscriptions. At his accession he sets order in place of disorder and, later, whenever there is a threat to order, he instantly counters it (Hornung 1966, 1971, Otto 1964–6, Gundlach 1985). He may also enlarge order, notably by extending the frontiers of Egypt. For these actions only the immediate past is taken into account, and it may be surpassed. The king's role is ritualized, and there is no sharp distinction between his actions in the cult, which is presented in the definition cited, and in the world; the difference is in the location and the sanctity of what is done. 'Historical' actions have a more-obvious meaning for humanity, but human participation is seldom emphasized in accounts of royal deeds, which were set up in temples and accessible to few. Non-royal human ideology is therefore largely separate from royal, although most private inscriptions relate their owners' achievements to the king. By referring royal actions to the gods and to the future, royal inscriptions exempt them from conventional ethical norms.

The definition is so general that it need not be reflected even in official sources, such as royal inscriptions, that have more pragmatic purposes. In stating that the king judges mankind, it gives the king a moral role similar to that of the gods, which is no accident. Concern with the transient and the past is an explicitly moral dimension of thought and occupies a position slightly below the grandest statements about the cosmos, which lack a human scale. Despite their overarching context, Egyptian time concepts can be relatively small-scale, unsystematic and this-worldly in focus. This focus affects the king in turn: his position is relativized by his mythical and royal predecessors.

Early positive evaluation of the past

The decisive period for defining an absolute past must have been the centuries around 3000 BC, when the state was unified, writing was introduced and the presentation of the cosmos on the monuments was formulated. 'History' could now be separated from the indefinite past. Even then, the past was a significant 'dynastic' factor. In the 1st dynasty the capital of the country was moved from Abydos, the capital of the earlier united but not 'historic' state of Egypt (Kaiser 1964), to Memphis, where the highest officials had grand tombs, *Saqqara*. Kings continued to be buried at Abydos in remote, architecturally modest tombs next to their predecessors' cemetery (Kemp 1967, Kaiser & Dreyer 1982). Tradition and lineage were more powerful legitimations than scale or proximity to the centre of power.

Dynastic history began with the serial recording of year names used for administrative purposes. These names were gathered into lists or 'annals' (Redford 1986, pp. 65–96), of which a fragmentary version made about 500 years later survives; this included more extensive records from the 4th and 5th dynasties, when the system had been superseded by a partial numbering of years of reign (inscription probably a 1st millennium copy: Helck 1970, but see Fischer 1976: p. 48). The monument has a top line giving the names of earlier kings (without any details), who provided a transition between 'prehistory' and 'history'. Nothing mythical seems to have been included. Perhaps the time before the existence of the Egyptian state was 'uncreated', since it was not within the established order of things. Nevertheless, sources that were compiled later place before the first dynasty of kings – what we know as the 1st dynasty – not human rulers but a sequence of groups including gods, who had precise but very long reigns, and 'spirits, followers of (the god) Horus', some sort of demigods (Gardiner 1959, pl. 1, Waddell 1940, pp. 3–27, Helck 1956, pp. 1–8). This very fragmentary material is irreconcilable with the earlier annalistic listing: at some time between the mid-3rd millennium BC and the 18th dynasty (c. 1500 to 1300 BC), prehistory as a mythical time, and a golden time (Kákosy 1964a, b, Otto 1969), was integrated into the official chronology of rule. Later king lists included rival lines of kings and usurpers, so that annals must have been relatively 'value-free'. However, the annals may not have been abreast with contemporary and earlier thinking. Two types of evidence, 'archaeological' and written, can be cited for different, less pragmatic views.

The 'archaeological' material comes from the Step Pyramid of Djoser at Saqqara (c. 2650 BC), the earliest large stone monument and pyramidal structure (Edwards 1985, pp. 34–57, 289–91). This innovative complex commemorates the past on a vast scale. It is sited at the capital, not at Abydos, but includes a symbolic 'south tomb' probably alluding to the old burial in Upper Egypt. The 'conservatism' of design of the surrounding buildings, which are solid dummy reproductions of originals in flimsy materials, and the mimicking of mud brick in the enclosure wall, have been attributed to caution in using the new medium (for example, Edwards 1985, pp. 51–2), but this need not be the only motivation, and does not explain the stylistic, as opposed to technical, transformation of architecture in the following century. Apart from the need for a model, the new medium of stone could be an everlasting 'celebration' of past styles. Among the finds from the entrance area is a statue base that has been dated much earlier and may have been reused for 'antiquarian' reasons (Schäfer 1986, p. 15; there was also much contemporary sculpture). The most massive commemoration was in numerous underground galleries beneath the pyramid, where tens of thousands of stone vases were deposited, many inscribed for 1st and 2nd dynasty kings. Most of these bore single king's names, but some had sequences of up to three (for example, Lacau & Lauer 1959–61, pls 8–17). Such objects were probably not buried in royal tombs, but might have been used in cult or have been inherited palace equipment. The proportion of accumulated material that was buried is unknown, so that the action cannot be seen in context. Since it can hardly have been done for the sake of tidiness, the best explanation is some sort of *pietas*, whatever other factors, such as provision for the mortuary cult (perhaps of Djoser's ancestors as well as himself), were involved. For the hereafter and for contemporaries, this 'ancestral' material in the king's tomb may have legitimated his position and his exploitation of labour in constructing it. Djoser's complex mobilized the past for the present on the most grandiose scale, in both accessible and inaccessible areas. This mobilization shows a positive evaluation of the past, however much the present transcends it. The dynastic Egyptian state was 300 years old, and it is not surprising that respect for 'ancient' kings was exhibited, perhaps especially in a period of rapid change.

Under Djoser there was great development in writing, which could now record continuous language (Baines 1983, p. 577, 1988). Once 'texts' are written down, a monumental context is available for comments on the past, which can then be referred to in a second 'level' of discourse. A fragment probably from the mortuary temple of Khufu, the builder of the Great Pyramid (c. 2550 BC), is relevant here, for it says, apparently of the arrival of a boat shown alongside: '⌈never⌉ [had] the like [happened] under [any king] since ant[iquity . . .]' (Goedicke 1971, no. 6, see also no. 60). This is a standard formula in better-preserved texts of the next dynasty and later (Luft 1976, 1978, pp. 155–66). Thus, from the time when texts were written, their commemorative potential was exploited and they were measured against 'antiquity': to the élite they displayed status for the present, recorded the past and created an absolute, mythical past for the present to emulate or surpass. Because the Khufu text is formulaic, it may not have been the earliest inscribed instance, but a tradition of any length would go back to oral forms. If it is ultimately oral, it implies a continuity in evaluating the past from the time of Djoser. The achievements of the present – unremarkable in the case of the boat – are set against those of the past, but are not said to surpass them. Since the Great Pyramid visibly and probably explicitly surpassed earlier architectural achievements, such an estimate belongs in a different, non-realistic dimension: there exists a mythical, absolute past. If this past was the rule of the gods or the spirits on Earth, it is not reflected in the annals of the period, but the conception could have been parallel to them and have operated on a different plane, just as values ascribed to the past do not relate to achievements in this world, but set a standard outside and above it.

This material counters a widespread view that Old Kingdom Egyptians did not have a complex attitude to the past, being absorbed in the present and its achievements (for example, Wilson 1951, pp. 69, 78–9, cf. Hornung et al. 1982, pp. 90–1). The collapse of the Old Kingdom around 2150 BC, amid famine and the questioning of values, would have brought home the imperfection of human institutions and hence the superiority of antiquity, with its rule of the gods on Earth. This interpretation, which assumes remarkable naïveté in the Egyptians, survives in a recent treatment, despite a 5th dynasty example of the 'antiquity' formula (c. 2450 BC; Luft 1976, p. 75; earlier examples unavailable then). As Luft notes, this formula is closely related to 'since the time (rk) of the god (/name of a god)'. The word rk refers to a period of rule or reign, so that the concept of the rule of the gods on Earth was probably current in all accessible periods, even if it was not incorporated in official listings or narratives until the Middle or New Kingdom.

Ways of mobilizing the past

These phrases mobilize the past for the present and – if anyone reads them – create a secondary past as monuments endure; oral counterparts would reach more of the society and would relate to inaccessible 'folk' uses of the past. Texts may project the past as a 'golden age' of divine rule, as a mythical 'antiquity' – approaches implied by the Khufu material – or as a specific earlier time when some deed occurred or situation obtained. Of this last pair, the first is attested in a late Old Kingdom inscription, where a dwarf brought back from abroad is said to be 'the like of the dwarf whom Werdjdededba brought from Punt in the time (*rk*) of Izezy' (about a century earlier; Lichtheim 1973, pp. 26–7). A negative counterpart is a formula in which people say they could not 'find' that others had achieved what they themselves had (Vandier 1950, p. 196); they imply that they searched the records before stating this. The second is attested with literary texts in the Middle Kingdom (*c*. 1975 to 1700 BC), and might have occurred in their oral precursors. The model earlier time is a historical period, principally the Old Kingdom, which could hardly have been a global model for itself. At a more detailed level, the 4th dynasty reign of Snofru is the most prominent 'good time' in Middle Kingdom texts (Instruction for Kagemni, Prophecy of Neferti, Pap. Westcar: Lichtheim 1973, pp. 60, 140, 216–7), and, apart from the singling-out of this ruler through deification (Wildung 1969, pp. 117–40), must be based on an earlier tradition, probably formulated by contrast with his successors, who built the Giza pyramids and kept their bad reputation until the time of Herodotus (II, 124–8, 5th century BC). The obvious time of origin for such a tradition is the 5th dynasty. Both Middle Kingdom literary texts and later religious sources refer to 5th and 6th dynasty rulers (for example, Pap. Westcar, Instruction of Ptahhotpe: Lichtheim 1973, p. 62, Neferkarc and Sisenc: Posener 1957, pp. 124–5). Such allusions might relate to the incorporation of the rule of the gods in a list with reign lengths, so that literary texts based on human and divine events could be referred to the same complete enumeration. The list will have been 'literary', because high culture was transmitted as a single complex (Baines 1983, pp. 577–8), and could have been formulated in the Middle Kingdom or later (the gods were distinguished from 'human' kings and could be omitted: Mariette-Bey 1869, pl. 43). It illustrates uses of literature rather than new conceptions of the past. Records of kings' names, reign lengths and dynasties existed and survived to form the basis of later lists.

Literary texts are almost never sited in the present (as is widely true of premodern literature). The nearest approach to the present is in inscriptions recording a king's recent deeds, which probably originated after written literary texts and may be a special category of them. These texts were central to the official presentation of the State, and seldom related anything untoward. Critical discourse is mostly conducted in terms of the failings of the past, often the king's immediate predecessors. The king's role requires a response to threats, but these are almost all from abroad or are natural disasters, rather than social or political. One exception is a text of Senwosret I (1935 to 1890 BC, Helck 1985), among the earliest royal inscriptions; the rules of the genre may not yet have been completely formulated. The world abroad of many texts is almost a spatial 'past', outside the present order, like the temporal past. The normal categories of space and time are abrogated at the edge of the cosmos (for example, Shipwrecked Sailor; Lichtheim 1973, pp. 211–5, cf. Derchain-Urtel 1974).

The ascription of literary texts to particular past figures must affect their content. Several Middle Kingdom 'instruction' texts which advise how to conduct an élite life are ascribed to Old Kingdom notables, and were formerly thought to have been composed then (cf. Baines 1983, pp. 577–8, Assmann 1983a, p. 80–8). Two texts with more-pointed discussion of justice, injustice and rulership are placed in the succeeding 1st intermediate period (*c.* 2150 to 1980 BC; the Instruction for Merikare and the Eloquent Peasant; Lichtheim 1973, pp. 97–109 [Helck 1977], 169–84). This could sharpen the discussion but if, as is likely, the texts date from a later time of superficial peace, then such an effect might be minimized by distancing. Texts with a more immediate message for the day, or of a new and complex literary type, came still closer to the present: the Instruction of King Amenemhat (Lichtheim 1973, pp. 135–9) was probably composed under his successor Senwosret I, while the elaborate Story of Sinuhe (Lichtheim 1973, pp. 222–35) depicts events of the same reign and may date to its end. These works contrast with the pseudo-apocalyptic Prophecy of Neferti, which was probably written in the reign of Amenemhat I, whose coming it predicts from the time of Snofru (Lichtheim 1973, pp. 139–45). Here, the 'timeless' golden age of the archetypal good king relativizes the period between him and Amenemhat, no doubt attacking in particular the latter's immediate predecessors.

The Instruction for Merikare is almost a paradigm for literary uses of the past (cited by line no.). It is as if the exploitation of the past was especially negotiable when the potential of 'useless' writing was first being explored. This reflects the recording and reformulation of oral discourse more than written biographical tradition, although that may have been the stimulus to creating written literature (Assmann 1983a). The text refers to various legitimating forces, such as the 'ancestors', as well as citing a 'prophecy of the Residence' and a 'teaching' of Khety (a predecessor of the text's putative author). Within a short tradition it makes play with literary antecedents – apparently similar works to the one we have but possibly non-existent.

The text addresses both the past and the future, whose importance is presupposed by the context of a ruler giving advice to his successor. This point is emphasized by exhortations to 'act for the future' (75) and to surpass earlier achievements (for example, 35). The past is alternately idealized and problematized, as when the author says he captured a town which the founder of the dynasty (?) had not taken (73–4); this would be unusual in an inscription. The ancestors, in whose sayings 'order (*m3ʿt*)' was 'strained clear' (35), are both authors of texts that should be read (35–7) and prophets of perpetual unrest (68–9); their nearest horizon is not distant, since the author treated with them (75–6: earlier rulers of the other half of the country). There are also references to the 'time (*rk*)' of Horus (93) and of 'the Residence' (102, perhaps the Old Kingdom). Nomads have fought Egypt since the time of Horus and cannot win or be defeated (93–4). The texture of past, present and future is such that 'a blow is repaid with its like, that is, everything that is done is intertwined' (123) – a statement acknowledging ultimate responsibility for the recent destruction of the early royal necropolis (probably known to be such, but not admitted in so many words). The present is repeatedly devalued against the conflict-laden past, which the future may emulate or even surpass. Yet little reason is given for optimism and the general tone is harsh and often opportunistic. The text ends by evoking an ethical judgment after death (128–9, also 53–7) and the deity's role in creation. This latter minimizes the splendour of the past by saying that the world was created for mankind, the 'likenesses' of the god, who repelled the disorderly waters (of the uncreated world?), 'killed his enemies, and destroyed his children (probably also mankind, who did survive) because they plotted rebellion' (133–4). This statement, which has a parallel where mankind and not the creator brought evil into being (Lichtheim 1973, pp. 132), both alludes to myths of divine rule and gives the present world a bleak status (superficially reversed at the end).

The other texts cited, which present the Old Kingdom as a glorious past, read like romances in comparison with the Instruction for Merikare (Luft 1976, p. 75, compares inscriptional evidence). Another 'pessimistic' work, the Admonitions of Ipuwer (for example, Faulkner 1973, Fecht 1972), uses the structure of a funerary lament to say that the present is a travesty of past order (cf. Junge 1977). This varied use of the past in one text and between different texts is potentially paradigmatic for later periods, during which these works continued to be known. Despite the currency of myths of divine rule, with problematic exceptions (the Herdsman's Story; Lefebvre 1949, pp. 26–8, Horus and Seth fragment; Griffith 1898, p. 4) no narrative is preserved before the New Kingdom; even then, two important examples (Hornung *et al.* 1982, Borghouts 1978, pp. 51–5) are in non-literary contexts (for arguments for late origin see Assmann 1977a). In any case, the narratives will have had oral antecedents, so that the full range of treatments of the past, including the strictly mythical, should be posited for the Middle Kingdom. The reason for our not possessing earlier evidence may lie in genre and in rules of 'decorum' (Baines 1985, pp. 277–305) governing the inscription of texts, as much as in changing attitudes that written literary works may not simply reproduce oral forms or concepts. Apart from the fragmentary Old Kingdom textual evidence cited, artistic material points in the same direction.

Artistic uses of the past

Old Kingdom representational art contains much non-textual use of the past. This is a later parallel for the architectural *pietas* of Djoser, but needs also to be seen in more narrowly artistic terms and set in context, as concepts of the past relate to general time concepts. Egyptian representation integrates picture and text captions. Its hierarchies and organization present the ordered world and fuse representation with ideological statement (cf. Baines 1985, pp. 70–5, 277–305). They were defined when monumental writing was devised, at the beginning of the dynastic period, and most later art operates within them (a notable exception is the Amarna period, *c.* 1350 to 1340 BC). Stylistic development occurs within this framework, and so is not superficially as radical as in Western art. There remains much room for choice and meaningful recourse to different periods.

'Classic' Old Kingdom style was fully formulated in the 4th dynasty – also the time of the great pyramids. The dynasty began about 400 years of consistent development, during which styles could evolve from their immediate predecessors or look to more-distant models; the latter is an explicit, perhaps ideologically pointed use of the past. Fourth to early 6th dynasty style developed by enrichment of detail and composition. This enrichment ceased in the late 6th dynasty (c. 2200 BC) and development was no longer uniform. Some tombs look back to the barer 4th dynasty style, a reference made specific by such details as a wig treatment revealing small piece of natural hair or a skull cap (for example, Junker 1941, pl. 9 [6th dyn.], cf. Dunham & Simpson 1974, pls 17, 19 [4th dyn.]), or where the skull cap is worn by itself (for example, Junker 1941, p. 91, fig. 23 = pl. 5b, cf. Dunham & Simpson 1974, pls 7, 20); these details are so authentic that they have led scholars astray. Another tendency, visible in different tombs, is to use some very fine tombs as models. Compositions from Ti (late 5th dynasty, Épron et al. 1939–66) and Mereruka (6th dynasty) were adapted at Meir, as when a relief of Mereruka with two sons (Sakkarah Expedition 1938, pl. 1) was taken up for a different purpose at Meir (Blackman 1914–53, 5, pl. 16).

The recourse to 'classic' 4th dynasty style accompanies general impoverishment, and may combine a search for models for sparse and concentrated decoration with detailed emulation of the time when the models were produced. The revived features of dress and ornament are more likely to be artistic than to reflect fashion, so that they argue for 'archaism'. However, the use of fine tombs shows a developed style marking time and being imitated in inferior, mainly provincial, works; it looks more like stasis than a deliberate movement. The case of Meir is notable because a major 12th dynasty tomb there (c. 1825 BC) contains several Old Kingdom revivals, one again drawn from Mereruka (Sakkarah Expedition 1938, pls 6, 7, Blackman 1914–53, pp. 6, 30–1, pl. 13); here, revival is eclectic, deliberate and focused on distant times.

These strategies are general: artists may build on the work of their teachers, perpetuating a style or carrying it forward, or they may react against them and look to more-remote models. The latter approach is found in surprising cases, as in the training of Bernini, who might seem to continue baroque tradition, as a sculptor (Hibbard 1966, pp. 25–9). It is impossible to trace such occurrences without documentary evidence; otherwise, 'archaism' is identifiable only if the borrowing is clearly visible, or where there is evidence that a monument was copied (for example, Baines 1973). Rejection of the immediate past may be more artistic than ideological, in which case it is scarcely archaism. 'Archaism' describes instances where there is some extra meaning in these practices, aptly characterizing late 6th dynasty tombs that look back to the 4th, rather less so the imitation of 5th dynasty tombs in lesser ones of the 6th. It remains significant that, just as the absolute concept of 'antiquity' occurs in the Old Kingdom, programmatic archaism occurs both before it under Djoser and near its end.

In literate societies, an ancient model can be sited precisely. The late 6th dynasty Giza artists could know when the monuments they turned to were constructed. For later times, the overpowering presence of the pyramids could have made them and the surrounding necropolis an inevitable focus of inspiration, but it did not do so, for Giza is archaeologically blank for the next 600 years (see also Wildung 1969, pp. 162–4).

A corollary exists for this absence of archaism. The Middle Kingdom inherited a wide range of artistic uses of the past. Old Kingdom capital styles were imitated in details under the Middle Kingdom's founder, Nebhepetre Mentuhotpe (c. 2025 to 1975 BC, Fischer 1959) and relief carving revived in his reign and the next (for example, Bisson de la Roque 1937, pls 18–28), but this art built essentially on the Theban 1st intermediate period. In the following 12th dynasty the capital moved back to Memphis and capital styles were revived more widely, notably in the pyramid temples of Amenemhat I (1955 to 1925 BC) and Senwosret I (1935 to 1890 BC) nearby at el-Lisht. This is the time when literature's 'golden age' was the Old Kingdom and texts exploited antiquity. The pyramid of Amenemhat I re-used much stone from the Old Kingdom pyramid complexes. This intensified normal constructional practice, in which ready-cut stone was preferred to more-laborious quarrying, and any structure that stood in the way of new building, or was no longer used, was incorporated in its successor, but the reference to earlier kings is probably programmatic, if not to the degree suggested by Goedicke (1971, pp. 4–7). It runs counter to the Instruction for Merikare's exhortation that a king should 'not build (his) tomb from ruins (or) from what was made for [another purpose]' (ll. 78–9). Despite this re-use, principally of Giza material, the el-Lisht reliefs owe little to the early Old Kingdom, looking rather to the complex of Pepy II (c. 2260 to 2150 BC) at South Saqqara (Jéquier 1936–40; for el-Lisht see Hayes 1953, pp. 171–95). The 'archaism' of these works is their reference to Memphite models in opposition to the provincial continuity of the 11th dynasty. In another sense, the use of Pepy's complex, the latest of the Old Kingdom, asserts continuity as much as renewal, and is not archaism. Early 12th dynasty Theban monuments (for example, Lacau & Chevrier 1956–69) continue the style of the local 11th dynasty without a marked break; here a different form of legitimation – or of artistic model – was appropriate.

After the early 12th dynasty, royal works continue their predecessors or strike out in new directions, while private monuments, especially statues, seldom look to the Old Kingdom; these tendencies continued in the succeeding 2nd intermediate period (c. 1640 to 1530 BC). This continuity and non-exploitation of the distant past suggests that the period was considered to be a unity, rather as modern scholars consider it.

Periods: the Middle and New Kingdoms

In its public display, the Middle Kingdom, which was the 'classical' period for later times (although this is never stated thus), appears to have been absorbed in the present and projected itself as a unity; this contrasts with texts. The rhetoric of present and future may fully exploit the past. A striking example is an inscription ascribed to Senwosret I, which mobilizes the resources of myth and of associating the king with the primeval creator (Lichtheim 1973, p. 115–8). The more expansive stela of Neferhotep (*c.* 1700 BC) has the earliest detailed legitimating use of past texts, although this possibility is visible in the royal Pyramid Texts (*c.* 2350 BC; cf. Faulkner 1969, 129, no. 391). The king wishes to 'see the writings of the antiquity of Atum (the creator); spread out the great inventory for me!' – which is then done (Pieper 1929, pp. 8–17, Helck 1975, pp. 21–3). The 'writings' specify the form for a statue of Osiris, and have generalized parallels in Graeco-Roman period temple inscriptions; in both contexts, they are cited for their age (Daumas 1973, Osing 1975). Middle Kingdom private inscriptions similarly use lineage to assert status (for example, Luft 1976, no. 3, Sethe 1935, pp. 26–8), a strategy apparently absent from the more centripetal Old Kingdom texts, where royal favour is the key. Literary continuity is also important: a late 12th dynasty(?) text complains that everything has been said and there is no new way to express suffering – almost a parody of belonging in a tradition (Simpson 1973, p. 230–3, Ockinga 1983).

Although there is general evidence from the Middle Kingdom, texts do not show how major periods were classified; the New Kingdom (*c.* 1530 to 1070 BC) supplies such information. Reliefs and texts display a sense of period and present diverse views in different contexts, creating a more widespread debate than that of the Instruction for Merikare. Ancient rites were performed according to old prescriptions (for example, Epigraphic Survey 1980, p. 43, pl. 28 – said to surpass previous performances), 'classical' – here Middle Kingdom – sculptural forms were revived for the learned (Lange & Hirmer 1967, pls 158, 159), ancient monuments, principally Old Kingdom, were visited by princes (Helck 1961, p. 140–3) and others including 'schoolchildren' (Helck 1952, forthcoming study by A.K. Phillips). Khaemwese, a son of Ramesses II (1279 to 1213 BC), restored many monuments (Gomaà 1973). A very vivid use of the past is a 20th dynasty (*c.* 1100 BC) record of an inspection of looted royal tombs. In emphasizing the seriousness of the crime being investigated, an official says of the king – an ephemeral 2nd intermediate period ruler – that he was 'a great ruler who made ten significant achievements for Amon-Re king of the gods, the great god; his monuments endure in (the god's) courtyard to this very day' (Peet 1930, 2, pl. 3, pp. 6, 2–3). The point is not whether this is true or the speaker knew much about the king, which is unlikely; the past was drawn almost automatically into present argument, here a dispute between different official factions.

These usages do not imply a disinterested concern with the past. The 'deeds' of Egyptian kings, recorded notably in Herodotus, are exploits, not part of a process, while their self-presentation in their inscriptions is not meant to be objective. Rather, a substantial awareness of the past is mobilized for various purposes, often moral, in different contexts. Whereas in earlier times it is a 'scarce resource' (Appadurai 1981), in the New Kingdom scarcity is moderated, but this is part of a pluralization of written culture not confined to the use of the past. I sketch four developments.

Artistic 'periods'

The 'dynastic' temple of Amon-Re at Karnak goes back to the early Middle Kingdom, but it contained very ancient objects (Romano 1979, nos 4 & 10), one heavily worn by visitors (no. 10; Goyon & Traunecker 1980, pp. 132–5). Antiquity honoured the deity. New Kingdom structures, among which these objects were deposited, look to specific times. Reliefs of Ahmose (*c.* 1540 to 1514 BC; for example, Vandersleyen 1971, pl. 1), the founder of the New Kingdom, look to the early 12th dynasty, and his successor even built a copy of the 'White Chapel' of Senwosret I (Björkman 1971, pp. 58–9). In modelling itself on the 12th dynasty, the early 18th evaded the 11th, the previous reuniters of the country whose rule did not last. Early New Kingdom private sculpture uses 12th dynasty models (for example, Bothmer 1966–7, pp. 155–9). In both cases the inspiration is the earlier part of the first period, marking a break from the preceding style and referring to 'classical' art, language and literature. This reference has a personal twist in the mortuary temple of Hatshepsut (*c.* 1472 to 1468 BC), which is inspired by the adjacent one of the founder of the Middle Kingdom and contains texts in very pure classical Egyptian (Naville n.d.), some probably of great age (cf. Assmann 1969, pp. 113–64, 1970). Hatshepsut attacked the 2nd intermediate period Hyksos kings (Gardiner 1946). This may appear bizarre, since they had been expelled decades earlier, but it fits with the evocation of earlier times in her temple. Similarly, monuments of the Nubian 25th dynasty were mutilated 60 years after its expulsion (Yoyotte 1951). These distinctions in the use of models show awareness of precise periods, their monuments, and their associations.

Historical periods

By the 19th dynasty, the 18th was incorporated into a formulation of major periods visible in excerpted groups of depicted or listed kings, and in detail in the Turin Canon (Gardiner 1959), of whose tradition the Graeco-Egyptian writer Manetho is a descendant (3rd century BC; Waddell 1940, Helck 1956). The Canon singles out Djoser, whose name is written in red, and gives totals for some dynasties and for the 1st to 8th – the early dynastic period and Old Kingdom (Málek's 1982, pp. 105–6, ascription of these features to the document's format is unconvincing, cf. von Beckerath 1984). The intermediate periods had a separate status; the 2nd is absent at Abydos (Mariette-Bey 1869, pl. 43). Periodization of this sort could enhance the prominence of Snofru, the 'founder' of the Old Kingdom, in whose reign fuller annals began, but other factors have been cited above. The late period cult of Menes, the legendary founder of Egypt, and of other early kings (Wildung 1969, pp. 15–31, Otto 1957) must be seen in this light.

Some New Kingdom documents juxtapose Nebhepetre Mentuhotpe and Ahmose, the founders of the Middle and New Kingdoms. Mentuhotpe was the fourth king of his dynasty, so that he cannot be cited mechanically from a list; a 'historical' tradition is implied. Ahmose's status at the beginning of a dynasty may 'historicize' him, because he ruled from his predecessor's capital and was his son or nephew. This process of dividing history and acknowledging significant figures is visible in a list with an extra pair of names which juxtaposes Haremhab (*c.* 1320 to 1293 BC), the last king of the 18th dynasty, with Mentuhotpe (Philips 1977). In Manetho, Ramesses I begins the 19th dynasty, but the Theban tradition of succeeding decades seems to have honoured his predecessor. Because no ties of kinship were involved, either division is meaningful, but Haremhab is historically more prominent. This respect for rulers also appears in the 19th to 20th dynasty veneration of members of the early 18th dynasty royal family by workers on the royal tombs (for example, Lepsius n.d., pl. 2), partly in gratitude to their institution's founder, Amenhotpe I (*c.* 1514 to 1493 BC), but also perhaps because the group inaugurated the current historical period. Haremhab marks a more recent break, which has a linguistic correlate in the introduction of written Late Egyptian (cf. Assmann 1985, p. 46).

Discussion in texts

The Ramessid period (*c.* 1290 to 1070 BC; cf. Assmann 1985) produces examples of veneration and of cynicism concerning the most important Egyptian expenditure – provision for burial. This is future-oriented, but the arguments invoke the past. In literary texts and in songs inscribed in tombs, the value of mortuary provision may be denied (offerings to the gods could also be questioned; Fecht 1973). The 'Harpist's song from the tomb(?) of King Inyotef' proclaims its futility: no-one has returned to tell how it is; one should live for the day (Lichtheim 1945, pp. 192–5, Assmann 1977b, pp. 55–6; the text is ascribed to the Middle Kingdom, probably fictitiously, although it has a literary parallel, Lichtheim 1973, pp. 163–9). Another text elaborates that the tombs of the past, including those of sages whose names are extolled, are gone, but they and their wisdom live on in their works, which can be read by scribes (Lichtheim 1976, pp. 175–8). All but writing decays – but the passage comes in an exhortation to be a scribe. There is an additional irony in a Ramessid tomb where some of these sages are depicted with notable deceased officials and probably a group of kings, all of whom may be receiving a cult (Simpson 1973, pl. 6). The tomb-owner must have known the cynical literary attitude, which occurs in harpists' songs in numerous Ramessid tombs (one 18th dynasty forerunner); he may have reacted against it or have had a song on the opposite wall. The songs display a private discourse about central values cast in the form of high culture which sees the past as a source of both fame and decay (which often came through the mutilation of monuments of disgraced or dead enemies). They deny permanence, yet they look forward to the 1st millennium revival or creation of cults of ancient figures, including sages (Wildung 1977). Such a discourse may legitimate almost heretical doubts – which surely surfaced in all periods – and is displayed in future-oriented tombs decorated mainly with religious scenes, dramatizing uncertainty in the face of death. This ambivalence toward the past coexisted with significant Ramessid cultural innovation.

Depth of perspective

Ramessid restoration and reinscription of monuments relates to many earlier periods and shows a great time depth, also visible in king lists in temples, but some perspectives shrank. One text presents Haremhab as the founder of a period within a century of his death. A generation later, Ramesses III based his titulary on that of Ramesses II (Helck 1968, p. 193) and imitated the design of the latter's mortuary temple (Badawy 1968, pp. 354–60). His eight successors took Ramesses as a 'dynastic' name of hitherto unknown type. Legitimation could now be in the traditional terms of overcoming disorder and assuming the regalia of ancient gods (for example, Breasted 1906, pp. 198–200 = Erichsen 1933, pp. 91–3), but political credibility was sought nearer at hand. Scholars see this as a time of decline, in the shadow of Ramesses II (Helck 1968, pp. 179–205). The maximum depth of perspective was regained in the mid-1st millennium.

Conclusion

The Ramessid period is the most diverse and explicit of those reviewed in its use of the past, which is both integral to high culture and openly discussed; in contrast, the sparse and more uniform Old Kingdom evidence has often been passed over. The development of attitudes relates to the gradual expansion of writing and the possibilities it opens up, but writing does not account for the cultural stability and long duration of the material and its views of the past. Here, decorum is a more useful concept: only some of what was said and thought could be expressed in public contexts. A related, important problem is how far writing and the consequent increase in scope and precision of 'memory' creates attitudes, allows them to be recorded, or, more plausibly, interacts with oral discourse to create modalities that are neither oral nor exclusively literate. Some theoretically possible developments are not found: Egyptian records allow a partial history of ancient Egypt to be written, but such an enterprise is alien to the material itself and embedded in quite different cultures. The understanding of this diverse legacy will be advanced if it is seen in parallel with the testimony of non-literate cultures, both archaeologically attested and observed in the field.

Acknowledgements

I am most grateful to Yvonne Harpur, Rolf Krauss, Anthony and Lisa Leahy, Richard Parkinson, Gay Robins and Helen Whitehouse for comments, references, and reading drafts.

References

Allen, T.G. 1974. *The book of the dead or going forth by day.* Oriental Institute, University of Chicago, Studies in Ancient Oriental Civilization 37. Chicago: University of Chicago Press.

Appadurai, A. 1981. The past as a scarce resource. *Man (new series)* **16**, 201–19.

Assmann, J. 1969. *Liturgische Lieder an den Sonnengott: Untersuchungen zur altägyptischen Hymnik*, Vol. 1. Münchner ägptologische Studien 19. Berlin: Bruno Hessling.

Assmann, J. 1970. *Der König als Sonnenpriester. Ein kosmographischer Begleittext zur kultischen Sonnenhymnik in thebanischen Tempeln und Gräbern.* Abhandlungen des Deutschen Archäologischen Instituts, Abteilung Kairo 7. Glückstadt: J.J. Augustin.

Assmann, J. 1975. *Zeit und Ewigkeit im alten Ägypten.* Abhandlungen der Heidelberger Akademie der Wissenschaften, philosophisch-historische Klasse 1975. 1. Heidelberg: Carl Winter.

Assmann, J. 1977a. Die Verborgenheit des Mythos in Ägypten. *Göttinger Miszellen* **25**, 7–43.

Assmann, J. 1977b. Fest des Augenblicks – Verheissung der Dauer: die Kontroverse der ägyptischen Harfnerlieder. In *Fragen an die altägyptische Literatur: Studien zum Gedenken an Eberhard Otto*, J. Assmann, E. Feucht and R. Grieshammer (eds), 55–84. Wiesbaden: Dr Ludwig Reichert.

Assmann, J. 1983a. Schrift, Tod und Identität. Das Grab als Vorschule der Literatur im alten Ägypten. In *Schrift und Gedächtnis: Beiträge zur Archäologie der literarischen Kommunikation*, A. Assmann, J. Assmann and C. Hardmeier (eds), 64–93. München: Fink.

Assmann, J. 1983b. Das Doppelgesicht der Zeit im altägyptischen Denken. In *Die Zeit*, 189–223. Schriften der Karl-Friedrich von Siemens Stiftung 6. München: Oldenbourg.

Assmann, J. 1985. Gibt es eine Klassik in der ägyptischen Literaturgeschichte? Ein Beitrag zur Geistesgeschichte der Ramessidenzeit. *Zeitschrift der Deutschen Morgenländischen Gesellschaft, Supplement* **6**, 35–52.

Badawy, A. 1968. *A history of Egyptian architecture: the Empire (the New Kingdom).* Berkeley and Los Angeles: University of California Press.

Baines, J. 1973. The destruction of the pyramid temple of Saḥureʿ. *Göttinger Miszellen* **4**, 9–14.

Baines, J. 1983. Literacy and ancient Egyptian society. *Man (new series)* **18**, 572–99.

Baines, J. 1985. *Fecundity figures: Egyptian personification and the iconology of a genre.* Warminster: Aris and Phillips.

Baines, J. 1988. An Abydos list of gods and an Old Kingdom use of texts. In *Pyramid studies and other essays presented to I.E.S. Edwards*. J. Baines, T.G.H. James, A. Leahy and A.F. Shore (eds), 124–33. London: Egypt Exploration Society.

B[isson de la] R[oque], F. 1937. *Tôd (1934 à 1936).* Fouilles de l'Institut français d'archéologie orientale du Caire 17. Le Caire: Imprimerie de l'Institut français d'archéologie orientale.

Björkman, G. 1971. *Kings at Karnak: a study of the treatment of the monuments of royal predecessors in the early New Kingdom.* Acta Universiteit Upsaliensis, BOREAS: Uppsala Studies in Ancient Mediterranean and Near Eastern Civilization 2. Uppsala: (no publisher).

Blackman, A.M. 1914–53. *The rock tombs of Meir*, 6 Vols. Archaeological Survey of Egypt 23–6, 28–9. London: Egypt Exploration Society.

Bourghouts, J.F. 1978. *Ancient Egyptian magical texts*, NISABA 9. Leiden: E.J. Brill.

Bothmer, B.V. 1966–7. Private sculpture of dynasty XVIII in Brooklyn. *Brooklyn Museum Annual* **8**, 55–89.

Breasted, J.H. 1906. *Ancient records of Egypt*. Vol. 4: *The twentieth to the twenty-sixth dynasties*. Chicago: University of Chicago Press.

Daumas, F. 1973. Derechef Pépi Ier à Dendara. *Revue d'Égyptologie* **25**, 7–20.

Derchain-Urtel, M.T. 1974. Die Schlange des "Schiffbrüchigen". *Studien zur altägyptischen Kultur* 1, 83–104.

Dunham, D. and W.K. Simpson 1974. *The mastaba of Queen Mersyankh III G 7530–7540*. Giza Mastabas 1. Boston: Department of Egyptian and Ancient Near Eastern Art, Museum of Fine Arts.

Edwards, I.E.S. 1985. *The pyramids of Egypt*, revised edn. Harmondsworth: Penguin.

Epigraphic Survey 1980. *The tomb of Kheruef: Theban tomb 192*. University of Chicago, Oriental Institute Publication 102. Chicago: Oriental Institute.

Épron, L., F. Daumas (senior) and H. Wild 1939–66. *Le tombeau de Ti*, 3 Vols. Mémoires de l'Institut français d'archéologie orientale du Caire 65. Le Caire: Imprimerie de l'Institut français d'archéologie orientale.

Erichsen, W. 1933. *Papyrus Harris I: hieroglyphische Transkription*. Bibliotheca Aegyptiaca 5. Bruxelles: Fondation égyptologique Reine Élisabeth.

Faulkner, R.O. 1969. *The ancient Egyptian Pyramid Texts translated into English*. Oxford: Clarendon Press.

Faulkner, R.O. 1973. The Admonitions of an Egyptian Sage. In *The literature of ancient Egypt*, new edn, W.K. Simpson (ed.) 210–29. New Haven and London: Yale University Press.

Fecht, G. 1972. *Der Vorwurf an Gott in den "Mahnworten des Ipuwer"* . . . . Abhandlungen der Heidelberger Akademie der Wissenschaften, philosophisch-historische Klasse 1972, 1. Heidelberg: Carl Winter.

Fecht, G. 1973. Ägyptische Zweifel am Sinn des Opfers. *Zeitschrift für ägyptische Sprache und Altertumskunde* **100**, 6–16.

Fischer, H.G. 1959. An example of Memphite influence in a Theban stela of the eleventh dynasty. *Artibus Asiae* **22**, 240–52.

Fischer, H.G. 1976. Archaeological aspects of epigraphy and palaeography. In R. Caminos and H.G. Fischer, *Ancient Egyptian epigraphy and palaeography*, 29–50. New York: Metropolitan Museum of Art.

Gardiner, A.H. 1946. Davies' copy of the great Speos Artemidos inscription. *Journal of Egyptian Archaeology* **32**, 43–56.

Gardiner, A.H. 1959. *The Royal Canon of Turin*. Oxford: Griffith Institute.

Goedicke, H. 1971. *Re-used blocks from the pyramid of Amenemhet I at Lisht*. Metropolitan Museum of Art, Egyptian Expedition 20. New York: Metropolitan Museum of Art.

Gomaà, F. 1973. *Chaemwese, Sohn Ramses' II. und Hoherpriester von Memphis*. Ägyptologische Abhandlungen 27. Wiesbaden: Otto Harrassowitz.

Goyon, J.-C. and C. Traunecker 1980. Documents de l'allée des processions. In *Cahiers de Karnak*. Vol. 6: *1973–1977*, 129–52. Centre franco-égyptien d'étude des temples de Karnak. Le Caire: (no publisher).

Griffith, F.U. 1898. *The Petrie papyri: hieratic papyri from Kahun and Gurds (principally of the Middle Kingdom)*. 2 vols, text and plates. London: Bernard Quaritch.

Gundlach, R. 1985. Geschichtsdenken und Geschichtsbild im pharaonischen Ägypten. *Universitas* **40**, 443–55.

Hayes, W.C. 1953. *The scepter of Egypt: a background for the study of the Egyptian antiquities in the Metropolitan Museum of Art*. Vol. 1: *From the earliest times to the end of the Middle Kingdom*. New York: Harper with Metropolitan Museum of Art.

Helck, W. 1952. Die Bedeutung der ägyptischen Besucherinschriften. *Zeitschrift der Deutschen Morgenländischen Gesellschaft* **102**, 39–52.

Helck, W. 1956. *Untersuchungen zu Manetho und den ägyptischen Königslisten*. Untersuchungen zur Geschichte und Altertumskunde Aegyptens 18. Berlin: Akademie-Verlag.

Helck, W. 1961. *Urkunden der 18. Dynastie: Übersetzung zu den Heften 17–22*. Urkunden des ägyptischen Altertums: Deutsch. Berlin: Akademie-Verlag.

Helck, W. 1968. *Geschichte des alten Ägypten*. Handbuch der Orientalistik 1, 1, 3. Leiden and Köln: E.J. Brill.

Helck, W. 1970. Zwei Einzelprobleme der thinitischen Chronologie. *Mitteilungen des Deutschen Archäologischen Instituts, Abteilung Kairo* **26**, 83–5.

Helck, W. 1975. *Historisch-biographische Texte der 2. Zwischenzeit und neue Texte der 18. Dynastie*. Kleine Ägyptische Texte. Wiesbaden: Otto Harrassowitz.

Helck, W. 1977. *Die Lehre für König Merikare*. Kleine ägyptische Texte. Wiesbaden: Otto Harrassowitz.

Helck, W. 1985. Politische Spannungen zu Beginn des Mittleren Reiches. In *Ägypten: Dauer und Wandel*, 45–52. Deutsches Archäologisches Institut, Abteilung Kairo, Sonderschrift 18. Mainz: Philipp von Zabern.

Hibbard, H. 1966. *Bernini*. Harmondsworth: Penguin.

Hornung, E. 1966. *Geschichte als Fest: zwei Vorträge zum Geschichtsbild der frühen Menschheit*. Libelli 246. Darmstadt: Wissenschaftliche Buchgesellschaft.

Hornung, E. 1971. Politische Planung und Realität im alten Ägypten. *Saeculum* **22**, 48–58.

Hornung, E. 1982 [1971]. *Conceptions of god in ancient Egypt: the one and the many* (Transl. J. Baines). Ithaca and London: Cornell University Press.

Hornung, E., A. Brodbeck, H. Schlögl, E. Staehelin and G. Fecht 1982. *Der ägyptische Mythos von der Himmelskuh: eine Ätiologie des Unvollkommenen*. Orbis biblicus et orientalis 46. Freiburg: Universitätsverlag; Göttingen: Vandenhoeck und Ruprecht.

Jéquier, G. 1936–40. *Le monument funéraire de Pépy II*, 3 Vols. Service des Antiquités de l'Égypte, fouilles à Saqqarah. Le Caire: Imprimerie Institut français d'archéologie orientale.

Junge, F. 1977. Die Welt der Klagen. In *Fragen an die altägyptische Literatur: Studien zum Gedenken an Eberhard Otto*, J. Assmann et al. (eds), *op. cit.* 1977b, 275–84. Wiesbaden: Dr Ludwig Reichert.

Junker, H. 1941. *Gîza*, Vol. 5. Akademie der Wissenschaften in Wien, philosophisch-historische Klasse, Denkschriften 71, 2. Wien und Leipzig: Hölder–Pichler–Tempsky.

Kaiser, W. 1964. Einige Bemerkungen zur ägyptischen Frühzeit III. Die Reichseinigung. *Zeitschrift für ägyptische Sprache und Altertumskunde* **91**, 86–125.

Kaiser, W. and G. Dreyer 1982. Umm el-Qaab. Nachuntersuchungen im früzeitlichen Königsfriedhof. 2. Vorbericht. *Mitteilungen des Deutschen Archäologischen Instituts, Abteilung Kairo* 38, 211–69.

Kákosy, L. 1964a. Ideas about the fallen state of the world in Egyptian religion: decline of the golden age. *Acta orientalia Academiae Scientiarum Hungaricae* **17**, 206–16.

Kákosy, L. 1964b. Urzeitmythen und Historiographie im alten Ägypten. In *Neue Beitraäge zur Geschichte der alten Welt*. Vol. 1; *Alter Orient und Griechenland*, E.C. Welskopf, with H.-J. Diesner, R. Güntner, J. Mathwick and G. Schrot (eds), 57–68. Berlin: Akademie-Verlag.

Kemp, B.J. 1967. The Egyptian 1st dynasty royal cemetery. *Antiquity* **41**, 22–32.

Krauss, R. 1985. *Sothis und Monddaten: Studien zur astronomischen und technischen*

Chronologie Altägyptens. Hildesheime ägyptologische Beiträge **20**. Hildesheim: Gerstenberg.

Lacau, P. and H. Chevrier 1956–69. *Une chapelle de Sésostris Ier à Karnak*, 2 Vols. Service des Antiquités de l'Égypte. Le Caire: Imprimerie Institut français d'archéologie orientale.

Lacau, P. and J.P. Lauer 1959–61, *La pyramide à degrés*. Vol. 4; *Inscriptions graveés sur les vases*. Service des Antiquités de l'Égypte, Fouilles à Saqqarah. [Le Caire:] Institut français d'archéologie orientale.

Lange, K. and M. Hirmer 1967. *Ägypten: Architektur, Plastik, Malerei in drei Jahrtausenden*, 4th edn. München: Hirmer.

Lefebvre, G. 1949. *Romans et contes égyptiens de l'époque pharaonique*. Paris: Adrien-Maisonneuve.

Lepsius, C.R. n.d. *Denkmaeler aus Aegypten und Aethiopien . . .*, 3. Abteilung: *Denkmaeler des Neuen Reichs*, pls 1–90. Berlin: Nicolai.

Lichtheim, M. 1945. The songs of the harpers. *Journal of Near Eastern Studies* **4**, 178–212.

Lichtheim, M. 1976. *Ancient Egyptian literature: a book of readings*. Vol. 1: *The Old and Middle Kingdoms*. Berkeley: University of California Press.

Lichtheim, M. 1973. *Ancient Egyptian literature: a book of readings*. Vol. 2: *The New Kingdom*. Berkeley: University of California Press.

Luft, U. 1976. Seit der Zeit Gottes. *Studia Aegyptiaca* **2**, 47–78.

Luft, U. 1978. *Beiträge zur Historisierung der Götterwelt und der Mythenschreibung*. Studia Aegyptiaca 4. Budapest: (no publisher).

Málek, J. 1982. The original version of the Royal Canon of Turin. *Journal of Egyptian Archaeology* **68**, 93–106.

Mariette-Bey, A. 1869. *Abydos, description des fouilles exécutées sur l'emplacement de cette ville*, Vol. 1. Paris: Franck (Vieweg).

Naville, E. n.d. *The temple of Deir el Bahari*, 6 Vols. London: Egypt Exploration Fund.

Ockinga, B.G. 1983. The burden of Kha'kheperre'senbu. *Journal of Egyptian Archaeology* **69**, 88–95.

Osing, J. 1975. Alte Schriften. In *Lexikon der Ägyptologie*, Vol. 1, W. Helck and E. Otto (eds), 149–54. Wiesbaden: Otto Harrassowitz.

Otto, E. 1957. Zwei Bemerkungen zum Königskult der Spätzeit. *Mitteilungen des Deutschen Archäologischen Instituts, Abteilung Kairo* **15**, 192–207.

Otto, E. 1964–6. Geschichtsbild und Geschichtsschreibung im alten Ägypten. *Die Welt des Orients* **3**, 161–76.

Otto, E. 1969. Das "Goldene Zeitalter" in einem ägyptischen Text. In *Religions en Égypte hellénistique et romaine*, 93–108. Bibliothèque des Centres d'Études supérieures spécialisés, travaux du Centre d'Études supérieures spécialisé d'histoire des religions de Strasbourg. Paris: Presses Universitaires de France.

Otto, E. 1977. Zur Komposition von Coffin Texts Spell 1130. In *Fragen an die altägyptische Literatur: Studien zum Gedenken an Eberhard Otto*, J. Assmann *et al.* (eds), 1–18. Wiesbaden: Dr Ludwig Reichert.

Peet, T.E. 1930. *The great tomb-robberies of the twentieth Egyptian dynasty*, 2 Vols. Oxford: Clarendon Press.

Philips, A.K. 1977. Horemheb, founder of the XIXth dynasty? O. Cairo 25646 reconsidered. *Orientalia (new series)* **46**, 116–21.

Pieper, M. 1929. *Die Grosse Inschrift des Königs Neferhotep in Abydos*. Mitteilungen der vorderasiatisch-ägyptischen Gesellschaft 32, 2. Leipzig: J.C. Hinrichs.

Posener, G. 1957. Le conte de Néferkarè et du général Siséné (Recherches littéraires, VI). *Revue d'Égyptologie* **11**, 119–37.

Redford, D.B. 1986. *Pharaonic king-lists, annals and day-books: a contribution to the study of the Egyptian sense of history*. SSEA Publication 4. Mississauga (Ontario): Benben.

Romano, J.F. 1979. *Catalogue*. The Luxor Museum of Ancient Egyptian Art. Cairo: American Research Center in Egypt.

Sakkarah Expedition 1938. *The mastaba of Mereruka*, 2 Vols. University of Chicago, Oriental Institute Publications 31, 39. Chicago: University of Chicago Press.

Sauneron, S. and J. Yoyotte 1959. La naissance du monde dans l'Égypte ancienne. In *La naissance du monde*, 17–91. Sources orientales 1. Paris: Éditions du Seuil.

Schäfer, H. 1986. *Principles of Egyptian art*, revised reprint, E. Brunner-Traut (ed.) (transl. and ed. J. Baines). Oxford: Griffith Institute.

Sethe, K. (with W. Erichsen) 1935. *Historisch-biographische Urkunden des Mittleren Reiches*, fasc. 1. Leipzig: J.C. Hinrichs.

Simpson, W.K. (ed.) 1973. *The literature of ancient Egypt*, new edn. New Haven and London: Yale University Press.

Vandersleyen, C. 1971. *Les guerres d'Amosis, fondateur de la XVIIIe dynastie*. Monographies Reine Élisabeth 1. Bruxelles: Fondation égyptologique Reine Élisabeth.

Vandier, J. 1950. *Mo'alla*. Institut français d'archéologie orientale, Bibliothèque d'Étude 18. Le Caire: Imprimerie de l'Institut français d'archéologie orientale.

von Beckerath, J. 1984. Bemerkungen zum Turiner Königspapyrus und zu den Dynastien der ägyptischen Geschichte. *Studien zur altägyptischen Kultur* 11, 49–57.

Waddell, W.G. 1940. *Manetho*. Loeb Classical Library.

Wildung, D. 1969. *Die Rolle ägyptischer Könige im Bewusstsein ihrer Nachwelt*. Vol. 1: *Posthume Quellen über die Könige der ersten vier Dynastien*. Münchner ägyptologische Studien 17. Berlin: Bruno Hessling.

Wildung, D. 1977. *Imhoten und Amenhotep: Gottwerdung im alten Ägypten*. Münchner ägyptologische Studien 36. Berlin: Deutscher Kunstverlag.

Wilson, J.A. 1951. *The burden of Egypt: an interpretation of ancient Egyptian culture*. Chicago: University of Chicago Press.

Yoyotte, J. 1951. Le martelage des noms royaux éthiopiens par Psammétique II. *Revue d'Égyptologie* 8, 215–39.

12 Beginning of agriculture: a synchronism between Puranic and archaeological evidence

RAI GYAN NARAIN PRASAD

Editor's note: Readers should refer to my introduction for a summary of traditional Hindu chronology. Prasad regards *manvantara* as epochs of 12 000 years, the duration otherwise attributed to a *mahāyuga*.

Introduction

The first unit of the traditional Hindu calendar is the *Chaturyuga* or four-age cycle, which is equal to one *manvantara* (*mahāyuga*) period of 12 000 years. It is argued that the duration of a *manvantara* (or *mahāyuga*) can be equated with half of the period taken for the completion of the conical movement of the Earth's axis known as the precession of the equinoxes (the period is approximately 26 000 years; see Zeuner 1958, p. 136). Longer epochs in Hindu chronology may be equatable with larger phases in the Earth's geological history (see Table 12.1).

Hindu chronology locates the present within the seventh, or *Vaivaṣvata, manvantara*. It is argued that the start of this phase correlates with the onset of the Holocene epoch, and that the character of human existence ascribed to the four ages of the *manvantara* may be equated with archaeological evidence. According to the *Vāyu Purāṇa* (ch. 8, vv. 45–60) people roamed freely during the earliest or *Kṛta Yuga*, without houses, agriculture or other social and economic activities. This description may be compared with archaeological evidence of the Mesolithic. The *Vāyu Purāṇa* (ch. 8, vv. 77–123) further states that during the transition between the *Kṛta* and *Tretā Yugas* the temperature of the Earth rose to produce rain, which in turn created heavy primary vegetation. Much of this vegetation was burnt and destroyed during group battles. It is argued that the junction between the *Kṛta* and *Tretā Yugas* corresponds with the period 7548 to 7308 BC. Singh's pollen profile (Singh *et al.* 1974, pp. 467–501) gives *c.* 7000 BC for the accumulation of charred wood fragments in lake sediments of north India (his zone B, phase III). With the beginning of the second or *Tretā Yuga* people had collected the seeds of food-grains, and this may be equated with the Neolithic age in archaeology. The chronology given in ancient Indian texts is therefore corroborated by archaeological findings from the Mehargarh Neolithic culture, the

Table 12.1 Chronological details of 14 *manvantaras* of the present (71st) *mahāyuga*

Introductory dawn 87 468 – 86 268 BC

Name of *manvantara*	(1) *Swayāmbhuwa*	*twilight*	(2) *Swāroschisa*	*twilight*	(3) *Uttama*	*twilight*	(4) *Tāmas*
duration (Savana years)	12 000	960	12 000	960	12 000	960	12 000
Start and end of epoch	86 268–74 268 BC	74 268–73 308 BC	73 308–61 308 BC	61 308–60 348 BC	60 348–48 348 BC	48 348–47 388 BC	47 388–35 388 BC

name of *manvantara*	*twilight*	(5) *Raivata*	*twilight*	(6) *Chākshusha*	*twilight*	(7) *Vaivasvata*	*twilight*
duration	960	12 000	960	12 000	960	12 000	960
start and end of epoch	35 388–34 428 BC	34 428–22 428 BC	22 428–21 468 BC	21 468–9 468 BC	9 468–8 508 BC	8 508 BC–AD 3 492	AD 3 492–4 452

name of *manvantara*	(8) *Savarni*	*twilight*	(9) *Daksha Sāvarni*	*twilight*	(10) *Brahma Sāvarni*	*twilight*	(11) *Dharma Sāvarni*
duration	12 000	960	12 000	960	12 000	960	12 000
start and end of epoch	AD 4 452–16 452	AD 16 452–17 412	AD 16 412–29 412	AD 29 412–30 372	AD 30 372–42 372	AD 42 372–43 332	AD 43 332–55 332

name of *manvantara*	*twilight*	(12) *Rudra Sāvarni*	*twilight*	(13) *Ruchi*	*twilight*	(14) *Bhaom*	*twilight*
duration	960	12 000	960	12 000	960	12 000	960
start and end of epoch	AD 55 332–56 292	AD 56 292–68 292	AD 68 292–69 252	AD 69 252–81 252	AD 81 252–82 212	AD 82 212–94 212	AD 94 212–95 172

Vindhyagangeya culture of eastern Uttar Pradesh and pollen profiles from the Rajasthan salt lakes further west.

Accounts from the classical Hindu texts, or *Purāṇas*

The account of the Harivaṃsha Purāṇa (Acharya & Sharma 1979, I, pp. 93–4)

During the *Vaivaṣvata manvaṇtara* (8508 BC to AD 3492) the following conditions hold during the reign of King Prithu, the son of King Vaina (*Harivaṃsha Purāṇa*, ch. 10 v. 16). People chose to live on the bare ground (v. 17). Before the time of Prithu the only palatable foods were fruit and roots or tubers. Life was therefore arduous (v. 18). With the guidance of the Earth Goddess Prithivi, King Prithu made the ground fertile and cultivated all kinds of food grains as 'milk of the earth' (v. 19). From that time, people used cultivated grains as their foodstuff (v. 20).

The account of the Vāyu Purāṇa

During the Kṛta Yuga   In this way the present creation was made from the earlier one and by this means the world was repopulated (*Vāyu Purāṇa*, ch. 8, v. 45). The progeny of *Prajāpati* (the supreme father) dwelled freely on river sides, sea coasts, lake sides and mountain slopes. In that *yuga* (Age), people roamed everywhere freely, without suffering climatic extremes of heat and cold (v. 46). People lived according to their own choice without any external (social or economic) pressure and took their food from a kind of juice created from the earth (v. 47). In the *Kṛta Yuga* people were not differentiated by their longevity, happiness or personality (v. 48). People had no dwelling place or shelter. At that time people were happy and full of eternal bliss, and enjoyed complete loneliness (v. 52). There was no differentiation of good and evil deeds. The division of the four *varnas* (major caste categories) did not exist, and consequently there was no problem of inter-marriage between castes (v. 60).

At the junction of the Kṛta and Tretā Yugas   At the beginning of the *Tretā* (Second) *Yuga*, during the transitional phase between the *Kṛta* and *Tretā Yugas*, rain fell for the first time (*Vāyu Purāṇa*, ch. 8, v. 77). Due to this first rain the earth became very humid and consequently heavy vegetation rapidly sprang up around the people's dwelling places (v. 78). Because the *Kṛta Yuga* was on the wane, dialectical pairs such as pleasure and pain were created among the people (v. 91). In order to achieve protection against the opposed forces of pleasure and pain, heat and cold, people began to live in houses whereas, before that period, they had roamed freely without house or shelter (v. 93). Now, according to their personal capacity and choice, people made protective dwellings on the barren lands or lower places, in hilly caves or on river banks where running water was always available (v. 94). Wherever they built, houses were constructed to protect the people from heat and cold (v. 95). After that houses were grouped together into settlements, first smaller and then somewhat bigger (v. 96). Having done so, people began to be concerned about their hunger because, due to the close of the *Kṛta Yuga* and the onset of the *Tretā Yuga*, the climate had changed radically from cold to warm, causing the old sources of food, namely honey and *Kalpa* trees (wild fruit trees) to become scarce (v. 123).

At the beginning of the Tretā Yuga   With the beginning of the *Tretā Yuga* (7308 BC), people became acquisitive and greedy toward their earthly possessions (*Vāyu Purāṇa*, ch. 8, v. 130). They had taken control of riversides and mountain slopes as exclusive possessions. According to their capacity and power, people destroyed the neighbouring trees and shrubs (v. 131). After considerable destruction of vegetation people were seized by panic, confusion and hunger. Helpless, they went to the *Prajāpati*, or supreme father (v. 139). At the beginning of the *Tretā Yuga*, *Prajāpati* Brahmā knew about the desire of his progeny (v. 140). Aware, by virtue of his divine vision, that the Earth had been stripped of its vegetation, Brahmā made an arrangement to refertilize the Earth (v. 141). He created Sumeru the calf and re-invigorated all types of seed from the ground, yielding all the essential types of vegetation, and they bore fruit (vv. 142–3). In the beginning of the *Tretā Yuga* all the 14 types of cultivated cereals and pulses were created for the first time (vv. 144–9). On the unploughed land were various types of tree, shrub, herb, creeper and climbing plant (v. 150). The seeds created by the autochthonous *Prajāpati* when he re-invigorated the Earth gave shoots, roots, fruit and flowers (v. 151). Although the new vegetation gave fruit and flowers in their season, they did not grow again and again (v. 152). So *Prajāpati* made an arrangement that the profession of his progeny should take the form of agriculture and observed the result (v. 153). From that time agricultural produce was brought into being by the act of ploughing the field and sowing the seeds. This practice, once started and found suitable, was fixed by the *Prajāpati* to be the profession of his progeny (v. 154).

Archaeological evidence

It is instructive to survey the beginning of agriculture in Asia and then see how India compares.

Excavations at Cayonu (north Syria) show agriculture based on domestic emmer wheat, eincorn, peas, lentils and bitter vetch in *c.* 7000 BC. Pistachio, almond, acorn and hackberry were also collected. In the Levant, at Jericho, the pre-pottery Neolithic A culture (*c.* 8350 to 7350 BC) produced two-row hulled barley and emmer wheat. In the Zagros region, Tepe Guran (*c.* 6000 BC) has yielded two-row hulled barley. Catal Huyuk, in Anatolia (Turkey) has produced a variety of cereals: domestic emmer, eincorn, bread wheat, six-row naked barley from *c.* 6000 BC contexts. In Mesopotamia, from the Khuzistan plains, the Tepe Sabz culture (*c.* 5000 BC) also yielded evidence of agriculture. In Iran, from Tala-Iblis I (Kerman), bread wheat and emmer were found in an early Ubaid horizon (Mellart 1975). The above find prompted Darlington (1969) to say: 'What we see today is the decisive evidence that agriculture in the Old World arose in a single connected region, a nuclear zone, of Anatolia, Iran [the Levant] and Syria before 7000 B.C. and that it arose here at a time when no other region of the Old World shows evidence of any similar settled life' (Darlington 1969, p. 68).

However, recent discoveries in Siam and Formosa have shown that South-East Asia was not far behind. From Spirit Cave, on the bank of the river Salween, about 60 km north of Mae Hong Son, in Thailand, Gorman has reported finds of almond (*Prumes*), kotamba (*Terminalia*), betel-nut (*Areca*), broad beans (*Vicia*), pea (*Pisum*), bottle gourd (*Lagenaria*), water caltrop (*Trapa*), pepper (*Piper*), butter nut (*Madhuca*), Chinese olive (*Canarium*), candle nut (*Aleurite*) and cucumber (*Cucums*). These plants thus include not only nuts, spices, seeds and edible oil, but also food plants. Thus, the evidence suggests an economic development beyond simple food-gathering. Carbon-14 dates place these Hoabinian levels at this cave between 12 000 and 8000 BP. These levels have also produced cord-marked pottery which is the hallmark of the Southeastern and Eastern Asiatic Neolithic (Gorman 1969)*.

This evidence is corroborated from the recent findings from Formosa. Chang reported a Neolithic culture from there, marked by chipped and polished stone axes, adzes, chisels, etc., and cord-marked pottery (Chang 1970, pp. 175–85). There are no direct dates for this culture, but it appears to predate the third millennium BC. However Tsukada's pollen profile from lake Jih-Yueh-Tan shows that primary vegetation was disturbed around 12 000 BP and that it co-incided with an accumulation of charred-wood fragments in the lake sediments. Thus, it has been suggested that there is circumstantial evidence for early agricultural activity.

The evidence is therefore indicative of an early Holocene start for agriculture both in West and in Southeast and East Asia. In India the earliest evidence of cereal cultivation, beyond the Indus civilization (2400 to 1700 BC) and Neolithic culture (2500 to 1000 BC) came from Koldihawa, in Eastern Uttara Pradesh. Here paddy-husk impressions have been identified from a level yielding micro-liths and hand-made pottery (Misra 1977). Two carbon-14 dates ascribe these levels to c. 5000 BC (PRL 101, 4530 ± 185 BC; PRL 100, 5440 ± 240 BC). Some recent evidence for the inception of agriculture comes from the north-Rajasthana salt lakes, viz. Sāṃbher, Luṇkarnasar and Didwānā. It is interesting to note that at c. 7000 BC (zone B, phase III) a cerelia type of pollen occurs associated with an abundance of comminuted charcoal pieces (Singh *et al.* 1974, pp. 467–501). This has been interpreted by Singh *et al.* as indicative of forest clearance and the beginning of 'some sort of primitive agriculture'. As mentioned above, the Formosa lake also produced similar evidence. No Neolithic cultures are reported from Rajasthana, but microliths have been reported (Agrawal 1982, pp. 91–2) near the lakes.

*Editor's note: see Harris (1973, pp. 409–10) for a critical assessment of the evidence from Spirit Cave, which is now taken by many to show that all of the plants of the Hoabinian levels were, in fact, wild.

The discovery of Mehargarh in Baluchistan in fact proved to be another turning point in the history of Neolithic India (Randhawa 1981, chs 10–12). The excavations conducted here by Jarrige in 1979 demonstrated the developmental stages of various pre-Harappan cultures from the 7th to the 3rd millennium BC. It is therefore possible that northern Baluchistan was the nuclear zone where man seems to have effectively changed from the hunting–gathering stage to the food-producing and herding stage. This change was independent of the Neolithic cultures of Western Asia and the Levant, even though domestication of goats, sheep, cattle and wheat and barley appeared slightly earlier in the 'Fertile Crescent'. Thus, there is a possibility that the beginning of agriculture may go back to *c.* 7000 BC in India, too.

Puranic evidence for climatic fluctuation

It is proposed that the present *mahāyuga* began around 87 468 BC, and would therefore coincide approximately with the beginning of the Würm glaciation during the Pleistocene epoch. According to the traditional Hindu calendar six *manvantaras* (*mahāyugas*), each having a duration of 12 000 + 960 years, have already passed, and we now live in the seventh, or *Vaivaṣvata manvantara*, whose onset would therefore correspond to the beginning of the Holocene epoch, from 8508 BC (see Tables 12.1 and 12.2). The *Harivamsha Purāṇa* (ch. 10, vv. 12–20) describes the cultural state of India during the sixth, or preceding, *manvantara* as follows: 'In this way King Prithu, the son of King Vaina, made the land level in the beginning of the *Vaivaṣvata manvantara*. In *Chākshusha*, the sixth *manvantara* (21 468 to 9468 BC), due to the great roughness of the Earth there were no divisions of settlements into towns or villages, nor were cattle domesticated. Agricultural activity, trade, roads, the oppositions between truth and evil, greed and malice, were non-existent'. This statement clearly shows that conditions for the cultural development of human settlements in the northern hemisphere, specifically India, were at this time unfavourable and the people of the *Chākshusha manvantara* were no more advanced than the Mesolithic people of archaeology.

Chronology of the Vaivaṣvata manvantara

According to Hindu texts the *Vaivaṣvata manvantara* began with a worldwide flood. This may have been due to a post-glacial rise in sea level. It is suggested above that we can correlate the start of the *Kṛta Yuga*, the first *yuga* of the four-age cycle of the present *manvantara*, with 8508 BC, or the onset of the present interglacial. In support of this one may treat the geological record of climate statistically. An analysis of deep-sea cores shows that no Pleistocene interglacial has lasted more than 12 000 years, and that most have had a life of about 10 000 years. Statistically, the present interglacial, i.e. the Holocene, is already on its last legs, tottering along at the advanced age of 10 500 years and can be expected to end within the next 1500 years (Imbrie & Imbrie 1979, p. 178).

Table 12.2 Comparison between the six substages of the 4th (Würm) glaciation with the past six *manvaṇtaras* of the present *mahāyuga* of the ancient Hindu calendar.

Loess	Radiocarbon* (years BP)	Geological (years BP)	Equilibrium method† (years BP)	Hindu *manvaṇtara*	End of epoch (Christian calendar)
			Anthenes Kay		
6. Valders (advance)‡	11 400	11 000		*Chākshusha*	9 468 BC§
5. Mankato‖	12 000	15 000	12 000 25 000	*Raivata*	22 428 BC¶
4. Cary	14 000–13 000	26 000		*Tamas*	35 388 BC
3. Tazedvell (sediment)	19 000–15 000	37 000		*Uttama*	48 348 BC
2. Lowan (wood)	23 000–21 000	51 000		*Swāroschisa*	61 308 BC
1. Framdale (wood)	25 000–29 000	64 000		*Swayāmbhuwa*	74 268 BC

*The radiocarbon method gives low dates (about half of the geological dates). Therefore, in the meantime, respect is held for carefully documented stratigraphic work and sampling by geologists.

†Percentage of equilibrium for uranium, ionium and radium.

‡Sweden, 6839 BC. De Geers by the advance method (see Wheeler: *New techniques in archaeology*, 389, outlines of modern knowledge).

§The end of Valders, the 6th substage, or the end of the 6th *manvaṇtara*, the *Chākshusha*, of the ancient Hindu calendar exactly coincides in all the dating systems; viz. radiocarbon, geological and precession cycle.

‖The end of *Mankato* or *Raivata* (of Hindu calendar), the 5th, is estimated to a later epoch by radiocarbon and geological methods, but the epoch estimated by equilibrium method (by Kay) is exactly coincident with the Hindu system of calculation.

¶The interval between the 1st to 5th substages had an average of 12 000 years according to the geological method, which is approximately equal to half the precessional cycle of equinoxes and also to the duration of Hindu *manvaṇtaras*. The effect of the precessional cycles and their duration may easily be verified by the Milankovitch radiation curves for low latitudes, viz. 15°.

If we equate the Sanskrit term *Dharma-pāda* (from the *Sūrya-Siddhānta*, ch. 1, vv. 15–17) with modifications in the average global climate, then the Denton–Karlen plot (Imbrie & Imbrie 1979, pp. 178–9) parallels the start and end of epochs for the four individual *yugas*: *Kṛta, Tretā, Dvāpara* and *Kali* (see Table 12.3). This relationship shows a surprising coincidence with Eddy's solar-activity table (Eddy 1977), if Eddy's maxima group 16 and 17 are correlated with *Dvāpara I-pada*, his minima group 13, 14 and 15 are matched to *Dvāpara II-pada*, maxima group 10, 11 and 12 to *Dvāpara III* and minima group 7, 8 and 9 to *Kali Yuga I-pada*, as shown in Table 12.4. It also demonstrates a surprising coincidence with Singh's plot for the dry–humid climate of north-western India, reconstructed on the basis of cerelia type and fossilized pollen-grains obtained from the substrate of the salty-lakes of Sāmbher, Didwānā and Luṅkarnasar of Rajasthana (Singh *et al.* 1974). Note carefully, in Table 12.3, that humidity crossed the dry–humid dividing line in *c.* 8500 BC which it is here postulated marks the beginning of *Kṛta Yuga.* The highest humid condition in northwestern India occurred around 7600 BC, when, according to the *Vāyu purāṇa*, during the *Kṛta–Tretā* junction period, the first rain (corresponding to the interglacial Holocene epoch) fell. The *Tretā Yuga* experienced a constant, low-humidity climate. During the transition between the *Tretā* and *Dvāpara Yugas* (here assigned to 5388 to 4908 BC), humidity rose a little. The *Dvāpara Yuga* (4908 to 2028 BC) was marked by a state of high humidity, which attained a maximum in the *Dvāpara III-pada* (2508 to 1308 BC), in other words, the period of the Indus civilization. The *Kali–Dvāpara* transition was marked by a drastic change in the climate of northwestern India and, with the beginning of the fourth or *Kali Yuga*, the climate of northwestern India moved from humid to dry, entering a dry phase during the *Kali Yuga.*

Puranic statements concerning climatic conditions and the beginning of agriculture

The equation of the *Dharma-pāda* structure for the present four-age cycle, given in the *Sūrya Siddhānta* (ch. 1, vv. 15–17) with either direction of average global temperature fluctuation within 6°C, plotted by Denton and Karlen for the Holocene's little ice-age cycles, enables us to decode our traditional Hindu *chaturyuga* calendar, at least for the present *Vaivaṣvata manvantara*, in climatological terms with full scientific accuracy. Evaluated in terms of the average temperature changes, the cycle of little ice-ages (on which it is here argued the ancient Hindu calendar was based) has about one-tenth the impact of the cycle of great ice-ages. However, changes in the higher-frequency cycle occur much more rapidly than those due to orbital changes. Exactly how much cultural impact the recorded 6°C cyclic fluctuation in average global temperature has had is difficult to assess, but there is no doubt at all that the decrease in rainfall, which in most places has accompanied the cooling, has had a definite effect on patterns of agricultural production, and therefore on patterns of human settlements (Denton & Karlen 1973).

Table 12.3 Dry–humid climatic oscillations in northwestern India reconstructed on the basis of fossilized cerelia types of pollen grain obtained from the substrate of salty lakes by Professor G. Singh (Agrawal & Agrawal 1970, p. 13). This table shows clearly that the junction periods corresponding to the individual four *yugas* of present *Vaivaṣvata manvaṇtara* of the ancient Hindu calendar was precisely followed by considerable climatic changes.

Date		Pollen division	Climatic epoch	Local climatic oscillations		Cultures of NW India	Four yugas of Hindu calendar	Solar excursions of Eddy's table	
				Dry	Humid				
BP	AD							1	(minima
		E	VI				(III)	2	group)
							Kali	3 –––––
1000	1000					Culture of Rangmahal	(II)	4	(maxima
								5	group)
2000	BC						Yuga	6 –––––
								7	
		D	V				(I)		(minima
								8	group)
3000	1000								
		C-3	IVc			PGW		9	
		C-2	IVb			OCP	Dvāpara	10	
4000	2000					LHC	(III)	11	(maxima
		C-1	IVa			Harappan			group)
						Pre-	Yuga	12	
5000	3000					harappan		13	
							(II)	14	(minima group)
6000	4000							15 –––––
								16	(maxima group)
							(I)	17	
7000	5000					Microlith		18	
		B	III				Tretā		
8000	6000								
							Yuga		
9000	7000								
		A	II				Krta		
10000	8000						Yuga		
			I						

Table 12.4 Tabular representation of major solar excursions in the past 7400 years and the next 1500 years which is applied to depict the individual *yuga-pādas* of *Dvāpara* and *Kali Yugas* of the ancient Hindu calendar. Graphically, solar activity and carbon-14 production have an inverse relationship. Climatologically, solar maxima represent a warmer climate. This table is reconstructed on the basis of Eddy's table. (Courtesy: Eddy, J.A. 1977, *Climate and the changing sun, climatic change*, Vol. 1, 181. Dordrecht: D. Reidel Publishing Company.)

Major solar excursion groups in Eddy's table	Duration in C^{14} record	Individual *Yuga Dharma-pāda* of Hindu calendar	Duration of individual *Dharma-pāda*
maxima group (17, 16)	5050–3700 BC	*Dvāpara* I	4908–3708 BC
minima group (15, 14, 13)	3700–2700 BC	*Dvāpara* II	3708–2508 BC
maxima group (12, 11, 10)	2700–1400 BC	*Dvāpara* III	2508–1308 BC
minima group (9, 8, 7)	1400–300 BC	*Kali* I	1308–108 BC
maxima group (6, 5, 4)	300 BC – AD 1340	*Kali* II	108 BC– AD 1092
minima group (3, 2, ?)	AD 1340–2300	*Kali* III	AD 1092–2292
maxima group (?–?)	AD 2300–3500	*Kali* IV	AD 2292–3492

Conclusion

On the basis of the climatological cycle of equinoctial precession, we have shown that if the *Vaivaṣvata* (7th) *manvantara* (8508 BC to AD 3492) is equated with the geological Holocene, then this period corresponds to an interglacial. In the *Chākṣhusha* (6th) *manvantara* the northern hemisphere would then have experienced a glacial stage.

With the advent of the *Vaivaṣvata manvantara*, in 8508 BC, the northern hemisphere entered its interglacial phase with the great flood event related to the manu *Vaivaṣvata*. After that the climate began to become warmer and more humid (Imbrie & Imbrie 1979, p. 179, Singh 1963). During the *Kṛta Yuga* (8508 to 7548 BC) according to the *Vāyu Purāṇa*, people roamed freely without houses, agriculture, or any other social or economic restrictions. Although, from the spiritual point of view, this worry-free mental condition of the people might have seemed the ideal situation to the religious-minded compilers of the *purāṇa*, from a materialistic point of view the people of the *Kṛta Yuga*, as the *Vāyu Purāṇa* (ch. 8, vv. 45–60) describes, were not more advanced than the Mesolithic people of archaeology. At the beginning of *Kṛta–Tretā* transition (7548 to 7308 BC),

160   BEGINNING OF AGRICULTURE

according to the Denton–Karlen 6°C temperature fluctuation plot, the average global climate became sufficiently warm to produce rains. Singh's plot for northwestern India matches this date for the highest humid condition. As a result of this rain, heavy vegetation might have been created. However, due to their ignorance, malice and greed, when they plucked fruits for eating, people also plucked flowers and leaves. In group battles, they might damage and burn the useful vegetation controlled by enemy groups. In this manner, people destroyed and burnt a considerable amount of vegetation. Tsukada's pollen profile gives *c.* 10 000 BC, whereas Singh's pollen profile gives *c.* 7000 BC (zone B, phase III) for the accumulation of charred-wood fragments in the lake sediments. Thus, we have synchronized puranic and archaeological statements concerning the deliberate destruction of primary vegetation.

After that, when people were subject to starvation they searched for seeds to grow the vegetation again and again. Primitive but regular agriculture came into being from *c.* 7300 BC, which it is argued corresponds with the advent of the *Tretā Yuga* of the *purāṇas*; the Neolithic cultures of archaeology.

Thus, we may conclude that the chronology concerning the beginning of agriculture adopted by the ancient Indian texts is commensurate with the recent findings of archaeology from the excavations of pre-Harappan Neolithic cultures of Mehargarh (Baluchistan), the Vindhya-Gangaya culture of Eastern Uttara Pradesh and pollen profiles from the Rajasthana salt lakes.

References

Acharya, P. and S.R. Sharma 1979. *Vayu and matsya purāṇa*. Barelly: Sanskriti Sansthana.
Agrawal, D.P. 1982. *The archaeology of India*. London: Curzon Press.
Agrawal, D.P. and P.L. Agrawal 1975. *bhartiya puraitihasis puratattva*. Lucknow: Hindi Grantha Academy.
Chang, K.C. 1970. The beginning of agriculture in the Far East. *Antiquity* **XLIV**, 175–85.
Darlington, O.D. 1969. The silent millennia in the origin of agriculture. In *The domestication and exploitation of plants and animals*, P.J. Ucko and G.W. Dimbleby (eds) 67–72. London: Duckworth.
Denton, G.H. and W. Karlen 1973. Holocene climatic variations: their pattern and possible cause. *Quaternary Research* **3**, 155–205.
Eddy, J.A. 1977. *Climate and the changing sun*. Dordrecht: D. Reidel.
Gorman, C.F. 1969. Hoabinian: a pebble tool complex with early plant association in Southeast Asia. *Science* **163**, 671–3.
Harris, D.R. 1973. The prehistory of tropical agriculture: an ethnoecological model. In *The explanation of culture change*, C. Renfrew (ed.), 391–417. London: Duckworth.
Imbrie, J. and K.P. Imbrie 1979. *Ice-ages: solving the mystery*. London: Macmillan.
Mellart, J. 1975. *The neolithic of the Near East*. London: Thames and Hudson.
Misra, V.D. 1977. *Some aspects of Indian archaeology*. Allahabad: Abinash Prakashana.
Randhawa, M.S. 1981. *A history of agriculture in India*. Delhi: Council of Agricultural Research.

Singh, G. 1963. A preliminary survey of the postglacial vegetational history of Kashmir valley. *Palaeobotanist* **12**, 73–108.

Singh, G., R.D. Joshi, S.K. Chopra and A.B. Singh 1974. Late Quaternary history of vegetation and climate of the Rajasthana deserts. *Philosophical Transactions of the Royal Society of London, Biological Science* **269/889**, 467–501.

Wheeler, R.E.M. 1968. *Archaeology from the earth.* H. Trivedi (trans.). Delhi: Government of India, Scientific and Technical Dictionary Commission, Ministry of Education.

Zeuner, F.E. 1958. *Dating the past: an introduction to geochronology,* 4th edn. London: Methuen.

13 Holding on to emblems: Australian Aboriginal performances and the transmission of oral traditions

MARGARET CLUNIES ROSS

The film *Waiting for Harry* (McKenzie *et al.* 1980) records some of the events, ritual performances and conversations that took place at an Aboriginal mortuary ceremony in North Central Arnhem Land in July and August 1978. At one point Harry 'Diama' (Cockle) Mulumbuk, the oldest living man whose mother belonged to the clan of the deceased, began to outline a sand sculpture of an ancestral Hollow Tree.[1] The Tree, a Stringybark, was a totemic being with special affinities with the dead man's clan. Harry drew the audience's attention to the powerful conjunction of artistic media in which the totem was being celebrated: as he worked to produce the sand sculpture, two singers in the shade behind him sang about Hollow Tree and Wild Honey from the clan song series *Djambidj* (Clunies Ross & Wild 1982, especially pp. 40–5).

The following discussion then ensued between Harry (HM), Frank Gurrmanamana (FG), Willy Jolpa (WJ) and Les Hiatt (LH), an anthropologist who has known Harry and his people, the Anbarra, for more than 25 years. The Aboriginal participants in the discussion were senior men of the dead man's or related clans, and the dead man himself had been a ritual leader and singer of note. I present the text of their discourse in the English translation of L.R. Hiatt, giving passages significant to the argument also in the Burarra language. The archival 16 mm footage from which *Waiting for Harry* was made may be viewed at the Australian Institute of Aboriginal Studies.[2] The text in question is on Camera Rolls 66 and 67, and is based on the original translation and Burarra transcription.[3]

Camera Roll 66

WJ: This is the substance of the tree.

FG: The real Stringybark Tree sand sculpture is a huge one that lies under the sea. It was put there.

WJ: Put there by a supernatural being.

HM
(to
LH):   This sand sculpture is not a new one. They used to make it before the war [i.e. World War II]. My mother's father (who would be your 'father') used to sing for it.

HM: Yes, those men who begat my mother and Andrew's mother, they used to sing for this one. It's an old one. It's not something that's just been made up yesterday. They used to make it when I was a little boy. Before the War. They used to exchange it too [i.e. give it to other groups and receive different sculptures in return].

LH: Did you make it after the War?

HM: No, we didn't. When people died, we made sand sculptures, but your brother, the dead man, said that as he'd been given the Fish Trap sand sculpture, we should make that. There was a lot of trouble over that. Leo Wujal showed us how to make it, Wujal, your 'great uncle' [MMB]. He has a big say in the sand sculptures for this clan country.

LH: Is he coming to this ceremony?

HM: Yes, he's on his way. All those 'great uncles' of yours are coming. They wouldn't desert your brother [the dead man], or this sand sculpture. They gave it to him. Actually, a man who's now dead, gave it to him.

....

Camera Roll 67

HM: This sand sculpture represents a tree called Biyarriyarri or Golupanda. Only we whose mothers come from this country are allowed to make it. That is the law. You say in English 'allowed'. Our word is *joborr*. It means that we have the right to do this, and no-one can interfere.

    So only we are allowed to make it. We've got to hold on to this emblem. It was put here for us by the gods. When we make it, we must do it very carefully. We mustn't rush it, or we might leave something out. And we've got to keep our eyes open to make sure that others don't steal it.

This text reveals a number of ways in which traditional Aboriginal people use the idea of a past time to give meaning to the present and directions for future conduct. It exemplifies what has often been recognized as a fundamental disjunction in Aboriginal concepts of time and creativity between the remote period of creativity, often called The Dreaming (or Dreamtime) and the here-and-now. Maddock expresses this succinctly:

'The cosmology posits a metaphysical discontinuity, a duality, between men and powers: the latter shaped the landscape in which the former dwell, formed the species with which they share the earth and off which

they live, and laid down the plan of life to which they should conform. . . .
It is in keeping with the doctrine of the two kinds of existence – the
extraordinary existence of the powers and the ordinary existence of men
and other creatures – that men are ordinarily unable to experience the
powers, even though they may have powers alongside or nearby or within,
or may themselves be within powers

(Maddock 1982, p. 105).

In the *Waiting for Harry* text, the first two speakers give expression to the distinction between 'the real Stringybark Tree sand sculpture' and those which men
make now and have made in the recent past. The real Stringybark is both huge
(*wana*), a marker of its difference and also of its power, and lies in an unusual
place for a tree species, beneath the sea, where Aboriginal people of the Arnhem
Land coast believe the spirits of their dead reside. It had been put there by a
supernatural being:

gochilawa	*gu-barnja-rra*	*gu-yunya-rra*
out to the horizon (of sea and sky)	she/he–it put	it is lying down

'It is lying out to sea. [A being] put
    it there.'

gu-barnja-rra	*gu-yu-rra*	*wangarr*[4]
he–it put	it lies	deity

'A deity put it there.'

The term *wangarr*, used here for the supernatural being responsible for placing
Stringybark Tree under the sea, is generic and may be used for a variety of
totemic spirits. In the text, no expressed interest is shown by the speakers in why
or how the spirit acted as it did. Indeed, given the metaphysical discontinuity formulated above, this could not be known or even speculated upon. Nor is it clear
how men came to know how to execute the Stringybark sand sculpture that represents something of the totem's essence. The sand sculpture is, as Jolpa says, the
substance of the tree. He uses the Burarra word *gun-mama* to express the
relationship between design and essence; its basic meaning is 'bone (of a living
being)', or 'the frame of a structure', and seems to denote the totem's
inherent shape.

The metaphysical duality of Aboriginal thinking does not deter the men speaking here from undertaking a discriminating review of events of the recent past
that have affected the transmission and drawing of the Stringybark sand sculpture. Harry uses an event in global history, World War II, as a chronological distinguishing line between times long past (*wartime gojilapa yirrawa*, 'wartime
half-way [to] yesterday'), and the more recent time within the speakers'
experience. At the time of speaking (1978), these men were in their late-middle
age – before the War they were boys, whereas the Wartime corresponded to their
early adulthood. Many of them had then been in Darwin, and had worked for the
Australian Armed Forces. In their memories it is a time of excitement and vivid,
new and unusual events. Whether any comparable event could have been used in

former times for the same chronological purpose must remain an open question, but on a more limited scale it is quite possible.

Yet the War itself was not, it emerges, the main reason for the discontinuity in traditional sand sculpture drawing that the men discuss. Factors of an inter-personal and interclan nature were the major determinants of change. Harry mentions a very important matter: the exchange of ritual icons and designs which are regarded as the property of individual clans for other, comparable designs belonging to different groups. Thomson (1949) gives the clearest account of the importance of ritual exchange in the period before extensive European influence on Arnhem Land life-styles, and there is no doubt that this process is still one of major importance in the area. It functions to promote both individual and clan interests by enlarging their sphere of political and ritual influence. Men establish personal ties with particular trading partners, whereby they acquire new designs and songs and hence farther-ranging sociopolitical connections.

The dead man for whom the mortuary ceremony in question was being held in 1978 had at some time been given a Fish Trap sand sculpture by a trading partner. The inference to be drawn from Harry's remarks is that Fish Trap had not pre-viously been part of the Anbarra's iconic stock-in-trade. This gift gave the dead man prestige both within and outside his own community, but also brought with it some unspecified trouble. Perhaps, in line with Harry's warning at the end of the text here, someone may have accused the dead man of unauthorized theft of the Fish Trap design. Whether there was any substance to such an accusation or not, it would have been sufficient to promote bad feeling or even fighting. Pre-sumably, through the dead man's considerable influence in his community, the old Stringybark sand sculpture fell into disuse until the generation of the speakers came to maturity. They were taught to draw it by a man from another clan, whose estates lie on islands some distance to the east, near Milingimbi Mission. This man, Wujal, stood in the appropriate classificatory kinship relationship to the Anbarra clans (that of mother's mother's brother) to offer to teach and supervise the clans' designs (Hiatt 1965, p. 54). As Harry comments, 'He has a big say in the sand sculptures for this clan country'. It is worth noting that two versions of the Stringybark sand sculpture were drawn at the dead man's funeral – the Anbarra version executed by Harry, and the Kamalangga version from Milingimbi, drawn by Wujal. Moreover, at the end of the ceremony a Fish Trap sand sculpture was drawn around the standing hollow log containing the remains of the man who had introduced Fish Trap to the Anbarra.

The transmission of knowledge of the past and of ritual practice takes place among Arnhem Land Aborigines at the level of personal interactions between individuals. The obligation to hand on traditions is a general one, in that it is expected of all Aboriginal people, but it is felt and indeed takes effect as a per-sonal duty, based on kinship affiliations and trading links with individuals from other, often distant, clans. Hence, as in this case, the standard forms of ritual per-formance for a mortuary ceremony are known to all, and are repeated from one individual's funeral to another's, but the configuration of emblems represented in song, dance, sand sculpture and painting are unique to specific persons and, as with the dead man honoured by the *Waiting for Harry* funeral, are a way of giving them an individual memorial full of aesthetic richness and emotional effect. Morphy (1984) has documented a similar procedure in Eastern Arnhem Land. Furthermore, in this case there is a personal connection between an icon and the man who had been given the right to draw it, so that the very act of executing it is a way of honouring him.

The enactment of a song or dance and the drawing or manufacture of an icon give the occasion for the transmission of information about these designs and artistic entities by older to younger members of an Aboriginal society. This information may be of various kinds: the meaning of the song, dance or design; its association with particular persons and events of the past; ways of making or performing it; and advice on its place in the ritual process. Because most Aboriginal ceremonies devote many days, or even weeks, to singing and the manufacture of icons, there is ample opportunity to tell myths and recount incidents in people's lives associated with them. Thus, exegesis and interpretative instruction go hand-in-hand with ritual performance, and the one promotes the other.

Most Aboriginal artistic forms are dependent for their full realization on performance contexts. These may range from elaborate rituals to the performances of individuals for a small group. Particularly in eastern and southern Australia, individual musical compositions of an occasional kind have been common, and in some places they still are. Such songs, which often have accompanying dances, could be inspired by striking events in the composer's experience, such as the introduction of the railway or a child wandering off into the bush and getting lost (Donaldson 1987). These song genres, just as much as those performed in elaborate rituals, have recently been shown to have structures dependent on performance conventions.

For Aboriginal people, most of whom are both performers and audience for their own artistic forms, repeated performances of the same song or dance enrich their understanding of tradition. At the same time, because no performance is ever really the same, each performance also modifies both text and meaning. The *Waiting for Harry* ritual exemplifies this process of continuity and change in the semantics of Aboriginal oral forms. The men's conversation acknowledges the antiquity of their clan designs, yet comments on innovation and discontinuity. At the same time, their discourse itself creates new meanings for their cultural inheritance. Immediately after the text reproduced here, Harry gives a long narration of a myth which tells of how the Stringybark *wangarr* encountered other spirit-beings, who came to live in or on him or wanted to cut him down. For those who heard him, and for Harry himself, the circumstances of his telling the story gave it new meaning. The myth itself, being about an ancestral hollow tree, is particularly relevant to a mortuary rite in which the bones of the dead are placed inside hollow logs, which are themselves painted with the iconic representations of the spirit beings whose acts are the subject of the narrated myth. Also, the fact that this performance was being filmed for Aboriginal people, but in the knowledge that it would reach a wider audience, gave it a new dimension of meaning that it had never before had.

There is one final characteristic of Aboriginal oral forms to be discussed. It bears on the metaphysical discontinuity between the sphere of the powers and the sphere of men, which has already been mentioned. Because the powers are held to be the agents of creativity, men being their passive recipients – mostly through the medium of dreams – texts are held to be unchanging. In many cases songs, dances and icons are said to be directly given in form and content by the powers. Yet, as we have seen, Aborigines are not unaware of the process of change and innovation in the present and the recent past. How can the ideology of lack of change in the forms be reconciled with an awareness of innovation and reinterpretation?

The answer seems to lie in the symbiosis between texts and exegesis on the one hand, and certain characteristics of Aboriginal texts themselves on the other. In societies like that of Aboriginal Australia, which subscribe to an ideology of unchanging transmission of texts from the gods to mankind, exegetical traditions are often found whose purpose is to interpret the texts to humankind. In some systems, such as that of the Christian church, exegesis is formal and institutionalized, and is the preserve of a priestly class. In Aboriginal society exegesis is much more informal, though it takes on a formal quality at some secret ceremonies, and the role of teacher is assumed by the most forceful and knowledgeable members of the older generation who have acknowledged rights over the relevant texts or icons.

It may also be questioned whether, in fact, texts do remain unchanged over time. On the whole it is only very recently that scholars have begun to explore the qualities of Aboriginal texts that allow the ideology of an unchanging transmission of Dreamtime creativity to be maintained. In the visual arts it is frequently the case that the more abstract the design is, the greater its sacredness and the more it needs to be interpreted by the knowledgeable to the uninformed (Morphy 1977). When the texts of Aboriginal songs are examined, it is found that there are a variety of means used to distinguish them as a marked form of discourse and to protect them from being tied down to a particular place, time and constellation of interests, while leaving them open to changing exegesis and, sometimes, to controlled change of the texts themselves. In addition there are well-documented examples of quite sweeping changes and innovations in some Aboriginal traditions, which arise nowadays in response to gross social and political changes (Wild 1987). Although such changes were probably less extreme in the days before the arrival of Europeans in Australia, they are likely to have happened on some occasions.

Some of the characteristics of Aboriginal song that mark it as a special discourse mode were analysed by Strehlow (1971) and by C.H. & R.M. Berndt in several of their writings. These circumstances are the subject of close scrutiny in several papers of a recent collection (Clunies Ross et al. 1987). The authors examine the use of special song languages, the mixing of lexis from a variety of languages, the removal of some grammatical features to be found in the corresponding spoken languages, the use of polysemy, the lack of specific reference to sites, ritual practice or persons, except through *double entendre* and allusion.

All these and other characteristics allow songs to represent the archetypal and unchanging metaphysical dimension of the Aboriginal conceptual universe, while freeing ritual practitioners to get on with the ever-changing process of reinterpretation and re-enactment. It is precisely at this meeting of theory and practice that we pick up Harry and the other Anbarra men, captured on the *Waiting for Harry* footage, as they discuss the ancestral Stringybark sand sculpture.

Notes

1   Elsewhere (Clunies Ross & Hiatt 1977, p. 131) a sand sculpture has been described as 'a design, outlined in high or low relief by means of walls of earth or sand, which is executed upon a carefully prepared earthen surface'.
2   The Institute's address is Box 553, Canberra, ACT 2601, Australia.
3   The transcription and translation are deposited in the Institute of Aboriginal Studies' archive under the name of L.R. Hiatt, and may be consulted there. Several Burarra men assisted with the transcription, including Johnny Mundrugmundrug, Albert Nganmarra, Frank Gurrmanamana and Frank Malkorda. The translation was the work of L.R. Hiatt and myself.
4   Burarra orthography and lexis is here given with reference to Glasgow & Glasgow (1985).

References

Clunies Ross, M. and L.R. Hiatt 1977. Sand sculptures at a Gidjingali burial rite. In *Form in indigenous art*, P.J. Ucko (ed.), 131–46. Canberra: Australian Institute of Aboriginal Studies.

Clunies Ross, M. and S.A. Wild 1982. *Djambidj. An Aboriginal song series from Northern Australia*. Canberra: Australian Institute of Aboriginal Studies.

Clunies Ross, M., T. Donaldson and S.A. Wild (eds) 1987. *Songs of Aboriginal Australia*. Oceania monograph 32. Sydney.

Donaldson, T. 1987. Making a song (and dance?) in south east Australia. In *Songs of Aboriginal Australia*, M. Clunies Ross, T. Donaldson and S.A. Wild (eds), 43–62. Oceania Monograph 32. Sydney.

Glasgow, D. and K. Glasgow 1985. *Burarra–English bilingual dictionary*. Darwin: Summer Institute of Linguistics, Australian Aborigines Branch.

Hiatt, L.R. 1965. *Kinship and conflict*. Canberra: Australian National University Press.

McKenzie, K. (dir.) *et al.* 1980. *Waiting for Harry*. 16 mm film, 57 min, sd, col. Canberra: Australian Institute of Aboriginal Studies.

Maddock, K. 1982. *The Australian Aborigines. A portrait of their society*, 2nd edn. Blackburn, Victoria: Penguin.

Morphy, H. 1977. Too many meanings: an analysis of the artistic system of the Yolngu people of north-east Arnhem Land. Ph.D. thesis, Australian National University, Canberra (unpublished).

Morphy, H. 1984. *Journey to the crocodile's nest*. Canberra: Australian Institute of Aboriginal Studies.

Strehlow, T.G.H. 1971. *Songs of central Australia*. Sydney: Angus and Robertson.

Thomson, D. 1949. *Economic structure and the ceremonial exchange cycle in Arnhem Land*. Melbourne: Macmillan.

Wild, S. 1987. Recreating the Jukurrpa: adaptation and innovation of Warlpiri songs and ceremonies. In *Songs of Aboriginal Australia*, M. Clunies Ross, T. Donaldson and S.A. Wild (eds), 97–120. Oceania Monograph 32. Sydney.

14 *Perceptions of the past among north Queensland Aboriginal people: the intrusion of Europeans and consequent social change*

A.K. CHASE

To investigate perceptions of the past among any socially coherent group of people is, in effect, to carry out an historical investigation into social process. Furthermore, this investigation provides only one of several data sources potentially available to the investigator, other obvious sources being the observation of current social action together with investigation of their cognitive bases, the archaeological record, and the various written records which may be left either by the society under investigation or by an alien observer. For any anthropologist working among kin-based societies, there are limitations here: he or she is lucky indeed if detailed archaeological information is available for the region within which the study takes place, and the only written records will be those left by outside observers, usually European explorers, pioneering entrepreneurs in search of easily extracted wealth, missionaries or early governmental officials. In these situations reconstruction of social processes relies heavily upon current ethnography, including modern perceptions of the past.

For the Aboriginal people in north-east Queensland who are discussed below, there has been no archaeological investigation, and the written record by European observers is very sketchy. In contrast with other areas where missions were established, staff turnover here was high, and no single missioner felt obliged to leave behind a detailed record of the people he administered. Basic mission records – apart from some incomplete records of births, marriages and deaths – have not survived. In addition, and more frustrating for the historical investigator, this particular region produced no early entrepreneur or government official who had enough of a sense of history to keep a detailed journal or to attempt an excursion into literature in the form of memoirs. This was despite an extremely active contact period which involved many Europeans and other aliens who sought their fortunes on land by fossicking for gold and other precious minerals, and on sea along the coastline by luggering for pearl shell, trochus shell and the sea slug *trepang* or *bêche de mer*. The social scientist who wishes to understand past social processes in this region is therefore heavily dependent upon indigenous perceptions of the past, drawing upon present interpretations among the Aboriginal people of the continuities and changes which have taken place, especially during the critical and disruptive period of European exploration, domination and enforced Aboriginal resettlement. The process of investigation is very much that described by Oakeshott:

> . . . an historian's only entry into the past is by means of these survivals. And the first concern of an historical enquiry is to assemble them from where they lie scattered in the present, to recover what might have been lost, to impose some kind of order upon this confusion, to repair the damage they might have suffered, to abate their fragmentariness, to discern their relationships, to recognise a survival in terms of its provenance, and thus to determine its authentic character as a bygone practical or philosophical or artistic etc., performance
>
> (Oakeshott 1983, p. 32, quoted in Giddens 1984, p. 356).

To clarify this quotation a little, in the context of our discussion we assume, with Giddens (1984, pp. 355–60), that historical investigation is first of all a legitimate part of social science investigation, and an investigation into social processes through time and space. In this sense it is theoretically unified with the types of social science investigations of social phenomena which are usually carried out by sociologists and social anthropologists. There is, after all, no such thing as a 'timeless' and 'spaceless' society. Giddens (1979, 1984) has provided the most recent unified theory (structuration), which attempts to account for dimensions of time and space in any social investigation. All statements of social processes are specific on both of these dimensions, and it necessarily follows that an understanding of sociocultural dynamics involves historical perspectives (see also Hudson 1973, Kuhn 1962, Leach 1964).

Indigenous perceptions of the past are part of what is often referred to as 'tradition' – a nebulous category for most social scientists, often perceived as relatively resistant to alteration, and forming the blueprint for the replication of society and its actions in a mechanistic sense. Tradition is taken here to mean an extremely flexible mode of thinking about the past as it refers to specific regions and societies, and one that is largely interpretative in terms of justifying present routine social actions. In this way tradition, rather than being a largely fixed entity across time and space, relates to authorization for current routine actions in terms of maintenance of order and power structures; it can thus consist of quite recently created mythologies as well as those from a more distant past (see Colson 1975).

Aboriginal societies of north-east Cape York Peninsula, Queensland

The *kuuku ya'u*, *uuthalnganu* and *umpila* people are Aboriginal hunter–gatherers occupying a narrow coastal plain in north-east Cape York Peninsula in the extreme north-east of the Australian continent (see Fig. 14.1). Some 10 km offshore lies the Great Barrier Reef, and the inner reef waters (exploited by large

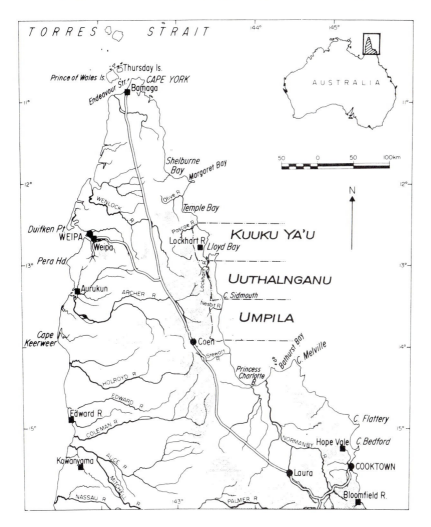

Figure 14.1 Cape York Peninsula.

outrigger canoes) together with this tropical coastal lowland provide resource bases among the most productive in the world (see Chase & Sutton 1981). These are societies of people who identify primarily with a language territory and, within it, with particular patrilineal estates. Each society most probably numbered only several hundred, and the three language territories occupied, in all, about 120 km of coastline, and extended inland, on average, some 10 km to the start of the mountain ranges. Territories extended out to sea to include the numerous islands, cays and reefs inside the main barrier reef, and the immediate shoreline and river estuaries contained many named sites, both sacred and secular.

Today the 300 or so survivors of these societies live at Lockhart River settlement, in Lloyd Bay. Until 1965 they were inhabitants of a mission which was formed in 1924 to minister to the spiritual and temporal needs of the groups which, at that time, were suffering the vicissitudes of some 50 years of continuous, if ever-changing, contact with Europeans and others drawn to the area to exploit the various marine and terrestrial resources. Unlike much of eastern Australia, this area was quite unsuitable for pastoral activities by Europeans, and while contact pressures were high, they did not involve displacement of Aboriginal people from land for this purpose. Permanent European possession of land, and its attendant competition with occupying Aboriginal groups, was not a major issue here. Consequently, because of this lack of pastoral occupation and due to the nature of the economic patterns of exploitation, contact and intrusion consisted of a very dense but ever-changing procession of individual aliens appearing and disappearing according to fluctuating markets or, at the mission, according to the strength of resolve among the Anglican overseers. Nor was the mission population sheltered from the great pulses of economic activity in the Peninsula–Torres Strait region. Because of their marine skills, the men were eagerly sought after as crews for the lugger boats from the 1880s to the 1930s, and it was not unusual for a man to have spent at least half of his life working around north Queensland coasts and the Torres Strait, even on occasions voyaging as far afield as New Guinea, the New Hebrides and Noumea. A parallel can, of course, be drawn with the peripatetic movements of cattle stockmen around the north of Australia on the great droving trips, but the marine situation was different: first, in the range of alien encounters (see Chase 1982), and secondly, in the high risk and adventurous nature of diving and sailing around the Coral Sea. Furthermore, boat work usually resulted in men returning to their own small societies at the end of the fishing season. They were not, in general, displaced permanently from their countries of origin, as so often happened in the cattle industry. Their societies remained coherent in terms of pre-contact continuities, but their views of the outside social and geographical worlds were expanded remarkably.

Present-day investigations of Lockhart perceptions of the past therefore delve into an historical perception of some complexity. A wide range of contact experience is woven into a perceived continuity from the creation period of the dreaming to modern times. This is done through the framework of episodic periods, each representing a transformation in the relationships of *pama malngkanichi* (the traditional category of 'sandbeach people' from this section of coast) with other indigenous people of the region, and with Europeans and the many other aliens who followed in their wake.

Aboriginal categories of the past

The *kuuku ya'u* people, whom we take as representative of the *pama malngkanichi* of this section of coastline, conceive of a 'beginning' period called *yilamu*, when the creator spirits of this region emerged from the Cosmos, creating the present landscape, its biological diversity, and its proper Aboriginal human occupants. As

Maddock (1973) described it, featureless entities became featured and specific. These creative events are celebrated in myth, song and ceremony, and in named sites where particular spirits either passed through and carried out certain acts, or came to rest and were metamorphosed into natural features. Site names of the former kind have the suffixal ending -*ngun(uma)*, and for the latter kind, the suffix -*mutha*. It is these sites which, through residual powers from these spirits, carry restrictions of use and behaviour, though these restrictions vary in intensity. *Mutha* sites are the more powerful. They are commonly referred to in the Australian anthropological literature as totemic sites. While people can argue over interpretations of later periods, *yilamu* interpretations are fixed by the properly authorized adults.

This spiritual transformation, which was responsible for the existence of authorized territorial groups and their speciated environment, gave rise to the next period of *anthanthama* or a 'long time before'. This is a period for which there are now no eye-witness accounts, nor is there any remembered first-hand experience of eye-witness accounts among living people, but it is commemorated in secular stories and songs, and certain sites. It can be thought of as the 'classical period' of Aboriginal life, before any alien intrusion, when people lived out their lives in the routine seasonal cycles within the known social universe of the region, disturbed only by internal disputes among individuals and groups who 'belonged' to the authoritatively socialized environment. Particular sites are remembered for famous battles between neighbouring groups, or between particular 'big men' (*pama mukkana*), or where particular events took place: a drowning, a traditional ceremonial performance area, an encounter with spiritual forces, or desperate encounters with half-human cannibalistic people who lived in territories just beyond the lands of neighbouring human groups with whom structured social interaction (trade, ceremony and marriage) took place. Designated fighting grounds where combat always took place relate to this period, as do the dugong bone mounds still visible along this coast, which are said to mark the gravesites of 'big men' renowned for their skill at the capture of dugong (*pama watayichi*). Some of the big men of this period have their names commemorated in territorial names or, perhaps more accurately, certain territorial names are interpreted today in this manner.

This period, in Lockhart historical perspective, may be seen as the old idyllic period – idyllic in the sense that there was no outside challenge to the authoritative presence of certain Aboriginal people for a specifically delineated geographic area. Importantly, for later archaeological investigation of the pre-contact past, this is the period of interpretative reconstruction by present Lockhart people, when an anthropologist investigates past economic use of the territories in the region by visiting sites and resource bases, and obtaining knowledge concerning routine traditional acquisition of resources in the seasonal schedule and the use of particular camping locations which I have referred to elsewhere as domicultural activity (see Hynes & Chase 1982). In the vivid creole of the modern population, this is *payten* ('fashion') time, a short-hand reference to 'old-fashioned' times.

This period is sometimes referred to additionally as *antha yi'achi* (literally, the 'middle period'), referring to its linear position between the creation period and the modern, European-influenced period. However, this episodic name is sometimes used specifically for the period of the next major transformation, which links the idyllic past with the present European era, which belongs to present people both experientially and through first-hand accounts from remembered ancestors. This specific use is for the time of the earliest European contacts: the time of the first explorers, the first arrival of tobacco, flour, boats, cattle and horses, and the initial Aboriginal reaction to these. Prominent among these people, as with other areas of northern Australia, are mythical accounts of the 'creator ancestor' of Australian Europeans – Captain Cook. Though his journal records that he travelled well to the east outside the main Barrier Reef along this northern section of the Peninsula, there are two specific sites which the *kuuku ya'u* attribute to him, but which are probably associated with the earliest survey ships in the region during the first half of the 19th century: a large rusting ship's anchor and a survey cairn. Cook is the symbolic representation of the coming of the Europeans to the area, as indeed he is to many Europeans who are not knowledgeable about his particular route through these seas.

In this sense, the 'middle period' of Captain Cook and Edmund Kennedy the explorer (the first European to enter this country in 1848, and who died at the hands of Aborigines; again a name learned through later European experience) forms a transformation period from *anthanthama* to the more recent period of European and other alien involvement. The coming of foreigners as resource exploiters in the 1870s and 1880s formed a pincer movement – by land Chinese and European miners fossicked the hills for gold and tin, by sea the boats explored the inner reef waters for pearlshell and trepang. This is the period of living memory – if not by people still alive, then by parents of people still alive. This major period is referred to as *kuma*, or within the time of present people. It covers all events which can be validated by eye-witness accounts. It consists again of a series of consecutive transformations in people's lives, each categorized either by an activity period, e.g. *'lugger-kuma'* (early luggering period before the mission, dominated by Japanese boat captains and divers, and crews from diverse South Sea ethnic groups), *'mission-kuma'* (the period of mission control and residence, 1924–65), *'government-kuma'* (1965–), or by the name of a focal European 'boss' who had direction over their lives, e.g. *'Giblet-kuma'* (from an influential sandalwooder who lived among them in the early 1900s), *'Rowan-kuma'* (a pre-World War II mission superintendent noted for his unremitting attack upon cultural continuities) and *'Warby-kuma'* (a post-World War II mission superintendent, much liked, who unsuccessfully attempted to form a Christian co-operative). These periods are indigenous 'eras', each representing a significant change of relationships among local Aboriginal people, European and other alien 'bosses', and the resource bases for continuing social life.

Each set of relationships in an era becomes accepted and routinized; and because the shifts in these relationships are not massively destructive in terms of people – land relationships, nor in terms of continuing social relationships and their institutional bases (birth, marriage, death, ceremonial activities, and so on), the transformations from one to another are seen retrospectively as 'normal' in the sense that the normative or authoritative base for society remains relatively untouched in the view of later members of the society. It is significant that, until the new administrative regime of the Queensland State Government from 1965, these Aboriginal people remained in constant, if intermittent, touch with their home territories. The early lugger period from the 1870s to about 1910 saw heavy recruitment for crews, and much seasonal absence. However, men returned in the wet season to their home camps (which by this time were concentrating into relatively permanent settlements at traditional wet-season sites, through the supplies of flour and other stores), or they attached themselves to the small shore processing stations along the coast which were an essential part of the trepang industry. It was in the interest of a boat entrepreneur to maintain relationships with his labour base, and there was no attempt to stop people from moving freely around their lands during the lay-off season (see Chase 1982).

It was this period which saw the mutually dependent relationships develop between both European and Aboriginal 'bosses', each exploiting the other for scarce resources – on the Aboriginal side, protection from malevolent Europeans, flour, sugar, tobacco, alcohol and various trade goods; on the European side a relatively dependable and inexpensive labour force, women, local knowledge and protection from malevolent Aboriginal people. This type of relationship became intensified into a permanent arrangement for many *kuuku ya'u* people from about 1910 to 1920, with the arrival and permanent settlement of the sandalwooder Hugh Giblet. He carefully maintained his relationships with the local Aboriginal people, drove off other entrepreneurs (particularly the Japanese) who tried to exploit the area, and provided the local population with large handouts of food, tobacco, clothes, alcohol and other desirable goods. He was responsible (according to people who lived in his camp) for the late arrival of missionaries, who had to wait for his death before they were confident to make plans for the area.

Similarly, the mission period, when it did arrive, was seen as unthreatening to the local cultural perspectives in its pre-World War II period. Despite harsh treatment for children speaking their indigenous language, participants in traditional ceremonies, and so on, men still got away for periods working on the luggers, and families returned to their home countries along the coast during the extended mission 'holidays' in the early dry season – a practice which seemed to be maintained by the missioners as much to relieve themselves from the Aboriginal presence and the constant drain on stores and resources, as for any charitable feelings for their charges. After a period of total abandonment during World War II in the face of a threatened Japanese invasion, the mission period struggled on until financial collapse brought in the State Government. Now, for the first time, there was an active attempt to keep inhabitants permanently attached to the settlement and away from their traditional homelands. To this end the government applied considerable financial resources, a stern European view about the need to 'raise' Aborigines to European levels of civilization, and a massive bureaucratic system administered from 3000 km away. Lockhart

Aborigines were now to become dark-skinned Queenslanders, no different from other Queenslanders, and any notions of local Aboriginal traditional ties were to be put firmly from their minds (Chase 1980).

Aboriginal perceptions of the past and social explanation

My initial proposition was that to investigate perceptions of the past as a conceptual category of human existence is to investigate social process. What I have discussed subsequently is a generalized and (necessarily) condensed framework of Aboriginal understanding for this region, together with some equally generalized conclusions from the European historical literature available. As an anthropologist working for some time in this area, I carried out very detailed ethnographic work recording individual life-histories, linguistic texts, ethno-classifications of species and environments, site and territorial information, economic and political dimensions, and so on. However, despite the wealth of ethnographic explanation recorded in the present, reconstructions of society and various political and economic processes must remain largely conjectural. There are, of course, certain validatory processes which can be followed. Seasonal resource sites can be visited, and information on social activity collected *in situ*. The now-abandoned mission can be visited and people's houses recorded, together with other activity areas. Some historical events can be cross-checked against European records. Care can be taken to sift out those verbal accounts which agree in substantive matters even if interpretation differs.

All of these past perceptions are, of course, extremely valuable in the explanation of the present society; here we have the framework of rules and social resources which are drawn upon in day-to-day social action – or rather, the logic of the framework, revealed in the explanatory continuities from the remote past to the present. However, how real are the reconstructions made by anthropologists concerning past social processes, where they do not have the advantage of archaeological interpretation or detailed historical records to guide them? My own work, for example, like that of others who have worked in Cape York Peninsula over the past 15 years, has presented explanatory models of the operation of local groups (pre-contact) in environments, placing heavy emphasis upon seasonal patterning of movement, camping and resource extraction. These explanatory models are built from present ethnographic information, augmented by (in some cases) observations and similar ethnographic data (including interpretations of the past) by the earlier generations of anthropologists who worked here in the 1930s. Are they – as Gorecki (1982) has suggested for similar reconstructions by Canneille among the Chaanba of the Sahara, among others – largely a product of the anthropologist's limited databases, bearing little relationship to the reality of long-term patterning of activities in time and space? At this point I wish to return to the eastern Peninsula Aboriginal people whose historical perspectives have been summarized above.

A reconsideration of the sequential periods or eras shows a marked differentiation between the latest categorical period of *kuma* (with its various subdivisions) and the periods of *anthanthama* and *yilamu* which precede it. *Kuma*, quite obviously, is differentiated into smaller and clearer episodic eras, which by their very titles indicate significant shifts in economic and political relationships with the dominant European state. It is also within the period of reportable experience. When I worked among these people in the early 1970s, some of the oldest residents were 80 years of age or more, and in some cases could remember a life-style free from any European presence, though, of course, this does not imply a life free from European influence. However, people of advanced years could go to sites and point out precise camping places for individuals and families, the location of the early European lugger and trepang processing camps, and numerous graves (often with almost no surface visibility to the outsider) along the coastal dunes. This division between the recent contact-dominated past and the more remote pre-contact past is obviously an important one for the present Aboriginal inhabitants of the area. The various sites and resource centres have a personalized value in terms of experience of living people and their immediate ancestors, as opposed to the *anthanthama* period of the distant past, even though this remote era is of profound importance in their cosmic viewpoint. For a social anthropologist the same division applies. He or she can reconstruct the contact history with more confidence, on the basis of eye-witness accounts, personal experience and the scattered European historical record. It must be acknowledged that anthropological reconstructions of the pre-contact past are much more conjectural. Without the benefit of detailed archaeological studies of this coastal area, economic regimes, local organization and territorial associations are extremely difficult to infer.

For archaeological research the same broad division between pre- and post-contact past is similarly important. Archaeologists, when they do carry out future research in this part of Australia, will be confronted by a narrow coastal area which has been under human occupation for thousands of years – almost certainly as long as the geomorphological history of the present littoral strip. Any surviving evidence in this tropical monsoonal climate will consist, in the top levels, of a series of occupation sites of great complexity, reflecting the many quite different uses made of the shoreline. The investigators will be dealing with indigenous campsites, temporary lugger camps, trepang treatment camps, mission locations, 'holiday' camps and sites from the very recent government period, all covering a period of about 100 years. It is in this situation that Aboriginal perceptions of the past, particularly of the contact past, will be of great value in making sense of the data. This will be so not just for the categorization of the eras discussed above, but also for the indigenous models of Aboriginal and European social action which explain people's lives during these eras. Inference of social action from incomplete material remains is, of course, a much argued matter in archaeology, as theoretical debate in the discipline testifies. I would contend that the material remains from the contact period probably complicates, rather than simplifies, the inferential process, especially where the contact period has been many-faceted, as we find in this area. However, the value of indigenous perceptions for the more remote pre-contact past in this area is less direct. Certainly current informants can present a detailed model of the seasonal use of environment, and of territorial divisions.

We can expect that the conceptual system of named sites, their totemic and other associations, estate and linguistic divisions, probably represents – as a system – a fairly accurate representation of pre-contact systems on the ground, allowing for minor variations which would have been part of any human dynamic social–land interaction, because these particular cultural phenomena were least penetrated by the dominant European-based control of the area over the past 100 years. The *kuuku ya'u* and *umpila* people can outline this system with considerable ethnographic detail. It is notable from work I have been involved with in the Northern Territory, where pastoralism formed the single major influence on the indigenous population, that site and territorial information today is far more obscure, and tends to be highly influenced by European property boundaries and European use sites. However, economic reconstruction of economic dimensions of the pre-contact past is less reflective of reality, due to the heavy European influence, both direct and indirect, upon the resource base and the perception of desirable resources. What emerges today from this type of reconstruction is most probably a model of seasonal use which, if true as an overall regional pattern, would present many anomalies for archaeological data from this particular area. The point about the general resource availability of this region is the high geographic diversity of the various seasonal resource bases. The vegetation communities are heavily mosaiced to the point where each small estate contained many options for food resources at any period of the year. In contrast with the western Peninsula coastline, for example, no single estate group could dominate a major survival resource base for certain times of the year, and thus control, to a major extent, the movements of others (see Chase 1982, 1984). Options for movement and resource extraction were very wide.

As a final point, I wish to touch briefly upon the matter of material culture. Part of the perception of the past deals with the 'traditional' artefacts and associated technologies which are seen to 'belong' to the particular language groups. Despite the obvious infiltration of European artefacts, these people can recreate a suite of these artefacts with great accuracy, and in a way that reveals their particular regional distinctiveness. Although in many cases certain forms of spears, containers, working tools, and so on, are no longer used, these items have become symbols of a local ethnic identity which is distinguished from those of neighbouring peoples in the region. Making a particular form of spear or spearthrower, or body decoration, is a current political statement, especially useful when groups meet as they do today to perform traditional dances. Knowledge about such matters, together with knowledge about the natural environment and its biotic species, forms a conservative information base which remains of current value for the purpose of ethnic distinctiveness, despite the fact that the application of this knowledge to routine economic activity no longer takes place. Such information has great relevance to ethno-archaeological research, as well as to current social research.

Ethno-archaeology then, in the form of indigenous perceptions of the past, provides two kinds of database which can be used in the interpretation of archaeological remains. First, there are data which relate to specific sites and which are accurate for the short-term past through eye-witness account or through reliable transmission from known immediate forbears. Secondly, there are data which relate to a generalized form of reconstruction belonging to the long-term past. This second category is not directly applicable to any specific site: it is, in effect, a model of social action against which routine social action is determined. The degree of divergence for particular groups in particular locations at particular times is a matter for archaeological investigation, but such an investigation can benefit considerably by consideration of the whole range of indigenous perceptions of the past.

References

Chase, A. 1980. Which way now? Tradition, continuity and change in a north Queensland Aboriginal community. PhD thesis, University of Queensland (unpublished).

Chase, A. 1982. 'All kind of nation': Aborigines and Asians in Cape York Peninsula. *Aboriginal History* **5**, 7–19.

Chase, A. 1984. Belonging to country: territory, identity and environment in Cape York Peninsula, northern Australia. In *Aboriginal landowners*, L.R. Hiatt (ed.), 104–122. Oceania Monograph No. 29. Sydney: University of Sydney.

Chase, A. and P. Sutton 1981. Hunter–gatherers in a rich environment: Aboriginal coastal exploitation in Cape York Peninsula. In *Ecological biogeography of Australia*, A. Keast (ed.), 1818–1852. The Hague: Junk.

Colson, E. 1975. *Tradition and contract: the problem of order*. London: Heinemann.

Giddens, A. 1979. *Central problems in social theory*. London: Macmillan.

Giddens, A. 1984. *The constitution of society*. Cambridge: Polity Press.

Gorecki, P.P. 1982. Ethnoarchaeology at Kuk: problems in site formation processes. PhD thesis, University of Sydney (unpublished).

Hudson, C. 1973. The historical approach in anthropology. In *Handbook of social and cultural anthropology*, J.J. Honigman (ed.), 111–41. Chicago: Rand McNally.

Hynes, R.A. and A. Chase 1982. Plants, sites and domiculture: Aboriginal influences upon plant communities in Cape York Peninsula. *Archaeology in Oceania* **17** (1), 38–50.

Kuhn, T. 1962. *The structure of scientific revolutions*. Chicago: University of Chicago Press.

Leach, E.R. 1964. *Political systems of highland Burma*. London: Bell.

Maddock, K.J. 1973. *The Australian Aborigines: a portrait of their society*. London: Allen Lane.

15 The past as perceived by the Bali Nyonga people of Cameroon

ELIAS NWANA

The Bali Chamba tribe of the North-West Province in Cameroon, Africa, are made up of a number of chiefdoms, including: Bali Nyonga, Bali Gham, Bali Kumbat, Bali Gashu and Bali Gansin. The discussion in this chapter is limited to the Bali Nyonga, who occupy the present Bali subdivision in Mezam Division of the North-West Province.

Location and social structure

Geographically, Bali Nyonga lies to the east of longitude 10°E and at latitude 6°N. It occupies a land area of 192 km², and has a population of more than 30 000 (1976 census).

The people are patrilineal, and they live in compounds of varying sizes depending on the size of the lineage that makes up the compound. Marriage is virilocal and polygamous, although with the advent of Christianity polygamy is gradually disappearing.

Bali people are mainly peasant farmers, growing such things as maize, groundnuts, plantains, cocoyams, sweet potatoes, a variety of yams, a variety of beans and a variety of vegetables. They rear fowl, goats and sheep, and keep dogs and cats as pets.

In the past the people used brass rods called *Chang* as currency. Sometimes cowries and traditionally made salt (*Chilum*) were also used as currency, as well as for bride wealth.

Bali men embroidered various types of gowns and knitted caps. They wove cloths out of local cotton thread, bags out of raffia and baskets out of bamboo. Bags, scabbards and belts were made out of leather or skin. They made spear heads, local razors, axes, hoes, cutlasses and knives out of scrap iron. They got fire out of flint, stone and steel. Some men shaped grinding stones. The raffia palm bamboo was a very useful plant. Out of it people made all types of furniture, such as beds, tables, chairs, cupboards, mats for fencing, local rain covers, ceiling mats and wall mats. The women made their own pots, bowls and pipes from clay. They also made straw bowls and trays, using the spear grass. They strung beads and decorated their calabashes by branding.

For the Bali Nyonga the world was a man's world. Men were regarded as superior to women in hierarchy. Thus, out of respect and courtesy, women never walked upright where their husbands or elders were assembled. They squatted or stooped low before drinking in the presence of men. They never called their husbands by name, and it was taboo for them to eat gizzards of fowl or eggs.

As a general principle the Bali Nyonga man's society was a stratified one, with those in the upper rank of the social strata highly honoured. Juniors never called their superiors by name.

History

Historically, Bali Nyonga belongs to the Chamba Leko-speaking people, who claim to have migrated between 1825 and 1835 from Chamba, a Sudanese tribe whose territory borders between Nigeria and Cameroon to the north, near Yola in Nigeria and Garoua in Cameroon, to the Bamenda grasslands. They are said to have been driven southwards by Fulani invaders during the second quarter of the 19th century. Zintgraff, the famous German explorer, dated the migration to 75 years before he visited Bali Nyonga in 1889 (Hunt n.d.).

The first recorded monarch of the Bali Chamba people was Ga-Wolbe I. He had two sons who reigned one after the other. They were called Ga-Tumjang and Ga-Banjang. On dying, Ga-Banjang was succeeded by his son Ga-Nyama who begot Ga-Gansin. Ga-Gansin begot Ga-Wolbe II who led the Bali Chamba people to the western grasslands and was killed at Bafufundong, near Dschang, in the present Western Province of Cameroon.

After the death of Ga-Wolbe II the struggle for succession started and the tribe was split into seven groups, each under a prince or a powerful leader. Nyongpasi was the leader with the greatest following. The mother of Nyongpasi was princess Nyonga, daughter of Ga-Wolbe II, who if she were a male would have been heir apparent. She was a powerful woman, and her son grew up to be very powerful and influential too. Nyonga's mother was a Bati woman. On the death of Ga-Wolbe II and the struggle for succession that followed, princess Nyonga decided to stay away from any of the other contestants, and asked her son to found a chiefdom. She and her son had a large following from not only the Balis but also the Batis (her mother's people), the Tikari, the Peli, the Kufad and the Buti people (Fomuso 1976). Thus was founded the present Bali Nyonga dynasty, named after Nyongpasi's mother, Nyonga. This is also the origin of the dual sovereignty which characterizes succession in Bali. Nyongpasi became the first monarch of Bali Nyonga, and was called Fonyonga I, and his mother became the first Queen mother (*Kah*) in Bali Nyonga.

When Fonyonga I left Bafufundong, he and his people migrated to Foumban, where they were welcomed by the Batis, a section of his mother's people who were constantly in conflict with the Bamoums. The social interaction that resulted among the Batis, Balis and Bamoum peoples gave rise to the present Bali Nyonga language, known as *Mungaka*, a language of diplomacy, war and commerce.

Nyongpasi's stay with the Bamoums was short-lived, as he was constantly under attack from king Mbuo-Mbuo Njoya. Between 1845 and 1848 Nyongpasi and his people were driven across the Nun river to Bagham, where they regrouped and moved towards Bamenda. After staying in Nkwen for a while, they moved to Kufon, near the present Protestant college Bali, defeated the Bali Kontan and incorporated them into the Bali army. During the long journey from Foumban to Kufom, Nyongpasi and his people subdued and incorporated many other people. These were the Won, the Set, the Ngiam, the Sang, the Ngod, the Sangam, the Fuleng and the Munyam people, who today form a great part of Bali Nyonga. These people are usually referred to as Bani Bantem or Bani Balolo, because they were not part of the original Bali group that broke off from Bafufundong under Nyongpasi.

When Nyongpasi or Fonyonga I died in c. 1856, he was succeeded by his son Ga-Lega I, who concluded a treaty with the Germans in 1891 (Chilver 1966). Ga-Lega I died in 1901, and was succeeded in that year by his son Fonyonga II, who reigned until 1940. Fonyonga II, before becoming ruler, was known as Tita Gwenjang. It was Tita Gwenjang's compound that housed the Bali armoury. Fonyonga II died in 1940, and was succeeded by his son Ga-Lega II on 30 August 1940. Ga-Lega II died on 18 September 1985, and is succeeded by his son Ga-Nyonga III, who was enthroned on 26 September 1985. The line of succession in Bali Nyonga is presented diagrammatically in Figure 15.1.

The political system

Before Fonyonga I died in c. 1856 he had set up a very powerful centralized political system and government in Bali Nyonga. This centred around him, the ruler (*Mfon*), his sub-chiefs (*Mfonteh*), his ministers (*Nkom*), the Queen mother (*Ka-Mamfon*) and the Queen (*Mfongwi*).

Apart from these, certain institutions played very important parts in the political set-up of Bali Nyonga. They included a unifying institution called *Lela*; the religious institution called *Voma*; an executive organ of the government, known as *Ngumba*; the Scouts who spied on other tribes during intertribal wars, called *Gweis*; and the palace courtiers, called *Tchindas*. This political system and government have lasted from Nyongpasi's days to the present.

Comments on the past by a cross section of the Bali Nyonga population

In recent years many changes have taken place within Bali Nyonga. Everywhere one goes cement-block houses and dried sun-block houses with corrugated iron sheets have taken the place of bamboo houses thatched with grass. The pattern of settlement has changed greatly. Instead of building in compounds, streets have been constructed with houses built on both sides. Polyga-

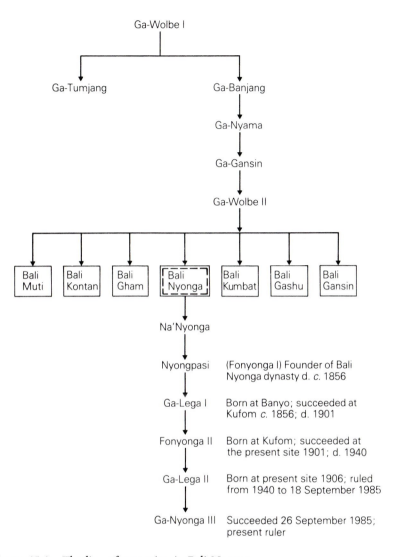

Figure 15.1 The line of succession in Bali Nyonga.

mous marriages are gradually being replaced by monogamous Christian marriages.

The grinding machine has appeared, to relieve women of the tedious problem of grinding corn on stones. Whereas in the past it took a woman about four hours to prepare a *foo-foo* corn meal, it now takes less than 30 minutes. Very many children have been sent to school, and many are graduating with degrees in various fields from various universities, and are returning with new ideas.

Despite all of these changes, some of the traditional institutions and customs of the people, such as those described above, still linger.

Interviews with a cross section of the Bali Nyonga population reveal that the social and cultural changes that are now taking place within the society are viewed with mixed feelings. Some among the older generation think that the past was better than the present. The youth think that many of the traditional institutions in Bali are now old-fashioned and ought to change with the times.

The dry season is the harvesting season, as well as being the *Lela* season. During this time, when people gather together after meals or in drinking bars, they tell stories or discuss issues of the day and life in general. During one of these occasions an old man of about 65 years lamented 'These days children are impolite. They no longer say "good morning" even to their parents. The few that do just say "morning" or "hi". They have no time for others. They always look very busy'. 'Very true', replied his colleague of about the same age, 'they even call their parents by name. I grew up not knowing the name of my father, who was the head of our compound, because we always referred to him as *Bah* [father]'. Talking about the *Lela* festival, a male university student aged 27 years remarked that '*Lela* is a good thing, because it has a unifying effect among the Bali Nyonga people. During the *Lela* season Bali people of all walks of life congregate at home and are in top form. They bring part of their wealth home and share it with their kith and kin. The drink sellers at Ntanfoghang [the town centre] maximize their profits from sales'. A female grade II teacher aged about 43 years emphasized that 'The *Lela* is another school where Bali youths are taught warfare. What they do here is equivalent to the pre-military training offered to the youths by the State'.

A *Mfonteh*, discussing the same institution, thinks that '*Lela* is a time for stocktaking. It is the time we [the *Mfonteh*] pledge our loyalty to the *mfon* and to Bali as a whole'.

On the importance of the *Voma* cult to the society, people's opinions are divided. An 85-year-old member of the *Voma* cult said '*Voma* was able to bring rain in the past, and so saved the people from drought and famine. It blessed the crops and they grew well. It blessed barren women and they bore children. So *Voma* is a good thing'. Asked by this author why *Voma* no longer brings rain nowadays, the old man replied: 'Your generation is one of unbelievers and a wicked generation. You people question everything and you may not keep the rules of *Voma*. You want to know the chemistry of every herb or root before you believe in its importance. I tell you herbs have power'.

A senior police officer aged 62 years advocated that *Voma* should be abolished. 'It is of no more use. The *Voma* has no right to stand on the road and ask people not to pass by. You cannot impose your tradition on a town with many different people living in it. Bali is no longer a village' (Green 1982, p. 22).

'*Voma* is retarding the village because people cannot go outside and do what they want to do, and the money they would have earned is lost', argued a 20-year-old male student.

Bali is a Subdivision, with a Divisional Officer representing the Head of State and government, and acting as the chief administrator of the Subdivision.

At the head of the traditional government is the *mfon*, who works closely with the Divisional Officer. The *mfon* is a political and spiritual leader. When asked who the most important person in Bali is, a 27-year-old businessman replied, 'The *mfon*, of course. We in Bali respect the *mfon* more than the Divisional Officer because, after all, a Divisional Officer is a commoner who can be transferred or dismissed from his post at any time, but our *mfon* stays with us forever. We hold him in high esteem'.

It is reported that a few years ago a newly arrived Divisional Officer ordered a clean-up campaign in Bali. He did not consult with the traditional authorities. On the appointed day very few people turned up for the work. In fact, only civil servants in the Subdivision responded to the Divisional Officer's call. However, a retired police officer advised the Divisional Officer to confer with the *mfon*. He did so, and that evening the *Ngumba* went through the town and advertised the clean-up campaign. The following morning the whole town turned up and before 11 a.m. the whole place was clean. This is one situation where a traditional institution has been of help to modern administration. There are many instances like this one that can be quoted to support the view that tradition and modernism can march hand-in-hand.

Writing about justice in Bali, Green (1982) states:

> The old folks say that there were fewer crimes in the past. People feared the ever watchful eye of their ancestors. In the small, close settlement that Bali is, people invariably knew who was guilty. Within the family crimes were settled by the family head. More serious offences were taken to the quarter head and if a matter was beyond his power, it would go to the Gate of the Palace. Here the person would be tried by commoners who deputising for the *mfon* act as magistrate for the day. It was considered a very fair system, as the disputants were judged by ordinary people like themselves.

In a situation like this the guilty party was usually told to make a payment in kind. Today many Bali people think that the traditional system was fairer than the present court system, where lawyers, policemen and magistrates draw out cases, sometimes for months.

The traditional week in Bali lasted for eight days, in contrast with our modern seven-day week. There was a traditional Sunday, known as *Foncham*, and a big market-day known as *Njinbufung*. In other words, if a market-day did not fall on a Sunday since the Bali weekdays were rotatory, the people would have to observe three days in the week as free days. These were the modern Sunday, *Foncham* and the market-day. Recently the new *mfon* of Bali announced a cut in one of the traditional weekdays to conform with the modern seven-day week. He appears to be meeting a lot of opposition on this decision, as his decision has affected all other market-days in the neighbouring villages in the north-west province that run the same traditional eight-day week.

As was mentioned above, titles in Bali are important, and commoners or even slaves could become titlemen on merit. Most university graduates who have made substantial contributions have been raised to the rank of *Nkoma* by the *mfon*. Asked what he thinks about securing one of these titles for himself, a top accountant working with one of the state corporations said: 'I care for wealth and not titles. I like to ride a Mercedes-Benz and live in a modern, comfortable house and command respect from my professional colleagues, rather than securing a title from the *mfon*'.

Discussing the pros and cons of the extended family, a university professor aged about 52 years made the following remarks:

> 'I think that the extended family is good. I was born and bred in a polygamous home. My uncle sent me to school. Had he not done this I probably would have been a wine tapper in the village like my age-mates. I owe a lot to the extended family and I do not think that one can bite the finger that feeds him'.

Comments like these are made in Bali daily. They show that people still admire their traditions, and that the past cannot be easily forgotten. However, there are a few people who think that the past was bad, and that the remnants of the traditional institutions still existing should be scrapped.

The relationship between the past in Bali Nyonga and archaeology

The history of the Bali Nyonga people that is outlined above has some implication for archaeology. Archaeologists can be seen as people who are interested in finding out the history of ancestors or the aborigines of a place. They do this by systematically studying the remains of the peoples' material culture. These remains are either buried underneath the soil or found on the surface. The archaeologist gathers information either by digging deeply into the various layers of the earth and systematically examining the material remains that lie buried, or by scientifically observing the features of old settlements or abandoned sites and comparing these with the features of the present.

The history of the Bali Chamba people of the grasslands of Cameroon is the most recent. They arrived in this part of the country roughly between 1825 and 1830. It is certain that, since they were warriors with superior weapons, they drove the original inhabitants of their present site to the slopes of the mountain ranges that surround them, but the Widikum people, as these refugees are called, are known to have migrated to the present Bali area from Tatkum, in the Batibo area. The questions that the archaeologist can ask here are the following: 'Who were the aborigines of the present site now occupied by the Bali Nyonga people before the advent of the Widikum people? What language did these people speak? What foods did they eat? What tools did they use?' etc. These are questions that can be answered only through archaeological studies.

It is difficult to assess the impact of the Bali Nyonga raids on the local chiefdoms that existed in the present North-West and West Provinces before their arrival. One feature stands out clearly: the Bali Nyonga raids produced a drastic change in the settlement patterns of the people of this area. Before the arrival of the Bali people the grassland chiefdoms consisted of small, scattered hamlets around a core of settlements that made up the chief's palace. The Bali raids compelled people to congregate in dense settlements protected by a system of deep moats or rivers, or both, or to find naturally protected sites in the mountain ranges.

These changes in settlement patterns produced two results. First, the abandoned sites of the old settlement offer challenges for archaeologists to exploit. Examples of such abandoned sites are numerous. Within the present Bali area abandoned settlements can easily be traced by the presence of certain important trees and plants, such as fig trees, the older palm trees and the draceana plant. They are all live plants. Huge fig trees with dense foliage provided shade for the community assembling during ceremonial or important occasions. They mark abandoned palaces or compounds of large lineage heads.

There are two species of the fig tree. One species grows very large with dense foliage, the other remains small with fewer leaves. The smaller species of fig tree was used for demarcating territorial boundaries. Where a truce or treaty was being made between two warring chiefdoms following a boundary dispute, before the fig tree was planted to mark the boundary, each side had to provide a slave. These slaves were killed and buried at the place where the boundary was being marked, and the fig tree was planted between the two graves.

The draceana (*Nkukeng*) is a multi-purpose plant. It is used for making peace. If two factions were warring and a mother of twins arrived at the spot and raised the plant with her two hands, the men would lay down their arms and get ready for peace.

Secondly, the changes in settlement patterns also brought significant changes in the social and political organization of the people. Whereas the original chiefdoms were based simply on lineage organizations, the new chiefdoms came to be based on wards, with fairly mixed lineages made up of refugees from other tribes and people from other cultural backgrounds. Sub-chiefs became ward heads under a powerful ruler or *mfon*.

A comparison of the old settlement sites and lineage organization with the new centralized chiefdoms based on wards would be of interest not only to the archaeologist, but also to historians and anthropologists.

A comparative study of the burial styles and sites and ceremonial shrines may also reveal something about the beliefs and changes that have taken place within the Bali Nyonga chiefdom over the years. This comparison can also be extended to other tribes of the western grassland.

As stated in the early part of this chapter, there are five other Balis in the North-West Province of Cameroon besides Bali Nyonga. A study of the *Lela* and *Voma* insignia in the other Balis could be undertaken, and a comparison could be made with those of Bali Nyonga. Since most non-Bali tribes in the North-West Province claim to have the *Lela* also, a comparative study of this institution in them may reveal some evidence of cross-cultural borrowing which is so important to anthropology and archaeology.

At Kufom, where the Bali Nyonga people first settled, farmers have traced such things as old grindstones, axe heads, crude razors, old hoes and clay pots. These can also be systematically collected, classified and stored in the museums or cultural houses that are now appearing in the province. Children from schools within Bali Nyonga could also be brought to these old sites to study the surroundings, and to discover for themselves some of the evidence of human settlement here.

Another problem of interest, despite the fact that the history of the Bali people is so drastically different from the history of the Tikari people, is that Bali art structures cannot be distinguished from those of the Tikari. This presents another problem which needs investigation.

One section of the Widikum people who were driven out by the Bali Nyonga people are the Baforchu (Mbu) people. These people escaped to find refuge around a cave that is known today as Shum Laka. Nkwi & Warnier report that, 'In one of the test pits that was dug at *Shum Laka*, the remains lying 20 cm below the surface date back 6000 years ago. At 55 cm below the surface, the remains date back 8700 years ago. The remains were mainly ashes mixed with organic matter, kitchen debris, stones, sand and earth' (Nkwi & Warnier 1982, p. 22). This is an obvious archaeological problem which should be researched further.

The Bali *mfon*'s palace, as well as many other palaces in the North-West and West Provinces of Cameroon, is the repository of the people's material culture. Very few comparative studies of these cultures have been carried out by historians, anthropologists or archaeologists.

References

Chilver, E.M. 1966. *Zintgraff's explorations in Bamenda, Adamawa and the Benue lands 1889–1892*. Buea, Cameroon: Ministry of Primary Education and Social Welfare and West Cameroon Antiquities Commission.

Fomuso, B.F.H. 1976. *Sacrifice among the Bali-Nyonga in Mezam, Northwest Province of Cameroon*. Yaounde: Cameroon.

Green, M. 1982. *Through the year in West Africa*. London: Batsford.

Hunt, W.E. n.d. *Assessment report*. Buea, Cameroon: Archives.

Nkwi, P.N. and J.P. Warnier 1982. *Elements for a history of the Western Grassfields*. Yaounde: University of Yaounde.

16 *Archaeology and oral traditions in the Mitongoa-Andrainjato area (Betsileo region of Madagascar)*

VICTOR RAHARIJAONA

(translated by S. Kus)

Introduction

This chapter is concerned with archaeological research carried out in areas where one finds traditional non-Western societies, in particular societies in which indigenous histories play a critical role in the creation and re-creation of social structures. If the archaeologist ignores the concerns and beliefs of local populations, he or she risks a misunderstanding on the part of both the archaeologist and the local people. This misunderstanding can result in a loss of time and information, and in more serious instances it can result in refusals by local populations to allow research to be undertaken in their areas. Given that an interest in history and the roots of cultural traditions is not the exclusive preoccupation of archaeologists, but can be a legitimate concern of any cultural group, there should be means to effect a complementarity of information and effort on the part of both archaeologists and local populations. Our research in the Mitongoa-Andrainjato area of Madagascar in 1984 and 1985 allowed us to appreciate the role that oral traditions can play in archaeological research (Kus 1984), and the responsibility that archaeologists have towards the communities that allow them to study their history and prehistory.

The region of our archaeological survey covers an area of approximately 60 km², located in the central highlands of Madagascar. It lies a short distance east of Fianarantsoa, the regional capital of one of the six provinces of the island. The Betsileo who inhabit this region are one of the 18 ethnic groups of Madagascar. They practise wet rice cultivation and cattle raising. Their social organization accords a critical role to the transmission of oral traditions from generation to generation (for previous studies of the Betsileo see Dubois 1938 and Rainihifina 1975a, 1975b).

Contact with the local population

Upon arriving in the region of Mitongoa-Andrainjato for the purpose of undertaking an archaeological survey of the region, we met with much reserve and even a certain amount of distrust on the part of the local population. Administrative authorization to travel and work within this region, although necessary, did not automatically facilitate our work. The more it became known that we were interested in studying the history of the region through archaeological investigation, the more sceptical the local inhabitants became. Their conception of history is highly personalized and localized. What could non-locals pretend to understand of such history, never mind contribute to it? To combat this scepticism we spent time explaining our methods and their purposes, and giving examples of similar work carried out in other regions of Madagascar.

Archaeological sites and their histories belong to the ancestors (*razana*) and to their living descendants who continue to occupy the surrounding areas. Both archaeological sites and oral traditions are considered sacred, and the major archaeological sites of the area, Mitongoa and Andrainjato, as well as other minor sites, still function as places of ritual activity where local inhabitants solicit the benediction and protection of their ancestors and various deities.

Such a situation at first would seem to be quite problematic for the archaeologist. However, the local Betsileo, rather than refusing to allow archaeological investigation in their region, were willing to share with archaeologists knowledge of their past – a past which is considered both highly intimate and non-profane. However, there are conditions that must be observed in order to make possible such a sharing of information. One such condition is that the local population be continuously and sufficiently informed about any research project, including its results. This condition is, in part, a concern for the accurate presentation of their history and tradition. In one instance certain Betsileo, after being shown how to read aerial photographs and maps, were astonished and upset to find spatial and orthographic mistakes in the location and recording of villages on published maps. These individuals were concerned to see the correction of such errors, so as to present a more accurate version of their past and present society, since spatial as well as temporal concerns are critical elements of their history. Betsileo history is traced through site occupation and abandonment, as well as through a temporal sequence of events.

Such groups as the Betsileo have a complex and coherent indigenous version of history. The archaeologist is often presented with an alternative version of history that gives different weight to historical events and materials. For instance, local populations accord value and prestige to archaeological sites according to their own cultural criteria. Thus, the importance of a site in local versions of history is not necessarily correlated with its size or its age, and certain sites of interest to the archaeologist do not find a corresponding interest on the part of local populations.

Given such possible divergence of historical interpretation between the archaeologist and the local population, it is critical for archaeologists to examine the attitude and role of archaeological research in such a cultural context. It is important for archaeologists to respect the fact that indigenous concepts of history are valid alternative versions of history. Such versions of history not only need to be recorded, but also need to be understood in relation to the role they play in the creation and reaffirmation of cultural identity. Archaeologists also need to pose the question: what is the nature of the co-operative effort between archaeologists and the local population in the study of culture history? More specifically, what is it exactly that archaeologists have to offer to a cultural group already in possession of a sufficient and valid version of their own history?

Initiating a co-operative study of history

Ritual of acceptance

The senior male of the village near Mitongoa accepted the responsibility of introducing us to the local population. However, it was the demonstration of our respect for local traditions and ritual that was critical in allowing us both to reside and to work in the area. It was further necessary for us to obtain the authorization of the ancestors for beginning fieldwork. Accompanied by the responsible senior males of the community, we climbed to the summit of Mitongoa. Mitongoa is considered by the locals to be the site of the original occupants of the region. Mitongoa thus serves as a site of ritual activity consecrated to the ancestors. With our bottle of rum as an offering, we participated in the performance of the rites necessary to introduce us to the ancestors and to obtain their blessings. Assembled on the point of highest elevation at the site of Mitongoa, one individual was responsible for the invocation while the other participants knelt facing the north-east, attentive to the address to the ancestors. The offering of rum was also accompanied by a modest sum of money, called *tandram-bava*. These symbolic offerings are necessary to initiate any important discourse, especially when such speech is directed toward the ancestors and deities.

To open the ritual address to the ancestors at Mitongoa, a sprinkling of rum was made in the four cardinal directions. The invocations that followed included the enumeration of various individuals and villages. Later in our research the importance of these names became apparent; they are the names of common ancestors, village founders and early villages. Our presence in the area and our research project, including details of scientific procedure, were presented to the ancestors during the course of this ceremony. The blessing of the ancestors was also sought to allow us to carry out a productive and successful project, a project that was viewed by the locals as a co-operative effort wherein they were available to offer counselling and explanation to help us to understand and appreciate their history. After the address to the ancestors, all of the participants in the ceremony shared the bottle of rum as a final symbol of the beginning of a co-operative venture in the study of the history of the area. This acceptance of the archaeologists into the local community helped to put aside earlier sentiments of reticence and wariness.

The 'right of speech'

Not all individuals have the 'right of speech' in this traditional society, even though there are no 'professional' spokespeople, historians or genealogists as are sometimes found in African societies. Speech is powerful, and there is the fear that the inadequately instructed individual will utter inaccuracies that might offend the ancestors and bring about some social or physical harm.

Among the Betsileo the 'right of speech' is accorded to the eldest male in most circumstances. At the household level it is the grandfather or the father that holds this right. In some cases, by default, it is the eldest son or the son considered as the 'protector' of the family that retains this right. At the level of the village the right of speech is accorded to the eldest male. Women do not normally have the right to speak about important matters of group history or identity. Given a pattern of virilocal residence, women find themselves both distanced from their family groups and strangers to the group with whom they reside. Thus, according to male informants, women have only a fragmentary and incomplete understanding of their own history. Women should therefore not speak of their group's history, for an incomplete version of history endangers the legitimacy and identity of the group.

Each recounting of history should be carefully controlled so as to conform to the accepted tradition. Individuals having the right of speech do not exercise it indiscriminately. Rather, there are appropriate places and situations to speak of history. If the history is that of a village or a territory, then the person who speaks does so in the central public space, or *kianja*, in the presence of the heads of families concerned. If it is the history of a family, then it is recounted in the ancestral home in the presence of important family members. Such oral traditions serve to define, preserve and valorize a group's identity and customs within a more englobing cultural context. Thus, the collection of oral traditions is a delicate matter among the Betsileo.

These oral traditions are not necessarily transmitted in a systematic manner. They are recited during the course of daily affairs, as well as during important ceremonial occasions such as birth, circumcision, marriage and death. The apprentice historian follows his father or his elder, and listens attentively to the histories recounted. The apprentice does not have the right to modify the content of the traditions. He is engaged rather in committing to memory the names and origins of different social groups, as well as the history of their settlement in the area and successive site occupations. The apprentice must be aware of not only the temporal and spatial history of groups, but also of the contemporary sociospatial map of group distributions and alliances. Thus, archaeological sites as well as contemporary villages are critical elements of oral historical accounts. One might say that as an individual proceeds to learn of his group's history, the individual comes to master an increasingly wide spatial and temporal network of information. However, it is also important to note that such knowledge has bounds. Individuals do not have the right to speak of a history that is not a history of their group.

Archaeology, oral history and the collaborative study of history

Collaboration with local guides and discussions with local historians, as well as the typical archaeological paraphernalia such as topographic maps and aerial photographs, allowed an effective archaeological survey of the Mitongoa-Andrainjato area to be carried out, which included the identification of 140 sites. Sites that were not located on maps or visible on aerial photographs were quickly and easily located with the help of local guides. One could say that the time spent in ceremonies of introduction to both the ancestors and their living representatives was largely compensated for, not only by rapid identification of sites, but also by an effective and economic coverage of the survey area, guided by individuals who knew their home territory and the most effective way to walk or drive between areas.

Oral traditions and local knowledge also contributed to the interpretation of the archaeological vestiges discovered. The local Betsileo have names for each site, as well as building remnants and other features in a site. These names suggest the function and significance of sites and their features, both in a utilitarian context and in a symbolic context. Such information can contribute to our archaeological interpretations of material culture, in that this information can suggest hypotheses not necessarily generated from simple visual inspection of archaeological remains.

Conclusions

The Betsileo are not only proud of their traditions, they are also interested in adding to their understanding of their own history. Memory, even collective memory, has a limit on its ability to record history. Consequently, the Betsileo are interested in the contribution that archaeology can make to their knowledge of their past. Archaeologists can benefit from this interest if they approach their research as a *co-operative* venture between themselves and the local population.

The Betsileo are also concerned not only about their own knowledge of their history, but also about the manner in which this history is presented to the non-Betsileo. This concern for the accurate presentation of their culture and history to the outsider implies that archaeologists carry the responsibility of satisfying this concern of the Betsileo when, as researchers and academicians, they speak of the results of their research to non-Betsileo audiences.

Like most of their African colleagues, Malagasy archaeologists do not always have written historical documents at their disposal. However, they often have access to oral traditions. The research undertaken in the Mitongoa-Andrainjato area of Madagascar suggests that an interdisciplinary approach that involves both archaeological investigation *and* the collection of oral traditions can prove fruitful in the investigation of indigenous cultural development.

However, research experiences in the Mitongoa-Andrainjato region also show that obtaining access to archaeological sites and oral traditions is not always easy. The archaeologist needs to be sensitive to the customs and concerns of the local population, if he or she is to carry out any successful programme of research. Local populations are often willing to collaborate with archaeological researchers if such researchers adopt a 'proper' attitude: i.e. an attitude which not only demonstrates a respect for local traditions, but also a respect for local knowledge. It is a respect that encourages the archaeologist to view his or her research project as a collaborative effort between the archaeologist and the local population. Research that is carried out as a specialized private professional concern may result in the speaking of inaccuracies and inadequacies concerning the history of 'others'. Such speech runs the risk not only of offending the ancestors, but also of offending sensitive professionals such as those contributing to this book.

References

Dubois, R. P. 1938. *Monographie des Betsileo*. Paris: Institut d'Ethnologie.
Kus, S. 1984. Time as space and space as time in nineteenth century Imerina, Madagascar. Paper presented at the 83rd Annual Meeting of the American Anthropological Association, Denver, Colorado.
Rainihifina, J. 1975a. *Lovantisaina I – Tantara Betsileo*. Fianarantsoa: Ambozontany.
Rainihifina, J. 1975b. *Lovantisaina II – Fomba Betsileo*. Fianarantsoa: Ambozontany.

17 Interpretations and uses of the past in modern Britain and Europe. Why are people interested in the past? Do the experts know or care? A plea for further study

PETER G. STONE

This chapter argues that professional archaeologists in Britain (both academic and field-based) do not take enough notice of the perceptions of the past held by the public. Drawing on information from a number of sources, including data gathered from a survey co-organized by the author, it argues that there are a number of potentially conflicting attitudes to the past held within contemporary Britain and mainland Europe, and that these differences can only be ignored to the detriment of archaeology as a discipline and, implicitly, to the actual physical archaeological heritage. The chapter further argues that the provision of school-based archaeological projects is one very important way of making archaeological material and ideas available to the public.

The problem defined

In 1985 and 1986 there were major disturbances at the prehistoric monument of Stonehenge when the National Trust and the Historic Buildings and Monuments Commission for England (HBMCE) were granted an injunction banning an unofficial festival that was to be held at the site. The festival had been held annually at Stonehenge since 1974 and increasing damage since then convinced the authorities to take strong action. The television news in Britain and throughout Europe showed scenes of police fighting running battles with would-be festival-goers, and a tremendous amount of damage to property was done. In 1985, on the day before the festival was due to take place, many people in the nearby village of Avebury (which also boasts major prehistoric remains) expressed their fears that the trouble at Stonehenge would spread to involve them, and a police 'monitoring room' was set up in the Alexander Keiller Museum in the village. At the same time local farmers were asked by the police to block-off access to prehistoric sites on their land. This was done by parking farm machinery at the access to such land. Similar action was taken in 1986.

The distinct problems that face those in charge of the Stonehenge complex have already been the subject of a number of popular and academic reports (for example Chippindale 1983, HBMCE 1985, Michell 1985). These problems only concern us here because they represent some of the extreme interpretations and uses of archaeological data that are invoked today. The National Trust, the HBMCE, the police, the would-be festival-goers and the Druids all had (and doubtless still have) different views on the use, and therefore presumably implied interpretation, of the Stonehenge complex. It is clear that over the past two years, in a small area of southern Britain, there have been a number of quite different attitudes to the monuments of the past – and through these monuments, to the past itself.

It has been argued elsewhere that archaeologists in Britain have little under-standing (or even regard) for what the public thinks about the past or archae-ology (Bewley 1983, Stone 1986a). It has also been suggested that the 'experts' deliberately hide archaeological information in high-flying academic jargon in a, to date, successful attempt to maintain their high-status position in a society where the control of knowledge is seen as synonymous with the control of power (Hodder 1984). It has also been argued that the increasing popularity of metal-detectors in Britain is, to a large extent, due to the failure of archaeology to communicate with the non-academic audience (Gregory 1983).

At about the same time the 1985 disturbances were going on at Stonehenge, the Council of Europe organized the first meeting on 'Making children aware of the existence, study and conservation of the archaeological cultural heritage' (at the European University Centre for the Cultural Heritage, Ravello, Italy). The meeting was stimulated by the need for a response to the increasing threat of damage done to archaeological monuments by metal-detectors (Hackens pers. comm., June 1985). Nearly 50 papers were presented by participants, who included archaeologists, educationalists, teachers, museum officers and politicians.

Most of the papers reported on the work that was being carried out, in the various countries represented at the meeting, to teach children about the 'archaeological cultural heritage'. *Not one* of the speakers defined what he or she actually meant by the 'cultural heritage'. Indeed, it was blatantly clear that participants were talking about different things when they referred to the 'cultural heritage' – a point that came across very clearly when the methods and content of teaching were described (see, for example, Oborn 1985, Conticello 1985). What was not at all clear was whether many of the participants had ever *really* thought about what they meant when they talked about the 'cultural heri-tage' (Stone 1985). It was also clear from the papers presented that few of the speakers had taken much notice about what children or other members of the public really thought about, or wanted from, the past.

A survey of public attitudes to the past

In an attempt to find out what the public think about the past and about archaeology, a survey was organized in Britain in 1983–4. A questionnaire was devised and first tested in Cambridge in 1983 by members of the Department of Archaeology at the University of Cambridge (Cambridge Research Co-operative 1983). As a result of this pilot testing, and in co-operation with the author, the questionnaire was modified and extended. In 1984 four urban centres were chosen in Britain for a much wider survey, and some initial personal conclusions were drawn (Stone 1986a).

Aims and scope of the survey

The survey attempted to:

> . . . collect information on the general public's conception of the past, together with the extent to which this conception is affected by the public's social context. The survey attempts to (1) collect information on how people's concept of the past is formed (e.g. from museums, the media, the family, education, work) and (2) collect information on people's archaeological interests, attitudes, and awareness. It is concerned with what interests people in the past
>
> (from page 1 of notes for those helping with the survey).

The time taken for completion of the questionnaire averaged 30 minutes which, as this time was always mentioned at the start of every interview, reflected quite a high level of commitment to helping with the survey.

The full survey was carried out in four urban centres (Cambridge, Lancaster, Southampton and York). It was intended to collect 100 responses from each centre. By the end of the survey more than 500 members of the public had been approached by one of a team of nearly 40 interviewers, and 301 responses had been gathered. The conclusions drawn from the survey are not seen as fully conclusive. The survey did not completely cover all of the possible areas of interest; it was not free from problems (for example, of size, bias and coverage); nor can the results be used, with absolute confidence, to make categoric statements about the public's attitudes to, or interest in, the past. However, the aims stated above are an important aspect of archaeology that has long been neglected by those concerned with the study of the past. If such aims continue to be neglected, this can only do archaeology and, implicitly, the archaeological heritage (however defined) harm. The results do begin to point out differences in attitudes towards archaeology within the population. These, often conflicting, attitudes could and perhaps should have an extremely important effect on the development and continued existence of archaeology, both as an academic discipline and as a practical profession.

Problems associated with the survey

The organization and major problems associated with the survey have been dealt with elsewhere (Stone 1986a). However, some problems need to be referred to here in order to put the survey, and conclusions, into perspective.

First, because there was no financial support for the work, the four centres chosen were all urban ones where enough help was forthcoming to complete the survey. In practice this meant towns with university archaeology departments that, by chance, all had fairly major archaeological excavations under way when the survey was carried out. Thus, the respondents' level of archaeological awareness *may* have been higher than that of an average member of the public. Again, many answers *may* have been influenced by the respondents' desire to give the 'correct' answer to the archaeology student asking the questions (despite an attempt to keep the interviewer's occupation a secret from the respondent, at least during the interview).

Secondly, more than 200 people refused to answer the questionnaire. The reasons given for refusal were many and varied, but most distressing (in terms of possible conclusions to be drawn from the survey) was the assertion that 'I don't know anything about the past, so I can't help'. This fairly widespread reaction sometimes resulted in no interview taking place or, more often, in the interviewer being passed on to another member of the family (usually from a female to a male). The response tended to support Hodder's (1984) claim that knowledge about the past is seen to be a specialist concern. Despite this worry, the response rate of just under 60 per cent is in line with other market research results, and it was noted by a number of interviewers that some people's generally negative reaction to surveys was more important in refusals than was hostility specific to the topic of the survey.

Thirdly, although the age and sex breakdown of the respondents does generally match that of Britain as a whole, the breakdown into social grouping is not properly representative of the country. This may be the result of the particular social make-up of the urban centres studied, or that those areas, within the four centres, selected as working class were not truly representative. Whatever the cause, there are proportionally more professional middle-class respondents than should be the case if the sample were to be representative of the national situation – a factor that should be taken into account when discussing the conclusions drawn from the survey (for the criteria used to define social class, see Goldthorpe 1980).

The scope of this analysis

It has already been argued that the results of the survey show a basic and wide-ranging interest in the past (Stone 1986a). More detailed analysis shows that the level and type of interest may differ between social groups and sexes (Hodder *et al.* n.d.). More recent work has certainly indicated that a bland uniformity in interest cannot be expected between those of different cultural backgrounds (Emmott, Ch. 1, this volume, Suffield 1986).

Knowledge of the past: television, films and books

Television and radio

Two undergraduate dissertations have recently been written on the theme of archaeology and the media (Frost 1983, Hoare 1983). Much of the statistical analysis in these dissertations has been criticized by members of the BBC for being based on misinterpretation of BBC data (at a seminar on Archaeology and the Media held in 1983). However, the basic message of both dissertations seems indisputable: after a honeymoon period between archaeology and the media in the late 1950s (a period also noted by Norman (1983), which saw two archaeologists being made BBC TV Personality of the Year), archaeology has been poorly represented on the television and, to a lesser extent, on the radio. Both Frost and Hoare put most of the blame for this on archaeologists.

However, whereas archaeologists must contribute ideas and impetus, the media themselves play a part in presenting a particular type of archaeology to the public. Although Norman thinks that 'wet planks, dead bodies, treasure and palm trees' (Norman 1983, p. 29) are what most viewers are interested in watching, archaeology on television is firmly linked to 'academic style' documentaries. Thus, while those respondents with less formal education say that they watch more television than do those with a high level of formal education, archaeology on television is aimed at, and attracts, the latter group. One respondent can be cited as an example of many of this latter group when he answered that he watched archaeology on television as part of a 'quest for knowledge' (25)[1]. A small audience of committed viewers is given the knowledge that it wants in a way that it finds interesting and acceptable. The trend to present archaeology in a tried-and-tested documentary format would seem to disregard a large proportion of those who watch a lot of television. Such potential viewers are ignored by archaeologists, and television producers, to their own disadvantage.

The same problem can be argued to exist on the radio. Of the respondents, 78 per cent answered that they had never listened to a radio programme about the past. The vast majority of archaeology programmes in Britain are broadcast on BBC Radio 4 (mainly in the *Origins* series) which is the station least frequently listened to by those with less formal education. Archaeology rarely gets air-space on the more popular national stations, and only really does so when the topic is spectacular or particularly controversial (for example, the raising of the *Mary Rose* or the finding of a preserved Iron Age body in the peat bogs in northern England.

The great exception to this is local radio, where archaeological topics of local importance, or even series concerning local archaeology, can be very successful (McWhirr 1980). This success has also been achieved on local television, where short series by individual archaeologists have captured much local imagination, and have achieved a surprisingly large following of confirmed viewers.

This emphasis on documentaries seems all the more incomprehensible when producers argue that those based on archaeology are 'the most difficult documentaries to make for television' (Norman 1983, p. 29). Archaeology is, by the very nature of its data, static, and audience interest is easily lost. 'You watch but do not learn' (43). 'Those who follow it are too academic. The presentation should change' (39). In order to reach the wider audience who claim to watch the most television, archaeology must be presented in a lively and exciting way. If programmes about archaeology and prehistory are not presented in a more acceptable way, then most people will turn to popular films about the subject.

Of the respondents, 59 per cent had seen one or more popular films about prehistory or archaeology, either on television or at the cinema. Forty-two per cent answered that many of these films gave reasonably accurate versions of the past. Included in the list were both *One Million Years BC* (where humans fight dinosaurs) and *Raiders of the Lost Ark* (where a heroic and handsome archaeologist comes up against both Nazi Germany and the supernatural powers of the Ark of the Covenant). '*One Million Years BC* gives a good representation of the past, but other films don't' (272). A number of people said that no-one, 'not even archaeologists', could know about the past and therefore, presumably, no-one could say whether a film was correct. Films 'do what they can with the available evidence. You always get it wrong anyway' (67). It is films such as *One Million Years BC* and *When Dinosaurs Ruled the Earth*, together with comic strips (such as *The Flintstones*), that principally contribute to the image of prehistory as a time when people lived in caves, fought dinosaurs and pulled women around by the hair. Unfortunately, it is also from programmes such as these that most people receive their understanding of the distant past.

Whereas the actual viewing figures for archaeology on television are really very low (for example, no archaeological programme has ever achieved figures comparable with televised snooker), television does remain the main medium for familiarizing the public with archaeology. If potentially large audiences are ignored, as seems to be the case at present, then archaeology will have missed a golden opportunity to influence the public.

Books

Less than half of the respondents showed any real interest in books on archaeology. Of those who claimed to read about archaeology (or history), the majority found it difficult to recall specific authors or titles of books. The normal response was versed in a period or thematic manner – thus respondent (151) enjoyed reading about the Egyptians and Romans, and (107) concentrated on New Zealand's history and anthropology. When authors were mentioned, it was striking that the most frequently named was Von Daniken.

The overriding impression of the type of books about the past that people read is that they should not be too 'heavy' or academic – respondent (9) only enjoyed reading books about the past if they had a lot of pictures and, along with a large number of others (of the group who did read), also enjoyed reading historical fiction. This desire to identify with the past – realized through illustration and fiction – seems to apply to all social classes.

Newspapers

Newspapers also maintain a distinction between archaeology as knowledge and archaeology as popular interest. 'Serious' archaeology is largely limited to reports in the 'quality' newspapers, *The Times*, *The Guardian*, *The Daily Telegraph* and *The Independent*. Yet, particularly at the local level, there is a popular story to be made out of mundane discoveries:

> Look at the press cuttings from the 1950s and 1960s and see the number of photographs and reports of the discoveries of what we might regard as insignificant items of information: rotary querns, a handful of medieval pottery or half a dozen coins. Put together the thrill of the finder of any of these, with the interest that they were found locally, and you have still got a good newspaper story. We may sometimes want to cringe at the puns of the headlines, the apparent naivety of the story or the cuteness of the photographs, and we may well regard them as unsuitable for archaeology – but they are unsuitable for the *Times*, not for the *Sun*. The style of local journalism is one that works and one that gets its message across, and we must be prepared to use it, or give journalists the material to use it. Feed your local papers with every little titbit you can and they will soon start to bite
>
> (Gregory 1983, p. 8).

Survey conclusions

The above paints a fairly dismal picture. Only those sections of the population who enjoy 'academic type' documentaries, listen to Radio 4, or who read the heavier academic books or quality press are exposed, on a regular basis, to high-quality (but not necessarily highly academic and jargon ridden) archaeological information. Yet the survey results indicate a strong desire, from all social classes, to identify with some form of a past. Archaeologists are just as much to blame for the lack of available material and information as are those involved in the media, and they have far more to lose.

Steps must be taken by archaeologists to rectify this situation. Archaeologists cannot expect others to protect either the physical heritage or their jobs if they do not disseminate their findings widely and in an acceptable form. The situation is a critical one, with resources (both physical and financial) under increasing pressure. If action is not taken, there will soon be no archaeological physical heritage to preserve or study.

The way forward

One of the most effective ways of reaching a wide cross section of the public is through working with children. Working with schools should be an important aspect of the work of any archaeological unit. Children are not only the adult public of tomorrow, they also have a direct influence, through their parents and teachers, on the adult public of today. A school-based archaeological project is probably the most effective way of influencing a large section of the population with the limited funds available.

One such project, usually carried out with primary school-children between the ages of seven and eleven years, is outlined below. The original project has been described elsewhere (Richardson 1987), as have some of the later organizational details and initial reactions to a somewhat developed project (Stone 1986b). It has formed part of the work of a team, called 'Archaeology and Education', especially brought together in the Department of Archaeology at the University of Southampton to assess the current presentation of prehistory and archaeology in schools and to the public, and to prepare, provide and test our own material. The team has four overall objectives that are incorporated into all of its projects:

(a) to demonstrate that there is evidence of the past in the physical environment everywhere around us;

(b) to show that this physical evidence of the past is under continual threat from ever-present and ever-changing human interaction with the environment;

(c) to integrate this unique category of evidence into the study of our past into local schools; and

(d) to develop material that is in keeping with the 'enquiry' based curricula now favoured in many schools.

The period chosen for the project is c. 5000 years BP, when society in Britain was in the early stages of sedentary farming. The children are taught through a variety of methodological approaches. Classroom teaching, visits to prehistoric monuments and days of 'experimental archaeology' all combine to present a picture of a past inhabited not by unintelligent 'grunter groaners' but by a highly organized, intelligent and skilful society. The children are able to learn through their individual (and group) first-hand experiences both of real prehistoric monuments and artefacts, and of experimental constructions of skills available in prehistory.

At no point do the children pretend to be living in the past, as has been attempted elsewhere (for example, Millar & Durston 1982, Cooper 1983, Bell 1984). They have lost too much and gained too much for such an approach to have any real educational value. Rather, it is the skills of the past, known or inferred from archaeological evidence, that form the basis of the children's understanding of, and empathetic relationship with, the past.

Children involved in the project have learnt a lot about the present state of knowledge concerning prehistory and the Avebury monuments in particular. For example, 82.2 per cent knew that West Kennet Long Barrow was a burial mound, and all but one of the children ascribed the building of the Avebury monuments to the Neolithic. Arguably more important than any measurable gain in factual knowledge, the children learnt about the use and interpretation of a number of different types of evidence. They were not fed stock responses or the 'correct' answer. They themselves had to learn by questioning, seeing and experimenting. The long-term benefits and value of such work can only be really measured after a number of years. Many children who have been through the project have certainly used information that was learnt during the project in later school work (see Richardson 1986).

Many have been provoked to thinking about the world they live in as a result of the work. When asked what advantages or disadvantages there were for people living in the Neolithic as opposed to today, a number of children talked (without prompting) of there being no pollution, it being more peaceful and there being no nuclear threat. However, most said they would miss, in one form or another, the technological achievements and luxuries of today. Not surprisingly, 76 per cent of children questioned said they would prefer to live in today's world. Whatever the responses, the crucial point is that all of the children had been made to think about their answers, rather than just repeating knowledge received from a textbook. It could be argued that the children were repeating perceived knowledge received from those teaching them. This possibility cannot be totally ruled out. However, the different conclusions arrived at by the children were always accepted, as long as they were based on correct evidence. Several of the children have also gone back to the Avebury monuments, taking with them parents who had never before visited prehistoric monuments.

Many teachers have initially expressed concern that some parts of the project are too difficult and too abstract for their children. However, in every school, by the end of the project, all of the teachers have been fully convinced of the worth of introducing teaching about the distant past into their curricula. Much of the teachers' initial concern stems from their own ignorance of the aims and techniques of modern archaeology. Once this ignorance has been partially overcome, teachers begin to see the potential worth of the subject. They begin to appreciate that the study of a prehistoric monument need not only develop historical skills (for example, writing, interpretation of evidence and empathy), but can also encompass subject areas such as geography, mathematics, art, craft, and even philosophy and religious study. Such multi-subject topic work is a very popular method of teaching in primary schools in Britain today. One of the great assets of archaeology in the university sector is that it has the potential to be a bridge discipline linking not only different departments, but also different faculties (Stone, forthcoming). Once this asset has been understood by school teachers, the demand, as already experienced in Hampshire, will be great.

Conclusions and recommendations

(a)   The complacent attitude of archaeologists and their apparent disregard of the opinions of the rest of the population is a near-suicidal stance. At a time when government funding can no longer be relied upon to produce even half of the finance required for excavation of sites threatened with destruction in the country, the public *must* be made aware of the importance of *all* archaeological work. This cannot be done in academic isolation, but must take into account public opinion about the past, and the different ways in which the public want to use and know about the past. Archaeology will only continue, or continue to develop, if it can show itself to be interesting and relevant to the public at large, a point recognized in America more than 15 years ago: 'We suspect that unless archaeologists find ways to make their research increasingly relevant to the modern world, the modern world will find itself increasingly capable of getting along without archaeologists' (Fritz & Plog 1970, p. 412).

At the recent first annual conference of the Institute of Field Archaeologists there was much positive indication that archaeologists had begun to address the public through displays and exhibitions at excavations and, in some cases, in 'high-profile' displays in urban centres. However, such work is almost entirely carried out by those employed on government schemes for the long-term unemployed and, while the development must be welcomed, it is usually seen as an 'extra frill' rather than as a major commitment.

(b)   In Ravello, the lack of uniformity or consensus regarding the definition of the 'cultural heritage' was isolated by the participants as being of major importance. It was agreed in discussion that a coherent policy for the creation and implementation of teaching about the 'archaeological cultural heritage' could only be achieved if what people (both those educating and those being educated) meant by the term was understood. The importance of the need for this understanding can be seen in the fact that the participants, in the conclusions adopted for laying before the Council of Europe, stated that:

> . . . The participants urge: A. The competent authorities of the Council of Europe member states to take appropriate measures in order to: 1. promote concerted research throughout Europe so as to further the understanding of the various attitudes or needs of the inhabitants of European countries and of their respective national and regional cultural heritage, of the European past and pre-historical past as well as of the means by which these ideas were developed and handed on. . . [*sic*]
>
> (Ravello 1985, p. 79).

Such a recommendation needs to be given the strongest support, and it was a matter of much concern to a number of the participants at the second meeting, in 1986, that no progress had been made in the attempts to set up such a study.

All of the above ideas should be developed alongside a far more imaginative and exciting liaison between archaeologists and media producers. Archaeology has a potentially huge audience of members of the public who want no more than to be entertained and informed in an interesting and exciting way. At present the vast majority of this public is ignored.

Acknowledgements

The survey discussed in this chapter was originally set up and tested in Cambridge by Ian Hodder and Mike Parker-Pearson. They remained responsible for the organization of the extended Cambridge survey while Val Turner organized the Lancaster survey and the author organized those in York and Southampton, in the latter city with much help from Jo Bailey. Many thanks must also go to all those who helped with the interviewing. The full results of the survey have not been published. They have been discussed in detail with Hodder and Parker-Pearson. While we agree on most conclusions, the present author takes full responsibility for all comments and conclusions in this chapter. The unpublished undergraduate dissertations have been cited with the permission of the authors and departments concerned.

Note

1.   Numbers in parentheses in the text refer to individuals who completed the survey.

References

Bell, R. 1984. A journey back into the past. *Teaching History* **39**, 5–7.
Bewley, R. 1983. Archaeology and the public: foreword. *Archaeological Review from Cambridge* **2** (1), 3–4.
Cambridge Research Co-operative 1983. The national survey of public opinion towards archaeology. *Archaeological Review from Cambridge* **2** (1), 24–7.
Chippindale, C. 1983. What future for Stonehenge? *Antiquity* **LVII**, 172–80.
Conticello, B. 1985. Relazione sezione didattica. Paper given at the first meeting of 'Making children aware of the existence, study and conservation of the archaeological cultural heritage' (Ravello, June 1985). *PACT News* **15**, 57.
Cooper, H. 1983. From marbles to murder. *Teaching History* **36**, 24–7.
Fritz, J. and F. Plog 1970. The nature of archaeological explanation. *American Antiquity* **35**, 405–12.
Frost, J. 1983. Archaeology and the media. Undergraduate dissertation, Institute of Archaeology, London (unpublished).
Goldthorpe, J. 1980. *Social mobility and class structure in modern Britain*. Oxford: Clarendon Press.
Gregory, A. 1983. The impact of metal detection on archaeology and the public. *Archaeological Review from Cambridge* **2** (1), 5–8.
HBMCE 1985. *Stonehenge Study Group report*. London: Historic Buildings and Monuments Commission for England.
Hoare, R. 1983. Archaeology, the public and the media. Undergraduate dissertation, Department of Archaeology, University of Edinburgh (unpublished).
Hodder, I. 1984. Archaeology in 1984. *Antiquity* **LVII**, 25–33.
Hodder, I., M. Parker-Pearson, N. Peck and P. Stone. n.d. *Archaeology, knowledge and society*. A detailed analysis of the general public survey.
McWhirr, A. 1980. Give it an airing! *Popular Archaeology* **1** (8), 45.

Michell, J. 1985. *Stonehenge, its Druids, custodians, festival and future*. London Radical–Traditionalist Paper 6.

Millar, S. and C. Durston 1982. Stepping back three hundred years: the Young National Trust Theatre sixth form day at Montacute. *Teaching History* **33**, 32–5.

Norman, B. 1983. Archaeology and television. *Archaeological Review from Cambridge* **2** (1), 27–33.

Oborn, G. 1985. 'Do it yourself. A way of discovering and preserving our rich cultural heritage'. Paper given in Ravello, June 1985. *PACT News* **15**, 54–6.

Ravello 1985. Conclusions adopted by the participants at the first meeting on 'Making children aware of the existence, study and conservation of the archaeological cultural heritage'. *PACT News* **16**, 78–80.

Richardson, W. 1986. Well, in the Neolithic . . . children's perceptions of the past, of learning about it, and of its relevance to them. In *Archaeological 'objectivity' in interpretation*. World Archaeological Congress, vol. 3 (mimeo).

Richardson, W. 1987. Isn't it all about dinosaurs? An experiment in a junior school. In *Degree, digging, dole . . . Our future?* S. Joyce, M. Newbury and P. Stone (eds), 69–77. University of Southampton.

Stone, P. G. 1985. Current research and work regarding the teaching of archaeology in primary schools in England. Paper given in Ravello, June 1985. PACT News **16**, 41–3.

Stone, P. G. 1986a. Are the public really interested? In *Archaeology, politics and the public*, C. Dobinson and R. Gilchrist (eds), 14–21. York: Department of Archaeology, Occasional Papers Series.

Stone, P. G. 1986b. Prehistory through ears, eyes and backs. *CBA Education Bulletin* **1**, 8–11.

Stone, P. G. in press. The present state of archaeology teaching in British universities. In *The excluded past: archaeology in education*, P. Stone & R. MacKenzie (eds). London: Unwin Hyman.

Suffield, F. 1986. Multicultural perceptions of the past by children and their parents in relation to teaching within schools. In *Archaeological 'objectivity' in interpretation*. World Archaeological Congress, vol. 3 (mimeo).

Index